MarketPlace: **AUK**	Order Number: **205-4841087-2529955**
Order Date: **2015-10-06**	Email: **bkqpb70vppcg379@marketplace.amazon.co.uk**

Items : 1

Item		**Locator**
Butterfly on a Wheel: The Great Rolling Stones Dru	OD	MUL-7-LD-064-04-1

ISBN : 1849389950

CW00402221

'our purchase and if so, ask you to leave positive feedback.
' will do our best to resolve any issues you may have.
By Sea, West Sussex, BN12 4QY. Tel:+44(0)1903 507544
vitter: @WorldofBooksltd | Web: www.worldofbooks.com

BUTTERFLY ON A WHEEL

THE GREAT ROLLING STONES DRUGS BUST

Youth culture
– Rock 'n' roll
– Drugs

THE GARDEN OF LOVE

I laid me down upon a bank,
Where Love lay sleeping;
I heard among the rushes dank
Weeping, weeping.

Then I went to the heath and the wild,
To the thistles and thorns of the waste;
And they told me how they were beguiled,
Driven out, and compelled to the chaste.

I went to the Garden of Love,
And saw what I never had seen;
A Chapel was built in the midst,
Where I used to play on the green.

And the gates of this Chapel were shut,
And 'Thou shalt not' writ over the door;
So I turned to the Garden of Love
That so many sweet flowers bore.

And I saw it was filled with graves,
And tombstones where flowers should be;
And Priests in black gowns were walking their rounds,
And binding with briars my joys & desires.

William Blake (1757–1827)

BUTTERFLY ON A WHEEL

THE GREAT ROLLING STONES DRUGS BUST

SIMON WELLS

OMNIBUS PRESS
London / New York / Paris / Sydney / Copenhagen / Berlin / Madrid / Tokyo

Copyright © 2011 Omnibus Press
(A Division of Music Sales Limited)

Cover designed by Fresh Lemon
Picture research by Jacqui Black & Simon Wells

ISBN: 978.1.84938.995.2
Order No: OP54043

The Author hereby asserts his right to be identified as the author of this work in accordance with Sections 77 to 78 of the Copyright, Designs and Patents Act 1988.

All rights reserved. No part of this book may be reproduced in any form or by any electronic or mechanical means, including information storage or retrieval systems, without permission in writing from the publisher, except by a reviewer who may quote brief passages.

Exclusive Distributors
Music Sales Limited,
14/15 Berners Street,
London, W1T 3LJ.

Music Sales Corporation,
257 Park Avenue South,
New York, NY 10010, USA.

Macmillan Distribution Services,
56 Parkwest Drive
Derrimut, Vic 3030,
Australia.

Every effort has been made to trace the copyright holders of the photographs in this book but one or two were unreachable. We would be grateful if the photographers concerned would contact us.

Extracts from the diaries of the late Sir Cecil Beaton used by kind permission of his Literary Executors and Rupert Crew Ltd. All rights reserved.

'Rainy Day Women #12 & 35'. Words & Music by Bob Dylan. © Copyright 1966, 1994 Dwarf Music. All rights reserved. International copyright secured.

'Butterfly On A Wheel' *The Times* article. © New International. Used by kind permission.

Typeset by Phoenix Photosetting, Chatham, Kent
Printed in the E.U.

A catalogue record for this book is available from the British Library.

Visit Omnibus Press on the web at www.omnibuspress.com

Contents

For Louisa – who put up with me during all of this

Introduction

"Who breaks a butterfly upon a wheel?
Yet let me flap this bug with gilded wings,
This painted child of dirt that stinks and stings;
Whose buzz the witty and the fair annoys,
Yet wit ne'er tastes, and beauty ne'r enjoys"
From Alexander Pope's *Epistle To Dr Arbuthnot*, 1735

With the 21st century more than a decade old, I find it strange that certain expressions of freedom still manage to provoke shock and outrage. While racial, sexual and gender rights have all been fully absorbed into the mainstream, there remains a large degree of uncertainty concerning recreational drug use. Add celebrities into the mix – especially pop stars – and the issue is elevated to hysterical levels.

In the last few years, the drug-related antics of Amy Winehouse, Boy George, Pete Doherty and, most recently, George Michael, have yet again highlighted the vexed subject of narcotic use by prominent pop musicians. Predictably, the crusty British right-wing press continues to act as moral arbitrator and lord high executioner. Though other world events clearly merit far greater coverage, it seems incongruous that methods of personal intoxication that are legal in other countries still receive so much column space in Britain.

Creativity and narcotic use have been intertwined for centuries, but during the mid-sixties a series of events in Britain raised the issue of drugs in the pop world to new and greater heights. Without doubt, the most famous of these cases was the trial and subsequent jailing in 1967 of Mick Jagger and Keith Richards of The Rolling Stones.

The case was the *cause celebre* of its era, raising issues of far greater significance than the simple possession of a bit of pot and a few pep pills. For several months it seemed that the entire establishment of Great Britain had taken up arms against the young, as represented by the singer and guitarist in the second most popular pop group in the land. The saga dominated popular opinion throughout 1967, prompting a fierce public debate over drug use and the laws that were meant to regulate it. Furthermore, it revived the old chestnut of the special responsibility that entertainers supposedly have with regard to the example they set to their audience. For the generation that remembered the war and stood to attention when the National Anthem was played in cinemas, the realisation that the nation's youth preferred pop stars as role models instead of army generals and navy admirals was deeply unsettling.

Equally disturbing to them was the popular revival of narcotics, notably LSD and marijuana. While previous generations had come to rely on tobacco and alcohol to soothe their traumas, recreational drugs (especially psychedelics) were becoming the binding agent that drove the sixties' creative explosion. A pioneering sense of discovery was abroad; from London to San Francisco, from Amsterdam to Paris, and those under the age of 25 challenged all that had gone before with a carefree audacity. The brilliant popular music that the period produced acted not just as a soundtrack to these cultural changes but also as a unifying factor.

Hence, whether they liked it or not, both The Beatles and The Rolling Stones found themselves as *de facto* leaders of this new movement. The Beatles, the first to cross the parapets, were obliged to adopt a clean if slightly cheeky image to progress but, the bridgehead having been established, The Rolling Stones were able to assume a different stance, anarchic and unconventional. Their music, too, had a whiff of danger, unpredictability and sex.

Behind this hyperbole, singer Mick Jagger presented a massive dichotomy; his rebelliousness was underpinned by a sharp intelligence. Guitarist Keith Richards' image was more definable, the embodiment of sneering dissent. More complex was founder member Brian Jones, a damaged Adonis forever running from anything that attempted to confine him. No less important were Bill Wyman and Charlie Watts, two necessary anchors holding their frighteningly disparate front line together.

Manager Andrew Loog Oldham's ambition to create a musical version of Frankenstein's monster certainly succeeded, pulling in a legion of youngsters looking for a sharper edge than the Merseyside groups who followed The Beatles example. In reality, of course, The Beatles were swearing, indulging in athletic sex and experimenting with drugs on a par with the Stones, but manager Brian Epstein's water-tight management and cosy relationship with the press ensured that his charges' shiny image was maintained as long as he drew breath. Oldham, meanwhile, portrayed his charges as having been dragged up from the gutter, a fabrication that was rewarded with copious column inches but which would come at a heavy price.

While Epstein was doubtless horrified at the negative publicity the Stones generated, huge swathes of British youth were unconvinced by The Beatles' sugar-coated manifesto of joy and celebration. Similarly, Britain's optimistic revival masked the nation's deep disquiet. The mods and rockers riots of 1964 served only to highlight the brutality of British working-class existence, a landscape where ballroom brawls and gangland violence loomed nationwide. Given their notoriety, the Stones were an obvious figurehead for this dissent and as a result riots accompanied their performances up and down the country. This would later spread through Europe and America, where the Stones' anarchic reputation was fast being cemented.

As the Stones' success took hold their music began to outgrow its primitive rhythm and blues structure. Led by songwriters Jagger and Richards, the group steered themselves easily through the shallow amateurism of the early sixties beat boom. By the tail end of 1964 and with Mersey Mania a tired phenomenon, the more creative musicians were looking beyond three-minute pop tunes towards something more challenging. The Stones – much like The Beatles – were at the forefront of this. Meanwhile, drugs were entering the scene, with a major amphetamine craze running in tandem with the growing interest in marijuana.

By 1966, the Stones had notched up six UK Top 10 singles and three chart albums. An intense schedule of touring had assured their ascendancy in Europe, securing for them a treasure chest of riches in the wine, women and song department that any young man would envy. A retreat from the road late in the year allowed for more creativity in the studio, all of it abetted by LSD and other mind-expanding drugs that blew open the narrow corridors of perception. The impact of acid was widespread, prompting a sea change in attitudes, fashion and direction.

This turn into left-field found many wondering what had occurred. While The Beatles and Stones grinned down from countless bedroom walls, there was little inkling what lay behind the glassy eyes and manic grins of their heroes. To the stars themselves, it was no one else's business, and while everyone in the industry was aware it went on, remarkably, prior to 1966 nobody saw fit to leak the news. As a result, the groups enjoyed a false sense of security, never believing for a second that their personal habits were being monitored by the forces of law and order.

By late 1966, talk of drug use by the nation's musicians was far too tempting to ignore. The *News Of The World*'s decision to blow the lid off this private party kick-started a series of events that led to a global reassessment of recreational drug use. The paper's series of articles, starting at the beginning of 1967, became one of the most famous exposés of celebrity behaviour of the 20th century. Headlined 'Pop Stars and Drugs – Facts That Will Shock You', the tabloid revealed the drug habits of unsuspecting musicians that had until then been kept strictly behind closed doors.

For the most part, the revelations paid deference to the popularity of the musicians, and although The Beatles were referenced, the articles never went as far as revealing that they took drugs. Fair game, though, were the likes of The Moody Blues, The Who, Donovan, The Move and, on February 5, 1967, Mick Jagger.

As a result of the paper's erroneous exposé of Jagger, a chain of events was set in motion that resulted in 18 police officers raiding Keith Richards' country home in Sussex on the evening of February 12. It was the first notable strike against pop's non-conformists, and while it was abundantly clear that the information fed to police came from the *News Of The World*, others believed there was a wider collusion, that this raid was an unequivocal directive from an establishment determined to pummel the Stones for their decadent behaviour and the example they were setting to the nation's youth.

The shock waves from the raid sent a wave of fear through British pop's tight-knit community. As tales of an undercover agent infiltrating the guest lists gathered momentum, London's party circle tightened and doors closed in the faces of the uninvited. With fingers pointing, a Kray Twins associate charged with determining who had tipped off the police brutally confronted one of the Redlands' attendees. Elsewhere, another shady character from the Stones' circle attempted to bribe a policeman to interfere with incriminating evidence. With these and other – more legitimate – acts being undertaken, it was obvious that every effort was being made to prevent the Rolling Stones from standing in the dock.

The trial of Mick Jagger and Keith Richards on drugs charges took place over a few sunny days in June 1967, during which the world's media witnessed a defining moment in history, the sight of two young celebrities lined up for summary execution. Sitting in judgement of them was a true bastion of the British establishment, Judge Leslie Block, whose understanding of and sympathy with pop culture could be measured in hundredths of milligrams. Clearly relishing the moment and with the world's press on hand to record every nuance of the trial, Block strutted his stuff before a retinue of landowners, local conservatives and forelock-tuggers, finally emerging as infamous as the two Rolling Stones themselves.

The summary prison sentences Block handed down to the two Stones provoked an avalanche of reaction from all quarters of British society. The publication of harrowing photographs showing the pair being driven to jail in handcuffs caused a wave of outrage across the land. Letters poured into newspapers, some in support of the jailing, others expressing deep unease at how two entertainers could be treated in such a fashion. Broadsheets hitherto uninterested in pop published thoughtful editorials on a saga fast enveloping the entire country. When their role in the story became known, the offices of the *News Of The World* were picketed for three nights in retaliation at what was evidently a stitch-up.

The most erudite opponent of the jail sentences was *The Times* newspaper. On July 1, its then editor, William Rees-Mogg, wrote one of the 20th century's most celebrated and impassioned editorials, challenging what he saw as exemplary treatment, likening Mick Jagger's fate to that of "breaking a butterfly on a wheel", a line borrowed from Alexander Pope's 1735 poem, *Epistle To Dr Arbuthnot.*

For a few weeks over the summer of 1967, the divide between opposing factions on the subject appeared unbridgeable. Recreational drug use was the issue and Paul McCartney's lively admission that he had taken LSD fanned the flames even more. While a few like-minded souls admired McCartney's honesty, it ensured that anyone in the pop business was likely to be scrutinised. This prompted an erudite group of cannabis sympathisers to call for the immediate decriminalisation of the drug, and with the reluctant assistance of Rees-Mogg, a full-page advertisement to this effect was placed in *The Times* during July.

The power of the advert was in the impeccable credentials of those that signed up to the cause. While the scientists and doctors on the list were known only within their profession, the names of all four Beatles and their manager Brian Epstein elevated interest globally. At the time Jagger and Richards were in the process of appealing against their convictions, and they wisely kept quiet on the issue although it was never in any doubt whose side they were on.

To the delight of their wide circle, Jagger and Richards' case was reassessed and their jail sentences quashed. Nonetheless, the residual energy from the case remained active. In what appeared to be a desperate act of revenge by salacious rumourmongers, totally untrue and crude canards were promoted through the bush network as to the exact nature of what was occurring when the police raided Richards' house. While Mick and Keith emerged from the saga with their reputations bolstered, the party's sole female guest, Marianne Faithfull, would forevermore endure a catalogue of lies and innuendo about what happened that evening. For everyone's sake, the rumour is completely debunked within these pages, with a finger pointed at the likely source of the slur.

Equally, I have been able to determine – as best as possible – the history and movements of the now legendary David 'Acid King' Schneiderman. Forever cast as *agent provocateur* of the Redlands saga, he has been the subject of considerable speculation in the four decades that have passed since the raid. With the help of unseen documents, photographs and assistance from some of his contacts, a broader picture of one of the sixties' most elusive personalities has finally been realised.

The close of the decade saw Jagger, Faithfull and Brian Jones face a further raking across the coals from the London drug squad. All of these raids left many unanswered questions, and caused considerable discomfort for those involved. While it is likely they were, in all probability, indulging in certain substances, the entrapment tactics utilised to bring the subjects to book points not just to malpractice but a vendetta against rock's premier practitioners.

Offering little respite, the death of Jones, the Altamont festival debacle and a catalogue of drug busts exhausted the inner circle of the Stones to the core. Personal issues, too, ensured the period would not be easily forgotten. Where others had been eager to wax lyrical about the era of peace, love, bells and flowers, it would take a long time for those intimately involved with the Stones to start re-assessing the sixties more favourably.

To try and present as correct a picture as possible of this remarkable time, I have steered clear of much of the received wisdom concerning both the Stones and the mythology of the sixties. While I have had the benefit of accessing numerous unpublished interviews and previously unseen documents, I have ignored the more sensational material unless it is absolutely relevant to the story. Despite their larger than life personas, the fact is that the protagonists of the story are human beings, and subject to the same feelings and emotions as the rest of us.

With the appeal of the sixties continually in vogue, it is of little surprise to me that a film is being prepared to dramatise the extraordinary events that engulfed Jagger and Richards in 1967. It's a timely proposition, and with today's pop stars still careful about what inspires their most creative moments, this remarkable period serves only to remind us of the need for understanding between authority and creativity. Forty years on, as the headlines of the tabloids still attest, drugs and pop stars remains an issue that provokes a lot of hot air. Similarly, the antics of some journalists remain as questionable as they were back in the sixties.

So let me take you back to a time when 'pop' music was still considered a passing fad, when Britain had only three black and white TV channels and the idea of mobile phones, satellite navigation and the Internet was stuff for sci-fi movies. It's a fascinating, energetic period and to this day we are still in awe of just how extraordinary it all was.

Simon Wells
Sussex, England, June 2011

CHAPTER 1

Dartford

"For many people, the 1960's ended in 1967... In 1967 the public started taking drugs, and it changed from being a quasi-private club; the whole world totally changed. There was another part of the revolution... suddenly we were not going to go away. In 1967, you still got Ken Dodd and Engelbert Humperdinck in the charts. So for the old guard there was a lot of hope that like Hula Hoops and Davy Crockett hats we would disappear and life would get back to Mantovani."

Rolling Stones manager Andrew Loog Oldham, 2007

The sixties. It's become a buzzword for unbridled fun, frivolity and a joyous optimism rarely witnessed in modern times. You will see it continually referenced in the popular media as a jolly, slightly potty time where seemingly everyone smiled, everybody appeared to hug each other and where young people especially enjoyed a new sense of liberation.

While it's more than apparent that the decade witnessed an enormous creative explosion, the era was equally pitted with poverty, war and famine, the likes of which tested the mettle of everyone involved. Equally, with the Second World War just a generation behind, the associated fall-out was still being felt in every corner of the United Kingdom. Nonetheless, a desire to change was in the air. However hard the nation's elders fought against it, the power base was shifting. With those under the age of 21 enjoying a sense of release, new freedoms were on the horizon.

Fads from Davy Crockett to hula hoops were shipped across from the States during the fifties and early sixties, but it was the beat boom of 1963 that arrested large swathes of Britain's youth. Irrespective of class, creed or colour, this first sizeable home-grown movement inspired many to reject their elders' prescribed attitudes, replacing them with a new sense of urgency and passion.

The Beatles' emergence onto the scene in 1963 both popularised and polarised this renewed sense of discovery. Whether they were aware of it or not, their music and cheeky grins offered a much needed antidote to the depression that had seemingly dressed every chapter of British life. In the Beatles' slipstream came a legion of others, all sharing in this new wave of excitement, all desperate to secure a slice of the fame and wealth the Fab Four were accruing after many years of effort.

While these lads from Liverpool re-branded their modest Merseyside beginnings into something romantic, The Rolling Stones' roots were less colourful, steeped in the cold, post-war modernity of the urban sprawl where London gives way to the county of Kent. With its overtly flat landscape matched by awkward place-names such as Thurrock, Bexley and Rochester, the band's chief protagonists, Mick Jagger and Keith Richards took their first steps in Dartford, situated some 20 miles south east of central London. With industrialism a solid bedrock of Dartford's history, there was little to convince an imaginative child growing up in the fifties of any great desire to stay put.

Nonetheless, despite the area's unremarkable atmosphere, Mick Jagger's respectable parentage elevated family life above what passed for the norm. His father Basil was a fitness teacher, whose army training had stood him in good stead for equipping youngsters in the locale with a structured PE regime. Known by his more palatable moniker Joe, Jagger senior had gained some minor celebrity through this unique brand of physical training, a trade he'd pass on to PE teachers worldwide.

Jagger's mother, Eva, was the epitome of a post-war housewife. Born in Australia and a hairdresser by trade, on the arrival of her two boys

Michael and Christopher she assumed a genial, yet matriarchal role in the household. With her husband's comfortable wage, the family enjoyed a rare sense of affluence denied to many in post-war Britain.

Born July 26, 1943, Michael Philip Jagger flourished under his parents' structured conventionality. With such a solid background, the youngster took well to academia, gravitating easily through the mandatory 11-plus to grammar school. With the Jagger household's all-encompassing interest in sport, he soon became absorbed in outdoor pursuits, especially cricket, a passion he'd maintain throughout his life.

If the crack of leather against willow would always bring a warm smile to Jagger's unusually fleshy lips, louder vibrations would serve to distract him as he approached his teenage years. Having passed his 11-plus exam with ease, Jagger's studies would take second best to the untutored, home-grown sound of skiffle music. With nothing other than the warbling of the likes of Johnny Ray and Sinatra to ignite teenagers, skiffle's thrown-together cult attracted huge rafts of British teenagers, all keen to emulate Lonnie Donegan, Britain's first garage-band star.

As quickly as it arrived, skiffle would give way to the more primal sonics of rock'n'roll. Though Bill Haley's reserved presence, generous girth and indeterminate age had alienated suspicious teenagers, Buddy Holly's shaky vocals and modest chord structures would prompt many pretenders to pick up a guitar. Engaged on interminable touring jaunts around the world, Holly would visit Britain in 1958, and though the nearest he came to Dartford was Croydon on March 12, his easygoing confidence and catchy blend of rockabilly and pop, not to mention his hitherto unseen solid-bodied Fender Stratocaster guitar, ignited the ambitions of suburban teenagers.

While paying deference to his studies, rock'n'roll's attendant culture of non-conformity certainly appealed to Jagger, who was quick to see the considerable gains to be made among his peers by buying into the craze. More unusual than attractive, the youngster compensated for his looks by adopting the fashion of the period, a dress sense designed to interest the fairer sex. As part of his teenage metamorphosis, the slightly conservative name Michael would give way to Mike. The cooler inversion of Mick would come a little later.

With the new movement indiscriminate of age or colour, rock'n'roll would act as a Trojan horse to usher in a variety of genres; some new, others already decades old. While Little Richard, Fats Domino and Elvis Presley encompassed all styles in their bid for popularity, the more discerning ear would gravitate towards the blues from America's Midwest upon which rock'n'roll was based, and in the process popularise the likes of Howlin' Wolf, John Lee Hooker and Muddy Waters.

One unashamed blues aficionado studying with Jagger at Dartford Grammar School was Dick Taylor. Though light years ahead of his peers in this regard, he formed an alliance with Jagger. "When we first met, rock'n'roll had had its first outburst, and was getting a little bit tame around the edges," says Taylor. "I was into jazz and blues and things like that, and then we discovered what was then called rhythm and blues, which was really sort of urban blues more like Muddy Waters and Elmore James and then Chuck Berry. Every time a new Chuck Berry record came out, you'd get an import or whatever. I mean we all would, all the trio or quartet of us at grammar school who were really into that sort of music."

With the blues movement calling on its listeners to engage beyond just listening, Taylor and Jagger gravitated beyond the predictable miming to attempt something approaching a sound. Meeting at each other's houses, and with several simpatico friends in on the vibe, they'd run through a few perfunctory musical steps. Rarely venturing out of the safety of the living room, they would occasionally tape their jam sessions, all the while dreaming of the sort of success that others were enjoying on TV and the radio. In honour of their fascination with the blues, the loose ensemble would name themselves 'Little Boy Blue & The Blue Boys', a pseudonym once employed by blues legend, Sonny Boy Williamson. 'Little Boy Blue' was also the name of a song by another early influence, Bobby 'Blue' Bland.

Despite these distractions and the lure of non-conformity stirred by the blues, Jagger and Taylor's academic performances at grammar school were good enough to see them transfer to higher education. Dick Taylor's more artistic bent led him to the nearby Sidcup Art College while Jagger, his sharp acumen suggesting a career in business, won a place at the London School of Economics, a prestigious achievement. It was a college with a tradition of politicising its students and while there Jagger would absorb a degree of radicalism or, at least, learn about left wing causes that were foreign to his upbringing. To embellish his hip credentials, it was here that Michael Jagger became Mick, the sharpened moniker defining his style for the rest of his life.

In pursuit of his studies, Jagger merged with hordes of commuters each morning on the 30-minute journey into London. On the train one morning in late 1961 was another Dartford teenager, Keith Richards, whom Jagger recognised from their time together at primary school. Although they'd grown up not far from each other, no friendship had ever developed, probably because Richards was from much more mundane stock than the Jaggers. An only child, he was born on December 18, 1943, and his family, like many of the post-war era, had been shunted into housing deemed suitable for the working classes. While Richards would later refer to their accommodation as "a fucking soul-destroying council estate", inside it was a warm and supportive unit; Keith's parents, Bert and Doris, clearly doting over their only son.

Richards' first steps in education were at Dartford's Wentworth Primary School. There, he'd mix with many of the area's pre-pubescent girls and boys, Michael Jagger amongst them, and attain a slight celebrity for his wacky, offbeat persona. Jagger remembered this young outsider, whose only desire in life it seemed was to be a cowboy. While they lived a stone's throw away from each other, their respective backgrounds denied them any sustained friendship.

Whatever interest Keith Richards ever displayed in academia and sport soon gave way to the all-consuming charms of music. As a child he'd enjoyed singing and was possessed with an angelic treble that saw him join his school choir which performed outside concerts when the occasion demanded. As a result, Keith would sing in such hallowed places as London's Royal Albert Hall, The Royal Festival Hall and, later, singing Handel's *Messiah* in front of the newly crowned Queen Elizabeth II at Westminster Abbey.

Puberty would rob Keith of his more dulcet tones, and with little else to distract him he'd fall hook, line and sinker for rock'n'roll, a diversion wholly encouraged by his grandmother, herself once a touring jazz musician. His mother too, would often fill the house with the music of Ella Fitzgerald, Billie Holiday and the Big Band music that was popular at the time. In this environment his immersion in rock'n'roll was wholeheartedly encouraged.

"In my mind the world went from black and white and into Technicolor," recalled Richards to the BBC in 2010. "There was a spark. Suddenly I heard this music from out of nowhere. It was as though everything had come into focus, and that's all you wanted to do."

Keith was simply swept up by it. His singing now took second place to a fascination with the guitar playing of Scotty Moore, who accompanied Elvis, and his greatest inspiration, Chuck Berry. The overwhelming attraction he felt for the sound of the instrument motivated Keith to pick up a guitar, an accoutrement that would rarely be less than a few feet from him for the remainder of his life.

With Keith's academic prowess insufficient to allow a transfer to grammar school, he ambled his way through the sub-division of technical college. With little interest in his studies, he was excluded for wilful absenteeism, and since gainful employment was unappealing, he opted to retrieve some semblance of an education at the nearby Sidcup Art College.

While Richards didn't know it at the time, Britain's art colleges were fast becoming a *de facto* breeding ground for many of the subsequent musical stars of the sixties. John Lennon, Pete Townshend, Ray Davies, David Bowie, Charlie Watts and Jimmy Page all worked their way through the system, the attendant freedom afforded at these institutions a vital component in germinating ideas and attitudes. Ironically, many of these, much like Richards, were also tapping into the sounds of the dispossessed from the Mississippi Delta.

Though Keith's interest in art was minimal compared to his overwhelming fascination with music, he would come into contact with a few like-minded souls at college. Coincidently, Jagger's musical sparring partner Dick Taylor was also studying at Sidcup, and considering a parallel career in art and music. He'd noted Richards' outlandish dress sense, and with music a binding component, the pair soon became buddies.

The typically lax timetable at college enabled them to supplement their studies with all manner of distractions around Dartford's otherwise drab environs. While rarely discussed, there was a modicum of drug use among Britain's youth during the fifties, but acquiring these substances required a fair amount of inventiveness, as Taylor recalled to Victor Bockris in 1992: "In order to stay up late with our music and still get to Sidcup in the morning, Keith and I were on a steady diet of pills, which not only kept us up, but gave us a lift. We took all kinds of things – pills girls took for menstruation, inhalers like Nostrilene and other stuff."

Attendance at college was expected, if not always maintained, and the most convenient transport to college was by train. The route to Sidcup fed the same line that took Jagger into central London, and so it was that Jagger and Richards recognised each other across a busy carriage. As fortune would have it, Jagger was carrying two highly desirable records with him: *Rockin' At The Hops* by Chuck Berry and *The Best Of Muddy Waters*. With his tutored sense of acquisition, Jagger had acquired these albums by mail order from Chess Records' base in Chicago. With these rare slabs of imported vinyl a point of mutual interest, the pair got talking.

"At the time there was a certain recognition suddenly between Mick and myself in that railway carriage," Richards would recount in 2010. "Something had brought us to a point of burning interest which was basically the blues, with rock'n'roll thrown in… I think it was kind of a shock to suddenly find that we were both into this music at the same time, and the fact that we should happen to meet again out of nowhere… And so from there, it went on."

Having discovered their mutual fondness for the blues, the conversation soon moved on to their own abilities; Jagger revealing his occasional involvement in a local, primitive blues unit and Keith mentioning his own guitar playing. As discussion mulled over the dearth of musicians into the same music, it soon transpired they had a mutual friend in roving guitarist Dick Taylor, and since Taylor had jammed independently with both Jagger and Richards, an alliance of talents was mooted. To Taylor's sharply honed senses, Mick and Keith's broader approach would lend the unit an extra dimension, adding doses of Chuck Berry, Buddy Holly and Elvis Presley into the mix.

It was while their jam sessions were taking on a greater urgency that word came through of a club exclusively dedicated to blues that was opening in Ealing in west London. The club's innovator was called Alexis Korner, born in Paris of Austrian and Greek parentage with an encyclopaedic knowledge of the genre and a performer of some repute. With interest in British blues barely operating above the level of cult, Korner had become a beacon for its appreciation in the UK. Along with his musical partner Cyril Davies, he had been enlivening trad nights in jazz clubs with blues covers. Playing support slots with the likes of Chris Barber and Acker Bilk, Korner and Davies had followed in the slipstream of jazz around the country. Nonetheless, despite the exposure afforded, Korner hankered for greater exposure, not just for himself and Davies but for the blues in general.

National radio in the UK in the early sixties was limited to the BBC whose Light Programme, its 'popular' music outlet, broadcast only what today can best be described as 'easy listening'. Blues, as foreign to the BBC's programmers in 1960 as punk was 15 years later, could be heard only by those lucky to have imported vinyl, or who ventured into Korner's orbit. In early 1962, weary of the intransigent machinations of the West End jazz and skiffle cartels, Korner was granted permission to host a dedicated blues night at the Ealing Jazz Club in basement premises opposite Ealing Broadway station. In tandem with this venture, Korner formed Blues Incorporated, a loose ensemble of like-minded musicians, its revolving membership reflecting the world of jazz. In time, the likes of Ginger Baker, Jack Bruce, Cyril Davies, Graham Bond and a drummer named Charlie Watts would pass through its ranks.

To promote Korner's club night, an advert was placed in *New Musical Express*, the UK's weekly Bible for fans. Propelled by the opportunity to engage with the modest blues explosion, Jagger, Richards and Dick Taylor sent a crude rehearsal tape to Korner for consideration and though it was returned with a polite deferral, the lads were inspired to make the 20-odd mile trip from Dartford to Ealing to witness blues in the raw.

Dick Taylor: "We saw that Alexis Korner was playing in the Ealing Club and we bundled in Mick's dad's car and went down there... We saw Alexis Korner, and were very impressed for a couple of weeks, and then with all the sort of cockiness of youth we said, 'Oh, we can do this. We could be up there!'"

A sense of camaraderie pervaded the club. As a result, anyone who wanted to share in the action could, with enough bluff, work their way onto the stage. In time, Jagger, Richards and Dick Taylor would all shamble up there, with Jagger's untutored, otherworldly swagger drawing most interest. He soon became one of the preferred vocalists in the Blues Incorporated roster, enlivening his vocal delivery with maracas, tambourine and occasional harmonica.

A multitude of other pretenders also appeared on the Ealing stage; some good, others simply eager to engage in the communal atmosphere. On April 7, three weeks after it had opened, one 'Elmore Jones' ventured on stage, augmenting a young singer on slide guitar. Watching him that night was Taylor, Richards and Jagger. Behind the pseudonym was Brian Jones, the applied moniker just one of a multitude of reasons to escape his past.

Born February 28, 1942, Jones' background was light years away from the dingy environs of Korner's basement dive. Brian's family were from Cheltenham, a genteel spa town enclave around 100 miles west of London. His parents were fairly atypical for the area; father Lewis an aeronautical engineer, mother Louisa a housewife and piano teacher. In tandem with his studies, Jones acquired a parallel interest in music, learning classical piano from his mother and then joining the school orchestra as a clarinet player. As puberty hit, a complex individuality began to assert itself. Like other curious souls of his generation, Brian had taken solace firstly in trad jazz and then in the blues, its mournful lyrics and cold sound resonating with unfulfilled ambition, repression and unrequited love. Jones soon took to playing the guitar, as well as the harmonica and saxophone.

Despite his musical aspirations, Jones had other reasons for escaping Cheltenham. His freely shared affections had already led him to father two children in the town. The first of these dalliances with a 14 year old had made the national press, and although the names of Brian and his conquest were never publicly revealed, he gained an undesirable reputation around Cheltenham. Brian's unpredictable personality had hardly endeared him to his peer group; his mercurial persona revolving from angelic cherub one minute to loathsome creep the next. Adding to this dichotomy, he excelled in his studies yet despised the conventions of schooling. Despite his sharp intelligence, he was drawn to more instinctive passions, allowing his academic studies to slip. With this complex array of issues, Jones was regularly threatened with expulsion from grammar school.

With Brian Jones' name referenced in dismissive tones around stuffy Cheltenham, his father arranged for him to move to London to take up a position with an optician. It was short-lived and he returned home to skulk around at a friend's flat before raising enough money to go on a hitchhiking holiday to Scandinavia where he hoped to broaden his knowledge of the fairer sex. Back in Cheltenham, music became his most sustained pursuit, his dedication winning him a parochial celebrity among his peers. Just when his musical aspirations hit stalemate, a chance encounter changed his life forever.

Such was the demand for trad jazz in the provinces that established acts such as Chris Barber and Kenny Ball could find a plentiful supply of work outside London. During December 1961, Barber's touring caravan was playing a gig at Cheltenham's Town Hall. While Alexis Korner and Cyril Davies playing blues between sets might have alienated a few of the purists, 19-year-old outsider Brian Jones was clearly enchanted by what he heard.

Following Korner and Davies' performance, Jones cornered Alexis at a bar close to the venue. There, he poured out his love for the music they had just played. Suitably intrigued by the young man's broad knowledge of their shared passion, Korner said that if Brian happened to be in London he should drop by and touch base and mentioned the possibilities within the burgeoning scene.

Aware that the 100-odd mile trip would incur a night in the capital, Korner offered floor space at his west London flat. This was entirely in character for Alexis, as he and his wife Bobbie were renowned for providing emergency accommodation for disposed musicians enchanted by the blues. High on the possibilities of escape from the stifling constraints of Cheltenham, Jones made the trip down to London during January 1962, lodging at Korner's flat for a few days. Smitten by everything the capital had to offer, he began visiting London frequently, all the while dreaming of forming his own blues group. In pursuit of determining the right personnel, he travelled around the South East looking for musicians, scanning the music press for any available action, and eventually came across an Oxford-based blues aficionado, singer Paul Pond. Later to become Paul Jones, the lead singer of hit R&B ensemble Manfred Mann, Brian was impressed by Pond's throaty delivery that belied his age.

It was a formality that Brian would get wind of Alexis Korner's dedicated blues venue in Ealing. Jones cobbled together a tape and sent it to Korner with a letter reminding him of their past meetings. With no definite response forthcoming, and with nothing to keep him in Cheltenham, Jones and Paul Pond attended several Sunday sessions at the club, and their persistence led Korner to grant the pair a slot in between Blues Incorporated sets on April 7.

Jones' unique style and presence certainly captivated the three youngsters from Dartford. "We were very impressed with Brian's slide playing," recounts Dick Taylor. "He was playing proper slide guitar. He had a Martin acoustic with a pick-up on it and it just sounded so good. We went and chatted to him and that's how it all started."

Paul Pond was evidently chasing a broader direction than pure blues, and when an opportunity arose to join a dance band in Slough he split with Jones who persisted in his ambitions, setting up an audition that brought together a few of the Ealing Club regulars. Others arrived via an advertisement in *Jazz News* on May 2. The auditions took place at an upstairs room in the Bricklayers Arms pub in London's Soho where the rent for the room was just 10 shillings (50 pence).

Keith Richards, his guitar skills duly noted by Jones, was invited to attend. Jagger and Dick Taylor came along as guests of Keith, both keen to engage in the proceedings. Another hopeful was boogie-woogie pianist Ian Stewart. The event resulted in the formation of Jones' new unit, and much like Blues Incorporated, it would feature revolving personnel. In the weeks following the audition, rehearsals would continue in Soho and elsewhere.

As was Brian's style, he had a serious falling out with two other members of his embryonic group, thus allowing Jagger and Taylor to fill the void. Jagger, his involvement with studies at LSE and with Blues Incorporated heavily dividing his time, would utilise these rehearsals to broaden his style. Whereas Korner's unit was strictly blues based, the more disparate entities in Brian's outfit allowed a morphing of styles. Permanent drummers were a rare commodity in London, and a handful of journeymen percussionists would attempt to anchor the band's sound, among them future Kink Mick Avory.

Though Brian's self-appointed leadership status went unchallenged, it was Jagger who first heard that due to a more pressing radio commitment Korner's Blues Incorporated had pulled out of a gig at London's Marquee Club. While Jagger's involvement with Korner's unit was peripatetic, the BBC's stipulation that they could accommodate only five members of the band ensured that he would not be required for the BBC session. The Marquee gig was handed over to another Ealing luminary, the lanky Long John Baldry, but the club's manager offered Jones' as yet untitled ensemble a support slot. Seizing the opportunity, the band grabbed the vacancy. The date for this historic moment in rock history was July 12, 1962.

Jones' scratch band was still without a name when an inspired choice came quite by chance. Eager to assert his impresario status, Brian took out an advert in *Jazz News* to publicise the Marquee gig and, requiring a name for the copy editor, he chanced upon a copy of a 1948 Muddy Waters album lying around his flat. The track 'Rollin' Stone' leapt out from the sleeve, so Jones swiftly appropriated it as a suitable name for the band's first gig. With this deft piece of synchronicity the name Rollin' Stones, albeit slightly truncated, was born.

Not surprisingly, the Marquee Club date was approached with a mixture of excitement and trepidation. Mick, Keith, Brian (as 'Elmore Jones') made up the frontline, while Ian Stewart on piano, Dick Taylor on bass and occasional drummer Tony Chapman formed the backline. With a blunt infusion of blues, rock'n'roll and nervous energy, it wasn't surprising that the group managed to affront some of the jazz purists present in the club.

Dick Taylor: "I remember the audience reaction was kind of mixed because I think there were a few people there who wanted to hear proper blues. I think there were quite a few people who really enjoyed it, but there were also people who were shouting, 'Play proper blues'. We certainly all got quite a buzz out of it. I know the cleaner didn't like it, she said, 'They'll never get anywhere.'"

Despite Taylor's recollections, it appeared that the Marquee's management weren't entirely in simpatico with the group's abrasive sound and presence. Although there were a couple of further gigs at the club, things turned sour when Keith accosted the manager with his guitar following comments about their appearance. Nonetheless, despite the Marquee episode gigs elsewhere started to trickle in. Booked and steered by Brian Jones, the rewards were minuscule, and yet such was the excitement at playing live, there was no desire to check Jones' creative bookkeeping.

With the need for a dedicated London base overriding dismal mornings spent on the Dartford commuter train, Mick found a two-room flat at 102 Edith Grove in Chelsea. It was situated at the less fashionable Earl's Court end of the King's Road where during the early sixties the big three and four-storey houses on either side had been converted into less than salubrious flats, all occupied by the flotsam and jetsam of London's bedsitter brigade. While students from nearby Chelsea Art College enjoyed the peppercorn rents, a legion of west London beatniks and itinerants were engaging in their version of Bohemia.

Though music was all-consuming, additional income was required to prop up the scant returns from gigging. Mick eked out what he could from his student grant while Keith had more or less waved goodbye to his Sidcup Art School ambitions, spending daylight hours strumming guitar and monitoring the rats that shared living space in the flat. Meanwhile Brian maintained his Kensington flat and had a job at Whiteleys department store in Bayswater, even though he spent the majority of his off-duty hours at Edith Grove. Jones' position at the department store would soon be terminated following irregularities in his till, and he'd find himself at home for most of the day. He'd been joined in London by Pat Andrews and her baby Mark, the result of another of Jones' flings back in Cheltenham. Andrews arrived in London hoping to raise the child with its father, and would endure Jones' mercurial and largely selfish behaviour for the best part of a year.

The situation at home ensured that Brian would travel over to Edith Grove most days. With Keith the only tenant present in the flat during the day, in between jamming, the pair cooked up scams to raise much needed finance. When he couldn't afford to pay his lodgings, Jones moved into the flat with Mick and Keith. With Jagger studying during the day, the unique cross-ply of Richards' and Jones' hugely idiosyncratic talents began to gel.

Housework was ignored. Despite its Chelsea location, the flat was typical of squalid bedsitter-land, with dirt and dust everywhere, its surfaces overrun with the detritus from occasional meals. To amuse themselves, Keith and Brian cheekily ran a microphone from a reel-to-reel tape recorder to the communal toilet, playing back the results to enliven the boredom. When their meagre funds dried up, they'd relieve their fellow tenants of a few essentials to eat. On other occasions, they'd exist from emergency rations sent up by Keith's mother Doris.

Despite talk of greater things, like all bands without a record contract securing gigs was the primary objective. With Britain's pop music tastes defined by the likes of Adam Faith, Cliff Richard and Frank Ifield, a dedicated rhythm and blues unit would find work thin on the ground, leaving Brian, Mick and Keith to hunker down in the Edith Grove garret during the winter of 1962–63 that saw the biggest freeze for over 200 years.

Outside, with Britain brought to a standstill by the weather, the country was changing its focus. In January The Beatles appeared on national TV for the first time, igniting the spark that would erupt in Beatlemania by the autumn. Meanwhile, Harold Macmillan's Tory government was about to implode over the Profumo scandal that forever dispelled the age-old British tradition of deference to upper-class elders. The UK's population was at 50,290,000 during 1961, with those under the age of 19 at their highest level since records began. National Service now abandoned, this generation was not required to prepare for war, and with British youth culture referencing American fads since the mid-fifties, it was clear that an indigenous response was bound to emerge at some point.

The territory was certainly receptive for this new gestation to occur. There were over 1,500 registered venues across Britain licensed to play music, so the scope was enormous for new talent to secure work. Union and immigration laws squeezed overseas performers, increasing the demand for local talent. With radio and television largely ignoring the new media of 'beat' music, let alone rhythm and blues, a band could nonetheless accrue a considerable following by playing live.

Despite their desire for success, life for Mick, Keith and Brian under the roof at 102 Edith Grove was still far from cosy. With the onset of Christmas provoking an assessment of the band's direction, Dick Taylor announced he was leaving the group to pursue his studies at the Royal College of Art. This threw the unit into a quandary. With no permanent drummer and with Taylor's defection, the need for a permanent rhythm section was paramount. To fill the bass slot in time for a predicted rush of festive gigs, a hastily organised audition was held at The Wetherby Arms, a popular Chelsea watering hole close to the lads' Edith Grove base.

Among those who turned up to the auditions was bass player William 'Bill' Perks who, at 26, was notably older than the others. Hailing from Sydenham, south London, he'd already seen out compulsory National Service, spending time in the Royal Air Force. During his time in the services, he met a fellow conscript called Lee Wyman. Duly impressed with his stylish moniker, Perks took the surname and with it, a sizeable amount of confidence. With marriage and home ownership part and parcel of a working class lad's life, Bill settled into both, fathering a son, Stephen, in March 1962.

Emancipated from the rigours of armed service, the newly branded Wyman embarked on a career that embodied his greatest passion, music. While never gifted in the more flowery adepts of lead or rhythm guitar, Bill found his niche with the bass and, since work for London-based bass players was plentiful, had worked his way through several outfits, at one point performing backup duties for one of Larry Parnes' discoveries, Dickie Pride. His job with The Cliftons provided little in the way of excitement, but he'd heard of the Stones audition through their then drummer, Tony Clifton, and then later from pianist Ian Stewart. Both men briefed Bill on the idiosyncrasies of the group, and he arrived for the audition fairly hopeful of a new direction.

Wyman's varied stage credentials caused a minor stir as he entered the pub, as did the massive Vox bass amplifier that had to be wheeled in. His bass playing was also fairly revolutionary for the time. With the instrument held upright, Wyman slid his fingers up and down a fretless board he'd adapted. Despite Bill's seniority on age, householder and marital status, his ability on bass was enough for him to fill Dick Taylor's vacant slot.

The role of drummer remained vacant and with none of the stand-ins gelling with the band, Mick, Keith and Brian sought out 21-year-old Charlie Watts. A minor legend within London's jazz and blues circles, Watts' versatility on the kit overrode any worries some may have held over his sullen persona. He was a graphic designer by trade, and had devoured jazz since the mid-fifties, possessing an encyclopaedic knowledge of the genre. After a hectic career in designing that saw him travel over Europe, he'd realised his passion for jazz by taking up the drums and was a frequent attendee at London's basement coffee bars and other musical haunts.

Sharing duties with Blues Incorporated and occasional stints with Soho-based Blues By Six, Watts had mentioned the Stones' offer to Alexis Korner. Already invited to join Blues By Six on a permanent basis, Watts was struck by the Stones' engaging personalities and boundless enthusiasm. Encouraged by Korner's savvy prediction that the Stones were destined for greater things, Watts made the decision to go with the unknown quantity, and in the process secured his own far greater destiny.

Coinciding with Watts' arrival, an audition at the BBC came as a result of one of Brian Jones' random tape dispatches. Although the Stones duly put themselves through their paces at the audition for the top-rated *Saturday Club* radio show, the corporation took a conservative view of Jagger's pseudo Negro swagger, decreeing the sound "too coloured".

Regardless of the BBC's rejection, work was gathering momentum on the London club circuit. Most of the bookings were secured by Jones, his founder status zealously underpinning a need to maintain control. But as is the way of burgeoning success, managerial interest soon appeared in the form of an energetic promoter, Russian émigré Giorgio Gomelsky, a blues aficionado who was always keen to seek out newcomers to the genre. Aware of his dilettante exploits in film as well as music, Jones charmed Gomelsky along to a Stones gig at The Red Lion pub in Sutton on February 22, 1963.

Suitably impressed by the Stones' ragged but exhilarating sound, Gomelsky secured the group a Sunday night residency in the back room at the Station Hotel in Richmond. Inspired by his blues obsessions, Gomelsky had named his Sunday night sessions the Crawdaddy Club, in honour of Bo Diddley's rollicking tune, 'Crawdad'. A following began to gather.

Word of the group soon filtered out beyond the leafy environs of Richmond, and queues for their Sunday night appearances began to form hours before the club opened. Sean O'Mahoney, soon-to-be publisher of the musician-centric publication *Beat Instrumental,* caught wind of the buzz and made a beeline to the Station Hotel to catch the excitement.

"The sound was so very different," recalls O'Mahoney today. "I remember it was a small room at the back of a pub with a low ceiling, and it was very, very hot and everyone was sweating like a pig. The most extraordinary thing was that they were wearing sweaters which in this very hot room seemed like a mad thing to do. Those young people were really getting into the music and they all looked like they knew they were onto something new and exciting."

Local press also bought into the frenzied scenes at the Station Hotel. A feature in the *Richmond & Twickenham Times* on April 17 told of "sweating dancers and those who are slumped on the floor". Historically, it was the first significant press notice for the group. In a matter of a few weeks, others would be lining up to cover them.

The first from a bona fide music paper was Norman Jopling from *Record Mirror* whose enthusiastic report of a show in May recorded the excitement shared by both fans and group at the Crawdaddy. "The fans quickly lose their inhibitions and contort themselves to truly exciting music. Fact is that, unlike all other R&B groups worthy of the name, The

Rolling Stones have a definite visual appeal. They aren't like the jazzmen who were doing trad a few months ago and who had converted their act to keep up with the times. They are genuine R&B fanatics themselves and they sing and play in a way that one would have expected more from a coloured US group than a bunch of wild, exciting white boys who have the fans screaming and listening to them."

With things bubbling nicely in west London, Gomelsky – now assuming a *de facto* manager status – began to spread the word about The Rolling Stones. His film work had brought him into loose contact with Beatles' manager Brian Epstein, fast becoming the most important impresario in British music. The Fab Four were booked for the television programme *Thank Your Lucky Stars* at Teddington on April 14. Somehow Gomelsky managed to squirrel out an invitation to attend the rehearsals.

Hobnobbing with The Beatles on the set of the popular chart programme *Thank Your Lucky Stars*, Gomelsky invited the group over to the Crawdaddy to witness the Stones play once filming was completed. Suitably intrigued by Gomelsky's ravings, The Beatles acquiesced and traipsed over to the club to see The Rolling Stones in action.

"We were playing this little club in Richmond," recalled Jagger in 1988. "I was doing this song, and then there they were in front of me, the Fab Four – John, Paul, George and Ringo. The four headed monster! They never went anywhere alone at this point. And they had on these beautiful, long black leather trench coats. I thought, 'Even if I have to write songs I'm gonna get these!'"

The urgency that the Stones brought to their show reminded The Beatles of their own formative days, especially George Harrison who told them they were the best new act he'd come across. Lennon was less effusive, and while he'd later succumb to their charms, his mercurial manner didn't offer much in the way of encouragement. McCartney, ever the opportunist and aware of the potential of the Stones, encouraged them to start writing their own material. While The Beatles, like everyone else, had started life as a covers band, the songwriting partnership of Lennon and McCartney had taken them to another level. Clearly this was the way forward for the Stones. Following this historic meeting, both groups would collide with each other on a regular basis at concert halls and nightclubs. Observing the Fab Four's extraordinary effect on their fans, the Stones – Brian Jones in particular – were eager to secure a slice for themselves.

By the summer of 1963, British Beat was invading the charts like a tidal wave. Record deals, previously the domain of the airbrushed and manufactured, were being handed out to anyone who looked or sounded remotely like The Beatles. Most signed away a big chunk of what was righfully theirs in the adrenaline rush to get into the recording studio, the few sherbets enjoyed by the musicians paling into insignificance compared to what their managers, music publishers and record companies were raking in. Throughout 1963, in every city and town in the UK, there were queues at the guitar shops of boys in their late teens, all of them growing their hair over their foreheads and practicing their chords in preparation for the big time.

While happy to buy into the trappings of the new movement, the Stones were markedly different to The Beatles. Lennon and co dressed in suits but the Stones were happy to wear informal clothes that displayed an affront to the etiquette of the pop star. The Stones' long hair was less coiffeured and combed than any of the Mersey Beat groups travelling the circuit. Only Brian Jones maintained a conventional presence, styling his hair into a blond version of the Beatle cut. His clothes too were impeccably cut, owing more to Savile Row than the downmarket look favoured by blues and jazz fans. The others in the group were tieless, and wore sweaters, cardigans and T-shirts without deferring to fashion trends.

Despite the rave reports of their shows around London and the patronage of The Beatles, a record deal still eluded them. Fate, in the form of the sudden passing of Giorgio Gomelsky's father, would remedy this. Temporarily without representation while Gomelsky attended to the obsequies, the group came to the attention of pop PR hustler Andrew Loog Oldham, whose instinctive nose for ferreting out saleable talent was unmatched at the time. Though only 19, Oldham had worked his way through Soho coffee bars to finding work with Carnaby Street shop legend John Stephen and fashion designer Mary Quant. Receptive to any vibe within Soho's media mile, Oldham was fully aware of the fortune to be made from the neophyte teen-centric pop industry. Oldham utilised any tactics to secure interest. "He was great at running around and meeting people and getting in," recalls publisher Sean O'Mahoney. "Often people used to say, 'Do I know him?' because he used to act as though as he was an old comrade."

Oldham's first brush with pop was as PR man for a small roster of artists associated with the innovative British record producer Joe Meek. He'd soon befriend American "wall of sound" production maestro Phil Spector and, inspired by his enigmatic personality, adopt the gifted producer's idiosyncratic business approach. Like many, Oldham beat a swift path to Brian Epstein's door once the Mersey shuttle docked in London, impressing The Beatles' rather naïve manager with his convincing patter and sizeable contact book. As a result, he was briefly taken on as an assistant, with a responsibility for promoting The Beatles' second single 'Please Please Me'. Oldham soon established other contacts in the entertainment business, one of whom was Tony Calder, who worked in promotion at Decca Records by day and as a DJ at night. Where Oldham's creativity was boundless but often impractical, Tony Calder was realistic in what could be achieved, with the dogged gumption to put his ideas into practice. Being similarly aged and driven, Calder latched onto Oldham's vision of the Stones immediately.

With an office in London's Regent Street, Oldham was perfectly positioned to pick up on any emerging signals coming up from street level. Schmoozing with the likes of Brian Epstein and Robert Stigwood, Oldham monitored their movements and employed many of their skills for himself. Another of his contacts at that time was Eric Easton, an established agent in his mid-thirties from the old school. While his clients were less threatening than the current crop of chart acts, Easton, unlike some in his profession, wasn't steeped in showbiz tradition and realised that this new wave was no overnight fad. More importantly to Andrew, he was officially licensed to promote artists – a vital prerequisite for ensuring sustained work and something Oldham at that point did not possess.

It was Peter Jones, a journalist then working for the highly respected *Record Mirror*, who encouraged Oldham to check out the Stones at one of their Sunday night slots at the Crawdaddy Club. Jones added further weight to his recommendation by mentioning that the band was as yet unsigned and without any tangible representation. Eager to catch the breeze, Oldham beat a swift path to the Stones' door.

As it happened, April 18 was an unusually quiet evening at Richmond, but Oldham's finely tuned senses recognised the uncut diamond before him, raw musical sex whipped up on stage by an untamed band of adolescent savages. An early acolyte of Anthony Burgess's cult novel *A Clockwork Orange,* he drew a connection between its delinquent protagonists and the understated fury of beat music. To his razor sharp understanding of pop sensibility, what acts like The Beatles, Searchers and Gerry & The Pacemakers merely hinted at, the Stones were freely evoking up there on stage. With many of the more popular groups having abandoned their initial rawness in favour of suits and smiles, Oldham saw a huge vacuum in the market waiting to be filled and seized the moment. "I knew what I was looking at," he'd later recall. "It was sex and I was 48 hours ahead of the pack."

Oldham made a second visit to Richmond a week later and was met at the station by his partner Eric Easton who was curious to see what this young upstart was raving about. While Easton had become familiar with Oldham's electrified ramblings, his predictions regarding The Beatles had all come to fruition, ensuring that he had to hear him out.

Following the show, Oldham and Easton approached the band in their dressing room and laid down his credentials. Such was the powerful presence of Mick on stage, Oldham assumed he was the leader and made his pitch to him before Brian Jones swiftly blocked his advances, announcing his leadership status. Tony Calder, privy to all of Oldham's movements, recalls his business partner's intuitive understanding of what made the band tick, especially that of their charismatic front man.

"Andrew saw the enormous, the absolutely phenomenal potential for Mick Jagger," recalls Calder. "And it was he who encouraged Mick; he goaded Mick; he prodded Mick to go to the edge of the envelope as we'd call it today. Andrew only wanted the very best for the band, and that meant projecting Mick... When I first met the Stones, Andrew told me that Brian Jones was the leader of the band. Andrew realised that Mick

Jagger was the star. Whether he was the leader of the band or not, it didn't mean a thing to Andrew. Everything had to be focused on Mick."

Collectively, the band were impressed with Oldham's youth, enthusiasm and unfettered sense of direction. Where they'd previously had to sell their blues aspirations, Oldham's implicit understanding of them won him an immediate thumb's up. Informed that their acting representative Giorgio Gomelsky was absent on personal duties abroad, Oldham's instinctive response was to offer the group a faster route to success than the Russian could ever hope to provide. With a promise of throwing the full weight of his promotional chutzpah behind them, Oldham persuaded the group to sign with him. With a swiftness that defied the rusty machinations of the era, Oldham promptly contracted the group for a three-year period.

Flexing his leadership credentials, Brian Jones oversaw the fine print of the contract. Unbeknownst to the rest of the group, Jones had previously managed to secure a £5 a week increment over his colleagues on account of his self-proclaimed leadership status. Presumably under Brian's influence, Easton would also suggest that Mick Jagger's presence be sidelined in favour of Jones's more mannered style. Aware of the value of Jagger's high voltage attributes, Oldham swiftly overrode the suggestion.

On his return from Switzerland, Gomelsky was duly informed by Jones of the group's switch of loyalties, the mischievous guitarist claiming that Andrew Oldham was an old school contact of his. Gomelsky ruefully accepted his fate and would go on to manage The Yardbirds. Oldham and Easton's most pressing commitment was securing a record contract for the Stones which, in the late spring of 1963, wasn't too difficult. The Mersey Sound now dominated the UK record industry, with the mighty EMI in close alliance with Brian Epstein's gilded stable of artists, leaving other labels desperate to sign anything that could cash in on the beat group craze.

In its own way, Decca Records was as established as EMI, but its historic, if in hindsight ludicrous, rejection of The Beatles in early 1962 had the industry echoing with howls of derision. The A&R man who'd famously turned down The Beatles was Richard 'Dick' Rowe who'd enjoyed a noteworthy production career in the fifties and early sixties with artists such as Billy Fury, The Bachelors and Jimmy Young. Normally, his opinion was trusted and valued by his peers, and a recommendation from Rowe was usually seen as a green-light to chart success.

Rowe's dismissal of the primitive Beatles' sound back in January 1962 was nonetheless backed with sound judgement, especially given the Liverpool group's substandard audition and bizarre choice of material. In this most unforgiving of industries, Rowe had gamely carried the weight of his decision, and was more than eager to make up for it if the opportunity ever arose again.

In the event it did, and ironically courtesy of a Beatle. With Mersey mania never more fanatical than in its home base of Liverpool, a talent contest in the city's Philharmonic Hall on May 5, 1963, drew Rowe and Beatle George Harrison to sit in judgement on a new roster of Liverpool hopefuls. Taking their respective places on a raised dais, Harrison and Rowe laughed off the slightly embarrassing reunion, their first meeting since The Beatles' ill-fated audition a year and a half previous. In tandem with judging the neophyte bands, Harrison mentioned to Rowe the unsigned status of The Rolling Stones. Raving about The Beatles' initiation to their sound just a few weeks earlier, he encouraged Rowe to catch up with them as soon as possible, mentioning their Sunday night residency in Richmond.

With Harrison's words ringing in his ears, Rowe was up and out of his chair before the talent show had drawn to a close. Driving to Richmond from Liverpool, he arrived as the Stones were just about to start their set. The club was packed to the rafters, and Rowe took in soundings from the crowd as well as what he saw on stage. Suitably impressed, Rowe decided against a meeting with the group in the dressing room, opting instead to liaise with their manager from the relative safety of his desk the next morning.

Following a raft of calls, Rowe was eventually directed to Oldham's business partner, Eric Easton. With time of the essence, the necessary paperwork to bring the group to the recording studio was swiftly prepared. By May 8, the Stones had signed an exclusive tape lease deal with the Decca Recording Company, elevating the company's hip and simultaneously salvaging Dick Rowe's disastrous rejection of The Beatles.

The deal wasn't as smooth as Rowe might have expected. Aware of the dangers of signing away every atom of control in the flush of a record deal, Andrew Oldham asserted that he should retain complete control (both musically and contractually) over the group's output. Conversations with auteur producer Phil Spector had armed Oldham with a cocky assurance that ran totally against the rigid machinations of show business etiquette. Given Decca's desperation to sign a group with as much potential as the Stones, they buckled to the demands of the 19 year old.

With a deal struck, the publicity machine began to turn. Patrick Doncaster, then the *Daily Mirror*'s entertainment correspondent, gave the group their first national newspaper coverage on June 13. Doncaster was positively fizzing with excitement at what he witnessed at a gig in Richmond. "In the half darkness," he wrote, "the guitar and the drums started to twang and bang... Shoulder to shoulder on the floor 500 youngsters, some in black leather, some in sweaters. You could have boiled an egg in the atmosphere."

In the early sixties the *Daily Mirror*'s circulation ran close to six million, making Doncaster's words all the more powerful. Fired by this publicity, Oldham approached his old employer Brian Epstein to assist with the Stones' ascendancy. Despite an offer of shared management, the Liverpudlian Svengali was heavily consumed with Beatles and other Mersey-Beat business, and he passed on Oldham's offer. Undeterred, Oldham would famously capitalise on the rebuff, drawing a distinct line between the Stones and Beatles. "If The Beatles are the Christ," he'd tell the Stones, "then you're the Anti-Christ."

Leaving no stone unturned to secure publicity, Oldham tailored a few other ragged ends of the group. Considering Keith Richards pluralised surname too clunky for delicate copy editors, he temporarily shortened it to 'Richard', hoping that the evergreen success of Cliff Richard might lend Keith some wider exposure. A more substantial edit was the ousting of pianist and co-founder Ian Stewart. While Stewart or 'Stew' was a much-liked member of the band, his age, conventional appearance and sizeable girth didn't fit into Oldham's fixed idea of the group. As a result, the genial Scot was delicately eased out, with the compensation that he would be kept on as roadie and occasional piano player. In the fullness of time he would not only become a key member of the Stones' entourage but a well-loved character on the British rock scene, forever available to offer sound professional advice to premier league rock stars in need of it.

Oldham accompanied the group into the studio for their first recordings. While they had cut some rough demos prior to this session, Oldham was now in charge of production and charged with selecting the most commercial song from their repertoire. From the half-dozen previewed at Olympic Studios, he picked Chuck Berry's 'Come On'. Despite their considerable enthusiasm, the Stones' version of Berry's composition was thrown together without any formal mixing. On hearing the results, Dick Rowe insisted that a more competent version was recorded at Decca Studios, with his engineers at the helm. With little room to manoeuvre, the group acquiesced to Rowe's demands, and a more polished reading of 'Come On' was captured.

Now that the release of a single was logged on Decca's schedule, the Stones underwent the perfunctory publicity afforded for a new act. With access to radio and especially television virtually guaranteed, interest from the teen and fan magazines would naturally follow. This in turn could lead to valuable space in the national newspapers. While Andrew Oldham had actively encouraged the group's unkempt deportment to act as a negative response to The Beatles' groomed appearance, he had ignored the fact that to win a place on coveted television shows, a certain measure of compromise – especially where dress was concerned – was required.

Programming these variety shows were men who'd forged their reputation in the fifties, producers and disk jockeys who'd been thoroughly charmed by the polished presentation of Brian Epstein's acts, but to whom the Stones might present something of a challenge. To facilitate much-needed exposure, Oldham nodded to convention with a reluctant sense of uniformity.

Keith Richards was not amused. "[Oldham] put us in those dog-tooth checked suits with the black velvet collars... For a month on the first said, 'All right. We'll do it. You know the game. We'll try it out.' ... en the Stones' thing started taking over. Charlie would leave his ... in some dressing room and I'd pull mine out and there would be wh..skey stains all over it or chocolate pudding."

This compromise was enough to secure their place on the top rated ITV pop show *Thank Your Lucky Stars*. Launched in 1961, the Saturday evening television programme was enormously successful, with viewing figures upwards of 20 million a week. Despite their lowly billing, the Stones appearance on the show was an historic moment in a medium still unsure about pop music, the group's presence easily provoking audience outrage. A plethora of calls were logged on the channel's switchboard, all conveying their disgust at the Stones' sneering persona. Others took to writing letters to register their outrage, one dissident accusing Jagger of wearing a "feather duster on his head". All of this condemnation made its way towards the press, which was exactly what Oldham was hoping for.

Despite the brouhaha, the groups' appearance was enough to send 'Come On' to number 21 in the national charts, a respectable position for a group that had yet to venture outside the London area. There was some skilful, if not entirely legitimate, manoeuvring of record sales. Savvy to the easily penetrable chart mechanisms, Oldham had targeted fan club members in the districts where the record sales were logged for chart purposes, and encouraged them to buy the single at the designated record shop.

Now that Mick had finally abandoned his studies at LSE, and with Bill Wyman terminating his daytime employment, the group was operating as a professional unit at last. Demonstrating this new sense of professionalism, the group began to wind down their west London commitments. One of their last appearances in Richmond was at the National Jazz Festival on August 11, 1963. At a gathering dominated by UK jazz bands, it was apparent that the Stones were destined for much greater things. Chris Welch, soon to become a feature writer on *Melody Maker*, witnessed the group's extraordinary performance that day. "We were all watching Acker Bilk on the main stage and all eyes were on this trad band," he recalls Welch. "Suddenly the announcer says, 'The

Rolling Stones are about to start playing at the back of the field in a tent.' We then heard the sound of electric guitars and drums playing against a clarinet and banjo. It was one of those historic moments when the whole audience who were all seated watching Acker Bilk, all turned around and ran across the field to get inside a marquee where the Stones were playing. There were people climbing on people's shoulders and pushing to the front to see them, it was so exciting."

The Stones were soon lined up for their first package tour of the UK. With little sense of logical geography, these rites of passage would test the stamina of all involved, often requiring two sets a night before travelling on to the next location. While these tours were a ritualised part of the music scene during the sixties, the promoters presented an imaginative package that didn't rely solely on Mersey Beat. Headlining at cinemas and ballrooms across Britain were the immensely popular Everly Brothers but also on the bill, and of far greater interest to the Stones, was Mississippi blues legend Bo Diddley. Watching him from the wings of venues in such provincial outposts as Doncaster, Bradford, Salisbury and Taunton made the otherwise tedious travelling somewhat sweeter. With poor attendances during the early part of the tour, Little Richard was flown over as an added attraction.

The more established acts on the bill presented a slick, energetic appearance on stage, and the youngsters were curious to know what drove these larger than life characters to keep their collective mojos working at all hours.

"A lot of those black bands we were touring with," recalled Keith Richards to Jeremy Vine in 2010, "they'd arrive at the gig and they've got suits and they looked so perfect and together and everything. They'd made the same journey that we had to make, and we'd be crawling in and not barely 20-years-old and we'd say: 'How do you guys do this?' and they'd say, 'Well son, take a bit of that, smoke a little of this.' So it was backstage secrets, basically that was the way they did it. To be able to make two shows a day and maybe 500 miles apart, you needed some substance and it wasn't just food and water."

Despite these occasional liveners from their fellow artists, the Stones still had to endure the squalid, unglamorous side of life on the road. With theatre, ballroom and cinema owners in 1963 paying scant interest to the well-being of performers, the group soon tired of maintaining their stage outfits. Dry-cleaners and launderettes were on wartime opening hours and their suits were quickly soiled. Andrew Oldham, ever the opportunist, decided that more interest could be generated by allowing the group to present themselves in their everyday clothes.

"Because of the way they were living at the time," recalls Tony Calder, "they would go to a gig, go home, sleep in the clothes, go back the next day, go to another gig. They did look pretty rough, and that was developed into their image."

Though strapped on the conveyer belt of touring for much of 1963, the Stones couldn't help but touch base with the social change that Britain was undergoing that year. Screaming girls at their concerts might not have cared but the Profumo scandal had fundamentally and irredeemably changed the status quo, ensuring that anyone, be it politician, priest, lord or even royalty, was no longer beyond scrutiny. Two of the female protagonists in the Profumo affair were under 21. A new generation was flexing its limbs and, in their own way, the Stones bought into this cocky arrogance. The establishment, threatened by what they didn't understand, would soon find ways of hitting back.

CHAPTER 2

Richmond

"If ever the parents of Britain are almost united, it must surely be in their general dislike of those shaggy haired discoveries... They are the anti-parent symbol."

The *Daily Mail,* August 1964

In tandem with their accumulating success, the Stones faced the kind of fan mania that was enveloping their contemporaries, but in their case it was of a rougher and harder variety. The group's message of shared dejection inspired a cathartic response that was more akin to sexual release than mere fantastical appreciation. The hard core within their audiences was much like the embodiment of the Stones themselves: untutored, instinctive and barely contained by society's expectations. Whether anyone noticed it at the time, the group were passing on a message that had previously been the domain of America's black underclass. For years Britain's politicians and intellectuals had similarly ignored the base interests of the country's dispossessed. Now The Rolling Stones were articulating this dissent.

Nonetheless, despite Andrew Oldham's practice of exploiting every opportunity to secure column space, in reality the group were cut from a different cloth to what the commentators imagined or implied.

Mick Jagger's private sophistication and keen intelligence contrasted sharply with the public's perception of the group.

Keith Altham, a music journalist at the hub of the beat explosion of 1963, recalls this strange paradox. "Jagger was always aspiring to be upper-class," he says. "The music they played indentified with poor, black immigrant workers from the cotton fields and chain gangs and all that kind of thing. The Stones thought, 'We can't sing chain gang songs and then dress up as Cliff Richard or Elvis in gold lamé; we have to look a bit more realistic and down to earth.' That in turn turned it into an almost inverted snobbery; to actually behave and look like people who were much more working class."

While their live act was polarising opinion and helping prise apart the generation gap, the Stones were having problems transferring the immediacy of their stage sound to disc. With no obvious follow-up single on the horizon and Decca desperately wanting a bigger hit, Andrew Oldham had the good fortune to chance upon John Lennon and Paul McCartney in London's West End one afternoon in September 1963. When Oldham mentioned the quandary that was facing his group, John and Paul offered them a new track they'd written as a vehicle for Ringo Starr entitled 'I Wanna Be Your Man'. Its ragged construction would easily fit the Stones' broader style, and they were happy to farm it off. Excited by the offer, Oldham brought Lennon and McCartney to the studio where the Stones were busily trying to conjure up their next hit.

Mick Jagger: "We were rehearsing and Andrew brought Paul and John down to the rehearsal... they were real hustlers then. I mean the way they used to hustle tunes was great. 'Hey Mick, we've got this great song.' So they played 'I Wanna Be Your Man' and we thought it sounded pretty commercial, which is what we were looking for. So we did it like Elmore James or something... It was completely crackers, but it was a hit and sounded great onstage."

'I Wanna Be Your Man' duly became the Stones' next single in November. Due in no small way to the Lennon/McCartney patronage, it rose to the respectable position of number 13 in the charts. Nonetheless, with insistence from all quarters, especially Oldham, Mick and Keith started to work at becoming songwriters.

With recording slotted in wherever possible, touring dominated the Stones' calendar, in the course of which it leaked out that Brian Jones had been insisting on a higher percentage due to his founder member status. The simmering resentment towards him manifested itself after a gig at the Cavern, Liverpool on November 5, 1963. "Everybody freaked out," recalled Keith Richards on hearing about Jones' deception. "That was the beginning of the decline of Brian. We said, 'Fuck you'."

In the ensuing weeks, Jones encountered retaliation from the band which enabled Oldham to elevate Jagger and Richards' standing in the group. The now compromised Jones reacted badly when his leadership status was being challenged.

Tony Calder: "He couldn't cope with the press coverage which was all centred on Mick, so little things happened. He wasn't told about recording sessions; he would be picked up late for a gig. If he pushed it the other way and decided not to be there and say, 'I will be an hour late,' they just left him behind."

Divisions aside, the early part of 1964 saw the Stones traipsing around the UK as before, slotting in recording sessions whenever they could. With home-grown compositions still eluding them, an EP of cover versions ensured their continued presence in the charts. Buddy Holly's 'Not Fade Away' was chosen as the Stones' third single, the group retuning Holly's Bo Diddley-style song into a suitably aggressive follow-on to 'I Wanna Be Your Man' and securing their first UK Top 5 hit.

An album was now a required formality. In between gigs, the group busied themselves at London's Regent Sound Studios with Oldham assuming a Phil Spector role in the control booth. Ironically, Spector happened to be in London on business, and he dropped by to give advice and play maracas on a few songs. In total, 11 tracks, the bulk of the Stones' live repertoire, were recorded, with just one Jagger/Richards track, the Mersey-flavoured 'Tell Me' among them. Though top-heavy with covers, the album was an instant success, selling 100,000 copies on its first day of release and knocking The Beatles off the top of the album charts. In a bold move that reflected Oldham's confidence in his boys, its front cover consisted solely of Nicholas Wright's photograph of the group looking surly, no artist name, no title, just the Decca logo in the top right hand corner.

Elsewhere, Oldham's machine was churning out publicity at every given opportunity. With the press lapping up the nation's first real bad boys of the beat scene, the adage 'any publicity is good publicity' was actively maintained. The *Melody Maker* headline of March 14 – 'Would you let your daughter go out with a Rolling Stone?' – exemplified this tactic, Oldham having fed the sound bite to reporter Ray Coleman. "It would make for a startling headline," he told Coleman, who agreed, although he softened Oldham's edge by substituting 'sister' for 'daughter'. It received enormous coverage.

For all this, the Stones' loutish arrogance as promoted by Oldham (and by extension the press) was less apparent to those who came into close contact with them. Gered Mankowitz, a young photographer employed by Oldham in 1964, was privy to this strange paradox. "When I first met them, they certainly weren't thuggish or in any sense difficult," recalls Mankowitz today. "They were very nice. I got on instantly with them. They were rather charming. We tried to exploit the mass media image of them. I think we were just playing up to it, and they were happy to get the column space, and I think it was probably all part of Andrew Oldham's plan."

Their busy timetable left them little time to maintain conventional romantic relationships. As the group's visual focus, Mick was singled out for questions about his love life, and while the press in those days maintained a discreet silence over the raunchier action occurring backstage and elsewhere, Jagger – wise to the crude machinations of the media – could be relied upon to offer up some carefully guarded remarks to defer further scrutiny. "We're on the road so much that we don't depend on girlfriends for relationships," he said, in the oblique manner that would characterise his interview style for decades. "It's not a barrier. Most men don't depend on their girlfriends for relationships. Besides, women never get on. If that sounds like an anti-feminist statement I'm sorry, but it's a product of practical experience."

When time allowed, Jagger was maintaining a fairly traditional relationship with Chrissie Shrimpton, the sister of top model Jean. Chrissie met Jagger at one of the Stones' west London performances in early 1963 and, following a brazen approach for a kiss on stage, the pair began dating.

Going out with Mick Jagger brought with it enormous issues. Like their Beatle counterparts, the women close to the Stones were sidelined for a variety of reasons, not least so their men could retain the appearance of marriageable eligibility. With the Stones rarely having a day off, the Jagger/Shrimpton relationship endured as best it could. "I used to go to clubs in London and I would have a bar bill that [Mick] would pay," Chrissie told an interviewer in 2004, "but I had to go home at a certain time. He would often phone up and I was told I had to go home now. I would be taken to the car and he would ring at home at three in the morning. I kind of liked that."

In the meantime the Jagger/Richards' creative partnership was starting to gather momentum, and though their first forays into songwriting were passable at best, their reputation courtesy of the Stones would nonetheless boost their confidence. Oldham's interests by now expanded beyond the Stones, and included promoting the precocious actor-singer Adrienne Posta, then known by her real surname Poster. At just 15, Posta's talent hinted at the sort of success that teen singers such as Lulu and Millie were enjoying so Oldham commissioned Mick and Keith to write a song for her, the largely forgettable 'Shang A Doo Lang'. Predictably, Oldham managed to milk some extra publicity by holding a launch party cum birthday bash for Posta at a location in Windsor. While 'Shang A Doo Lang' would ultimately fail to penetrate even the lower reaches of the charts, other, more fortuitous, results arose from the gathering.

Alongside Jagger and Richards, the launch brought together many luminaries from London's swinging crowd, among them Paul McCartney, his then girlfriend Jane Asher, her brother Peter and several of their friends. These included the artist John Dunbar and his softly spoken, 17-year-old girlfriend Marianne Faithfull. While Dunbar appeared seasoned to this sort of function, his petite date was wide-eyed at the outpouring of stardust around her.

In her own way, Faithfull was just as exotic as the company she was in. She was the daughter of Major Robert Glynn Faithfull and Viennese aristocrat Baroness Eva Von Sacher-Masoch, and further back in her mother's lineage was Leopold Baron von Sacher-Masoch, author of the classic novel *Venus In Furs,* who is credited with coining the word masochism. Marianne's education was split between several schools, some of it spent at Braziers Park in Oxford, an alternative commune her father had helped establish. Convent education in Reading from the age of eight turned her towards classical literature and drama. "It was tremendously strict," she'd recall in 1970. "We learned nothing about the outside world. After we bathed we quickly got into shifts, because it was thought shameful for us to look at our bodies. If heaven can impose that kind of restrictive practice, hell can look tempting. We were not only virgins, we were absolutely virginal. The one thing you come out with is a very strong conscience."

Schooling aside, she'd endured the break-up of her parents' marriage and a case of childhood tuberculosis, all of which contributed to a deep sense of detachment. Faithfull's immersion in the romantic arts soon gravitated to singing, where she accompanied her delicately rich voice on guitar, and as her confidence grew she enlivened the odd party and coffee bar with her talents. At just 16, she'd fallen for John Dunbar, a Cambridge fine arts undergraduate who spent most of his time in London building up contacts in the alternative culture. Dunbar's dilettante exploits around town brought his young girlfriend into contact with the artistic illuminati and she was soon absorbed onto the capital's swinging carousel. Dunbar's tentacles penetrated many avenues; he'd become friendly with singer Peter Asher and by association, Paul McCartney, and the invite to the record launch brought all of these entities together.

With the room bursting with raw talent and fragile egos, Dunbar steered his glamorous beau around the party. Oldham's mojo soon homed in on Marianne's extraordinary presence. Her stunning figure offset by an angelic aura and understated dress sense, the starmaker's marketing wheels began to turn. On hearing her surname that dripped propriety he remarked, "With a name like that you should be making records!" When Dunbar mentioned that Marianne could indeed sing, Oldham offered her a deal on the spot. He'd later crudely remark, "I saw an angel with big tits so I signed her."

Circling the room at the launch were Jagger and Chrissie Shrimpton, their relationship now veering from quiet domesticity to fractured discontent, and when sharp words between them left Shrimpton in tears Mick's roving eye soon detected Marianne's ethereal presence. Seeking an introduction, he 'accidentally' spilt champagne over her cream top. After a short, embarrassed silence, Mick attempted to wipe the alcohol off her blouse with his hand. Innocent of the vulgar machinations that drove much of the pop world, Marianne's introduction to The Rolling Stones proved something of a disappointment.

Andrew Oldham pursued Faithfull in a more conventional fashion. Within days, formal contracts for her singing career were drawn up and signed. Given that she was only 17, she had to have all the paperwork countersigned by her mother. With the only stipulation that she be chaperoned on any extended touring dates, Oldham's vision of a convent girl invading the pop scene was duly realised.

Oldham next contacted some of London's established writers to see if anyone had anything suitable for Marianne's first release. Lionel Bart, the Bard of popular musicals, had a tune that was deemed usable, but ultimately it didn't suit Faithfull's unusually low reach. In something of a dilemma, Oldham then turned to Jagger and Richards, compelling them to compose something that fitted his vision of Marianne. Oldham's edict was precise, demanding a song with "brick walls around it; high walls and no sex." To facilitate this, folklore has it that Oldham locked Jagger and Richards in the kitchen of the Hampstead flat they shared, refusing to let the pair out until a song was forthcoming.

Ultimately, Jagger and Richards would come up with the circular, hypnotic 'As Tears Goes By'. Displaying a maturity that was light years ahead of their experience, the composition simultaneously dovetailed Faithfull's reach and innocence. The sensitivity of the composition didn't extend to travel arrangements on the day of the recording, and young Marianne was left to find her own way back to Reading on public transport. Happily for all concerned 'As Tears Go By' entered the charts during the summer of 1964, reaching number nine in the UK and 22 in the US. With Oldham's well-oiled exploitation package in full swing, the convent girl was sucked out of her quiet Berkshire existence and propelled into the hectic itinerary of a sixties' pop lifestyle. In 1965, Marianne was shipped across to the States as part of the seemingly interminable conveyor belt of British acts crossing back and forth across the Atlantic. Such was her extraordinary presence she would be courted by Bob Dylan, his poetic persona resonating with her own erudite tastes.

Now a component part of Oldham's stable, Faithfull collided with the Stones' circle on numerous occasions. While Jagger's initially crude introduction had done little to impress her, she found the aloofness of Keith Richards far more attractive. "Keith was a sort of insecure person with a very reflective, intuitive side," she'd later recall. "I liked him. Very much." Absorbed deeper into the Stones circle, she also found Brian Jones' similarly mysterious persona much to her liking. Mick, however, was still somewhat lower in her appreciation. That in time, like a lot of things, would change dramatically.

The sensitivity of 'As Tears Go By' bore zero relation to the scenes at Stones concerts where violence and rioting occurred at every port of call. With most gigs during 1964 ending in varying degrees of riot, the London *Evening Standard* would articulate a growing feeling that the group's anarchic presence was sullying the otherwise effervescent pop field. "This horrible lot have done terrible things to the music scene, set it back eight years," ran a diary piece. "Just when we got our pop singers looking all neat, tidy and cheerful, along come the Stones looking like beatniks. They've wrecked the image of the pop singer in the Sixties."

In between their overwhelming diary of TV, radio and recording duties, in the summer of 1964 the Stones were more than ready to make their American debut. The Beatles' trailblazing visit in February 1964 ensured that all British entertainers, be it musicians, actors or artists, were afforded a greater amount of interest than ever before. With Beatles-coat tail acts like Gerry & The Pacemakers and Billy J. Kramer & The Dakotas making considerable inroads into the lucrative American market, it was a shoe-in that the Stones would be guaranteed considerable attention, despite not having a hit single to accompany them. Others in Britain weren't so sure. A government official talking with a *Daily Express* reporter offered the opinion that, "Our relations with America are bound to deteriorate. The Americans will assume that British youth have reached a new low in degradation."

Despite this and other brickbats, on June 1, 1964 the Stones assembled at London Airport to make the trip across the Atlantic. This first sortie onto American soil was more of an introductory visit, with less than a dozen concerts scheduled between press, radio and TV appearances. Nonetheless, to greet them in New York were over 400 fans; a presence that appeared to be permanently on duty at Kennedy Airport to welcome any new British act.

With several articles having paid particular attention to the group's casual style, an appearance on the top-rated *Hollywood Palace* TV show turned out to be nothing more than a send-up. After soused host Dean Martin aimed numerous pot shots towards the group, one guest was heard to mutter, "I didn't know whether to applaud them or set traps."

Elsewhere, the reaction from fan mags such as *Tiger Beat* and *16* was more favourable. Though the Stones' music had yet to penetrate America, their modish clothes and British provenance guaranteed them considerable coverage. While Oldham's tactics would ensure copious interest in their reputation, the band themselves were keen to advance their music. To this end Oldham arranged two days of recording sessions at the famed Chess Studios in Chicago. With engineers experienced from working with the likes of Chuck Berry, Muddy Waters and Bo Diddley, the sound that the Stones had been so desperate to transfer to disc back in England was captured with a greater clarity than before. Among a dozen numbers captured on tape was a Bobby Womack composition, 'It's All Over Now', which was reworked from Womack's soul-ridden original with The Valentinos into a raunchy rock song more in keeping with the Stones' image.

The highlight of the visit was two concerts at New York's Carnegie Hall. Since The Beatles had broken in pop audiences to the prestigious venue, the guardians had green-lighted promoter Sid Bernstein's every request to present other acts. The Stones booking at the staid arena was, perhaps, a gig too far since, unbeknownst to the guardians of the hall, Oldham had planted several *agent provocateurs* in the concert hall to "stir things up a bit."

Sid Bernstein: "The Rolling Stones' crowd was different. They had never had a rock and roll concert at Carnegie Hall prior to The Beatles, and that went very well, but the Stones crowd got them nervous.

The kids didn't do any damage, but they were older and more excited, so the people at Carnegie Hall asked me not to come back."

Energised by simultaneously enchanting and outraging America, the Stones returned to Britain to begin another round of touring. Musically, they were on a high, with 'It's All Over Now' scoring them their first UK number one in July. More importantly for their greater successes, the record earned them an important foothold on the States, reaching 26 in *Billboard*'s Hot 100 chart.

With success continuing unabated, Jagger found himself in court for three minor driving offences. In his defence speech Mick's solicitor, Dale Parkinson, spoke of his client's character in ways that reeked of Oldham's string pulling. "Put out of your mind this nonsense that is talked about these young men," said Parkinson. "They are not long-haired idiots, but highly intelligent university men... The Duke of Marlborough had much longer hair than my client and he won some famous battles. His hair was powdered, I think because of fleas, and my client has no fleas."

These guerrilla tactics with the press were starting to have a provocative effect on the Stones' British audiences. Much of the pent-up energy that fuelled the seaside battles between mods and rockers in 1964 spilled over into the group's live appearances which, for some, became nothing less than an excuse to cut loose. At a concert in Blackpool on July 24 the mania elevated itself into something else entirely.

While the majority of the 5,000 crammed into the Empress Ballroom weren't expecting anything other than a noisy evening, events got out of hand when a few fans attempted to climb onto the stage. When Keith Richards booted out at one of the main protagonists, all hell broke loose. Fights broke out with security staff but, heavily outnumbered, they retreated, and the ballroom's grand piano ended up being tipped into the orchestra pit.

Keith Richards: "It was like they had the Battle of Crimea going on, people gasping, tits hanging out, chicks choking, nurses running round with ambulances. A whole gang of them came to this ballroom and they didn't like us and they punched their way to the front, right though the whole 7,000 people, straight to the stage and started spitting at us. In those days, I had a temper and, 'You spit on me?' And I kicked his face in."

With scores of fans treated for injuries and the majority of the Stones' equipment broken beyond repair, they were swiftly ushered out of the back door well before the advertised close of the show. Under closer inspection, some of the efforts employed to engage with the group on stage had a strange provenance to them. Filmmaker Peter Whitehead, who later captured for posterity the hysterical reaction the Stones incited, was privy to events that occurred. "Mick once said to me, 'Some of the boys in the audience are drawn to you on stage. When they reach you, you can see they want to kiss you, but they feel so embarrassed they hit you instead.' But a few of them ended up kissing us!"

Regardless of the intent, the violence would continue. A concert in Northern Ireland provoked such mayhem that the gig was cancelled after only 12 minutes. An appearance in The Hague in August was met with heavy violence. Playing in the historic Kurhaus opera house, the Stones' performance was cut short after seven minutes when sections of the audience set about systematically destroying the ornate venue.

Leaving a trail of chaos around Europe in their wake, the group began their second tour of America in October. A prize slot on the prestigious *Ed Sullivan Show* was a highlight; The Beatles having notched up viewing figures of over 70 million on their first appearance, Oldham and the Stones were hoping to attract similar interest. The venerable Sullivan had relied solely on the advice of his scouts in England to book the Stones and, still intoxicated with the charm of The Beatles, he wrongly assumed that they'd probably engender the same cheekiness that the Fab Four had brought with them earlier in the year.

The famed Sullivan theatre on Broadway underwent a seismic shift in atmosphere the night of October 25, for while the Stones played only two songs, their gritty presence ignited the audience into an uncontrollable delirium. Despite a later, largely obtuse interview with Sullivan punctuated by manic screams, the bulky presenter was initially buoyed up with the reception the band received, and, there was no reason why their appearance would provoke a major controversy.

A few days later, however, Sullivan did a huge about-turn. A stream of complaints from conservative America denounced what they'd witnessed, and Sullivan, brittle when it came to public opinion despite his laconic image, issued a terse statement disowning any responsibility. "Frankly, I didn't see The Rolling Stones until the day before the broadcast," he reported. "I promise you they'll never be back on our show. It took me 17 years to build this show. I'm not going to have it destroyed in a matter of weeks."

Sullivan's rant served only to ratchet up the publicity, and when Oldham asked Sullivan about this embargo on future appearances he received a terse telegram from the presenter: "We were deluged with mail protesting the untidy appearance, clothes and hair of your Rolling Stones. Before even discussing the possibility of a contract, I would like to learn from you whether your young men have reformed in the matter of dress and shampoo."

Thanks to the enormous coverage generated by the *Sullivan* appearance, the Stones' reputation for outrage accompanied them across America. The writer Tom Wolfe, fast becoming the doyen of thinking America, crystallised the effect that the Stones were having by writing in *Esquire* magazine: "The Beatles want to hold your hand, but the Stones want to burn down your town."

Reaching California, the Stones topped the bill on the now legendary *T.A.M.I. Show* special, filmed at Santa Monica's Civic Auditorium, alongside an impressive line-up that included Chuck Berry, The Supremes, The Miracles and Marvin Gaye. The group had to follow, with great trepidation, an incendiary display from James Brown & His Famous Flames – Brown had reportedly claimed "I'm gonna make those Rolling Stones wish they'd never left England."

It was a largely successful tour but towards the end Brian Jones missed a number of Midwest dates and was hospitalised, officially for "bronchitis and exhaustion". In reality, while Jones did indeed suffer from periodic asthma, his penchant for living life to the extreme was beginning to take its toll. This was no more apparent than during recording sessions at Chess Records in Chicago, where the band were laying down tracks for their next release.

"He was certainly ill all right," recalled road manager Ian Stewart. "But he didn't do anything to help himself, he aggravated it by taking too much of something, and generally behaved very stupidly. I tell you what;

he nearly got hoofed out there and then. He hadn't really contributed anything on those record dates. He was either stoned or pissed or just sick and they got fed up with him."

Brian was given a brief moratorium from his roistering over the Christmas of 1964. Nonetheless, he was back on board early the following year as the Stones tsunami continued around the globe. In Australia the press, starved of any major scandal concerning pop stars, teased readers about the group's long-awaited trip with headlines such as 'Loved By The Kids, Hated By The Parents'. The media down under would mine further controversy when they gleefully reported that Mick, Keith, Brian and Andrew Oldham were involved in a fracas with some local Sydney "sharpies" when they'd attempted a spot of boating.

With the group enjoying larger audiences abroad, returning to Britain in early 1965 meant a largely redundant traipse around the provinces for two shows a night, a hugely exhaustive exercise with pallid returns that barely covered their expenses. While package tours were a formalised ritual during the early sixties, there was scant pleasure to be derived from such jaunts for the artists involved. Hospitality was dismal and meals more often than not snatched in transport cafés late at night.

Other perils lay in wait. Following the tour's final shows at the ABC Cinema in Romford on March 18, the band were driving the short journey back to their respective London bases. With the late 'house' finishing at 10:45 p.m., they were presumably fairly whacked out, the predictable rush to avoid the exiting crowds leaving them no chance to change, let alone attend to more personal demands, and on the way home Bill Wyman requested their driver to pull into the nearest service station so he could relieve his bladder.

This was undoubtedly a mercy dash for Wyman. According to Richards, Bill was renowned for his marathon urination. With time of the essence, the party detected the bright lights of the Francis Motor Service Centre at 176 Romford Road, in the Forest Gate area of east London. Pulling into the forecourt at around 11:30 p.m. and in something of a rush, Bill burst into the service station in search of a toilet. On duty that night was 41-year-old Charles Patrick Keeley, normally a mechanic but acting as a petrol attendant for the evening. As a matter of urgency, Wyman asked if he could use the establishment's convenience. Told by Keeley that they were being refurbished, Wyman then asked if he could use the staff toilet instead. Receiving a similar response, Bill allegedly turned on Keeley using "disgusting language".

Wyman, who Keeley would later describe as a "long-haired type with dark glasses", returned to the car and informed his fellow passengers of the situation. From then on, the scene descended into chaos. According to Keeley, around eight or nine men and women got out of the car and proceeded to shamble around the service station forecourt. What exaggerated their presence more dramatically for Keeley was that the group were still dressed in their stage attire and caked in stage make-up. Refused the use of the service station's toilets, Wyman, Jones and Jagger allegedly wandered around to the boundary wall that separated the garage with the adjoining Elm Road. There, they proceeded to relieve themselves "without taking steps to conceal this act", as Keeley would later describe.

When attempting to stop Jagger from urinating against the wall, the garage worker was allegedly brushed aside and told, "We'll piss anywhere man". Keeley then reportedly demanded that the trio get off "his forecourt". This order was adapted by those present as a sort of an impromptu chant, along the lines of "Get off my foreskin!" According to Keeley, the party started gyrating around the garage premises. Adding to the bizarreness of the incident, a few passers-by had recognised the Stones and were attempting to obtain autographs. With mirth from all quarters directed towards Keeley, things got further of hand. "We were laughing a lot," remarked Brian later, "because Mr. Keeley's behaviour was so comical."

Also filling his car up that night was 21-year-old youth worker Eric Lavender. He'd watched the events unfold, and on witnessing the scene decided to confront the troupe on their behaviour. The party allegedly barracked the youth worker before getting back into their car and driving off. As they left, Lavender duly noted the Stones' car number plate, as well as its occupants' deportment. If Lavender was as fastidious in his notation of the vehicle and said occupants, he would have equally been aware of the people inside proffering a "well-known gesture" as they left. Keeley and Lavender promptly called the police and insisted that a charge relating to events be formally raised by authorities. Keeley, it appears, was most adamant about this, saying, "If the police do not prosecute, I will press a private prosecution."

Such were the lines of communication between Scotland Yard and the press that word of the toilet encounter soon slipped out. By Saturday, March 20, the story had made front-page news of the *Daily Express* and other papers at the lower end of the media scale. Evidently, reporters were working around the clock and had already collared both Keeley and Lavender for their version of events. Since the urination allegation was presumably too sensitive to publish, there was no mention of anything other than suspected "insulting behaviour". Aware that speculation could easily run riot, the group's business manager, Eric Easton, issued an ambivalent response to a *Daily Express* reporter: "I am not denying or confirming what these people are saying happened at the garage. It was a great surprise to me to hear about this. None of the group mentioned it."

Nevertheless, the attendant and youth club leader demanded action, and charges were prepared against Mick, Brian and Bill. While Rolling Stones' duties involved further trips to Europe and America, the trio were forced to return to East Ham Magistrates Court on July 22, 1965 on charges of insulting behaviour. Dressed uniformly in suits, their presence appeared very much at odds with the media's perception. Albeit on relatively minor offences, those accused were adamant that the charges had been largely embellished. During a two-and-a-half-hour hearing, a succession of hysterical claims was made against the defendants, who were described as "long haired morons" and "shaggy haired monsters".

Denying the urination charge, the trio's solicitor, Dale Parkinson, described their actions as nothing more than, "riotous, adolescent, carefree, student-like behaviour". Nonetheless, prosecution lawyers championed the witnesses' version of events. Fearful of revenge attacks, the bench excused anyone giving evidence from verbalising their home addresses.

Outside, over 50 police vainly attempted to contain the 300 fans that had queued outside for hours to catch a glimpse of their idols. Inside, it was no less charged with police watching over the 50 fans installed inside the public gallery. Sitting among them was Charlie Watts, quietly watching proceedings. Keith Richards was also there as a character witness, claiming that the events of the night had been nothing more than a misunderstanding. Ultimately, Bill Wyman was found not guilty of using obscene language. On the charge of insulting behaviour however, the trio were found guilty and each of them was fined five pounds, with costs of 15 guineas.

Aware that their decision would be scrutinised by the media, the prosecution utilised the sort of semantics not unfamiliar in a period drama. Chairman Alderman Albert Moorey remarked that in his opinion the trio's behaviour was "conduct not becoming to young gentlemen". Furthermore, he'd invoke a responsibility the trio supposedly had on their audiences, a lecture that would be revived in years to come. "Whether it be The Rolling Stones, The Beatles or anyone else," said Moorey, "we will not tolerate this conduct. Because you have reached the exalted height in your particular profession, that does not give you the right to behave in the manner which you have been found guilty. On the contrary, you should set a standard of behaviour which should be a moral pattern for your large number of supporters."

The trio lodged an immediate appeal but with more pressing business to attend to, it was later deemed not worthy of pursuing. Perversely, the charge served to further embellish the anarchic credentials of the group, Oldham feeding the urination episode directly into the band's PR dossier. "The Rolling Stones have been responsible for a lot of controversial publicity," Oldham would write in a press brochure. "They have been known to use gas stations as toilets when nature couldn't hold herself any longer, and other such exploits have amused their fans the world over."

The Romford incident duly milked for all it was worth, the group concentrated on building their ascendancy in more conventional ways. Their fifth single, 'Little Red Rooster' (released November 1964), had followed 'It's All Over Now' to the top of the UK charts, as did the sixth, 'The Last Time', released in February 1965 and the first to be written by Jagger and Richards. Like Lennon and McCartney, Jagger and Richards could now look forward to accruing publishing royalties on top of what they made from record sales. Those newspaper columnists with the savvy to look beyond the headlines about hysteria were starting to comment on the earning potential of these young pop groups, an aspect of 'the British Invasion' that had aroused the interest of 33-year-old American music industry wheeler-dealer Allen Klein. An orphan of tough New York Jewish stock, Klein was an accountant turned music publisher whose speciality was extracting funds from record labels on behalf of his clients, becoming something of a pariah in the process.

With his street-level banter and confrontational approach, Klein had charmed the likes of The Shirelles and Sam Cooke onto his client list and got them lucrative deals that way overrode traditional royalty rates. With his wife, Betty, he established a business partnership (later named ABKCO – Allen & Betty Klein and Company), and set his sights on breaking into the burgeoning British market. In an attempt to secure a piece of the action, he'd flown over to London in the summer of 1964 and conferred with Beatles' manager Brian Epstein, offering the services of singer Sam Cooke as support for The Beatles' summer 1964 tour of the States. In return for his magnanimous gesture, he'd suggested being repaid with a slice of Epstein's pound-printing NEMS organisation. Taken aback by the raw, upfront approach of Klein, the sensitive Epstein asked the portly American to leave his premises.

Undeterred by Epstein's rebuff, Klein turned his attentions to other British acts, most notably The Rolling Stones. Criss-crossing back and forth across the Atlantic, Klein tracked Andrew Oldham to a record convention in Miami hosted by Decca's US subsidiary label, London. Despite Oldham's reputation as a shrewd hustler, Klein's detective work had revealed the meagre returns the Stones had secured from Decca and their associated interests. While to the public at large the group appeared to be coining it in at every opportunity, personally they weren't millionaires. This was not uncommon in the fledgling pop industry; even the Beatles' seemingly inexhaustible money machine hadn't as yet made them millionaires. However, others aligned to the industry were doing very well for themselves.

As was his style, Klein found numerous inconsistencies in the Stones' business affairs. Aware that Oldham and his partner Eric Easton were evidently from two different schools, Klein seized an opportunity to make an inroad into the band. Oozing broad semantics that fell well outside of management protocol, Klein asked Oldham if he'd like to be a millionaire, then promised him delivery of a brand new Rolls-Royce if he acquiesced to sharing a slice of the Stones. While clearly enchanted by Klein's promise of immediate riches, it was the opportunity to focus less on financial matters and more on the creative side of business that appealed to Oldham.

A deal struck, Klein promptly excised business manager Eric Easton from the partnership. Expecting an avalanche of legalities and bruised loyalties, Oldham removed himself abroad while Klein manoeuvred himself into a position of control over the Stones' financial affairs. Despite the predictable injunction from Easton, Klein took control.

On July 26, 1965, Mick's 22nd birthday, the Stones met Klein for the first time. The burly New Yorker welcomed the Stones to his suite at London's Hilton Hotel and made his customary overtures, referencing his own humble start in life, and how he identified with the brash base the Stones were operating from. With a well-rehearsed patter, Klein spoke about how their global successes had borne enormous riches, of which they had seen only a fraction. With a promise to renegotiate their contracts and radically elevate their meagre base rate to levels never previously envisaged before, the group were won over. Equally, with touring receipts barely covering their expenses, Klein promised greater returns from live shows and a reduction in appearances, especially in the UK where the group had tired of the endless round of one-night stands.

Despite Wyman and Jones' reservations, Klein won over the power base of Jagger, Richards and Oldham with his seemingly honest approach and gritty humour. Inclusive with the management arrangement was the promise of a five-film deal over a three-year period. The first demonstrable result of the deal was when Klein renegotiated the group's Decca recording contract for a sum approaching £2 million. News of this staggering feat made it into the lofty *Financial Times,* a journal not necessarily known for its coverage of pop music.

Jagger, his keen business acumen honed by studies at the London

School of Economics, was initially bowled over by Klein's approach. Worn as something of a badge of honour, Mick would boast Klein's remarkable dealings around clubland, embarrassing John Lennon and Paul McCartney who were still receiving derisory returns despite their success.

In all this, Brian Jones' founder status had been all but reduced to a footnote. Klein's takeover was achieved without any major involvement from Jones other than turning up to sign the paperwork, for he could do little other than go with the majority vote. Oldham had effectively taken control of the group's artistic presentation, thus further marginalising "the contradiction in blonde", as Richards described him. While due in part to his consuming drug use, Jones' fears regarding Mick and Keith's increasing dominance had reached fever pitch. Continually at war with himself, he'd talk to anyone about his disquiet over his diminished role. He consoled himself with the fact that he was still highly regarded by major peers like Bob Dylan and John Lennon, but there was little doubt that his paranoia over losing control was having a devastating effect on his well-being.

While amphetamine and marijuana use had become almost *de rigueur* among musicians, Jones had been upping his intake of every conceivable substance in an almost desperate need to escape reality. High on a variety of chemicals, he would often go missing for days on end, only to return looking sick and haunted. Jones' turn into chemical left-field served only to generate further resentment within the group. Mick and Keith were no strangers to drugs but stopped short of overindulgence that compromised the business of being Rolling Stones. Brian, however, was frequently becoming unable to function.

Women, too, were a constant source of problems for the tetchy and overtly chauvinistic Jones. With female company constantly in his slipstream, Brian was effectively on the run from his dalliances, and though further paternity claims did little to curb his insatiable libido, he still hadn't met anyone who could satisfy his complex nature. He articulated a benchmark for his perfect woman in one of the teen magazines of the period that fed off the interests and desires of pop stars.

"I haven't tied myself down to a girl yet," asserted Jones. "After all, how many girls could I find who would make my tea, cook my meal, tidy my house and talk intellectually to me while I sat watching with my feet up?"

In this regard, things changed dramatically for Jones on September 14, 1965 at Munich's Circus Krone Bau concert hall where among those hanging around backstage between shows was the girl of his fantasies, Anita Pallenberg. Despite her elfin presence, Anita had packed a lifetime of adventures into her 21 years. Expelled from school at 16, her puckish beauty gave her an entrée into the world of international modelling. In Rome she mingled with the Dolce Vita set before making her way to New York where she encountered Andy Warhol, Allen Ginsberg and others from the alternative arts scene. Back in Munich, she received an invite from a photographer friend to see the Stones in concert, easing herself backstage between performances with a supply of hashish and the potent chemical amyl nitrate, with which she attempted to engage Mick before he hit the stage.

Jagger passed on the offer but watching on the sidelines was Jones. Enchanted by Anita's startling aura, he saw much of himself in the leggy blonde with the pixie features. He approached her, saying, "I don't know who you are, but I need you." While this exchange was taking place, Pallenberg's photographer friend managed to record the historic meeting, the resulting image perfectly capturing the connection between them. Moments later the group were called to the stage, leaving Pallenberg to return to her seat in the auditorium. There, she witnessed Jones' slow burning enigma, as always set just a few paces back from the frontline of the group. After the predictable unruly audience scenes, Anita ended up with Brian backstage. "I asked Brian if he wanted a joint," she recalled. "He said yes, so he asked me back to his hotel and he cried all night. He was so upset about Mick and Keith… saying they had teamed up on him. I felt so sorry for him."

Jones evidently made his mind up there and then that Pallenberg was the key to a new direction for him and from that night on they became virtually inseparable. In the blink of an eye, Pallenberg hopped aboard the Stones caravan, filling a void in Jones' life and becoming a powerful advocate for his point of view. Almost immediately, the pair began to mirror each other's personalities, adopting an air of arrogance and an unconventional lifestyle that could occasionally manifest itself in dark ways. Pallenberg encouraged the quirkier side of Brian's personality and in turn, Jones would adopt her androgynous fashion sense, which was soon copied by others on the scene, Jagger and Richards included.

By the end of 1965 the pop world was evolving at a furious rate. Jagger's search for a higher level of acceptance brought him into contact with young, rich and intellectual men who were attracted to the Stones' dangerous aura. There were invites to dinner parties and society functions, all of which tended to diminish the Stones' association with their brash past. Jagger attended many of these gatherings independently, a gulf having appeared in his relationship with Chrissie Shrimpton. Mick had apparently assured Shrimpton that he'd marry her during a lull in the Stones' itinerary, but other distractions made this unlikely. While he'd reportedly demanded that she never touch marijuana, he'd imposed no such restrictions on himself.

It was a different matter when LSD started to gain a foothold on the pop scene. Mick kept the unpredictable drug at arms length and had warned Chrissie not to experiment. Brian, however, was immersed in an acid baptism that spanned several months, and he found the effects of LSD both challenging and provocative. In an attempt to provoke some sort of reaction, Jones had mischievously suggested to Chrissie Shrimpton that Mick had also been experimenting with LSD, and she became convinced that someone had slipped her a dose of the drug unawares.

With Shrimpton in a whirl of confusion over the direction their relationship was taking, Jagger was reportedly monitoring Marianne Faithfull's movements. In the social whirl of 'Swinging London', there were numerous occasions when they could meet, both professionally and socially. Meanwhile, she maintained her relationship with John Dunbar, the couple marrying on the heels of Marianne's discovering she was pregnant.

Still only 18 and very much in love, Marianne was hoping for a conventional bourgeois marriage. However, the couple's flat at Lennox Gardens, Knightsbridge, had become a popular meeting point for the pop fraternity while other characters on the fringes of Dunbar's world continually challenged Faithfull's innocent view of life. Her timetable was hectic, and with Dunbar pulled further into the burgeoning avant-garde scene and its attendant drug culture, Marianne started looking for distractions elsewhere. The entourage surrounding the Stones' grew ever more attractive.

Meanwhile, Mick had professional distractions to occupy his mind, not least the Stones' fourth tour of the United States, starting on October 27, which would take the group across the length and breadth of the continent. They brought enormous collateral with them. '(I Can't Get No) Satisfaction', their first real international hit, fed directly from the kind of frustration that was being experienced by youth worldwide. While The Who's 'My Generation' exemplified the angst felt by British working-class kids, the broader metaphor of 'Satisfaction' was far more accessible.

Under Allen Klein's stewardship, the US visit would take on a greater financial significance, with the price tag on the group's concerts rising considerably. Previous tours had barely scraped even, but this time they would return home in profit.

Hysterical scenes followed them at every juncture. Photographer Gered Mankowitz was commissioned to document the jaunt, and recalls that the excitement had long ago lost its shiny veneer. "The reality of touring was mundane, hard work and with an upside down timescale," he says. "That took the edge off it. So it wasn't as though it was a 24-hour rock'n'roll party, it was full of rather tedious periods where one was sitting on a plane for hours in the middle of the night, arriving at deserted townships and remote motels. It wasn't super glamorous and it wasn't super high-powered either."

During a requisite stay in New York, the Stones were ensconced in the Lincoln Square Motor Inn when, on the night of November 9, a major power cut affecting the Northeast plunged the city into darkness. A welcome visitor was Bob Dylan, who arrived with several of his retinue, a quantity of hashish and some of his trademark cheap wine. Out of all the Stones Dylan was closest to Brian, despite the uneasiness the latter felt over 'Ballad Of A Thin Man', off Dylan's recent *Highway 61 Revisited* with its recurring line, "Something is happening but you don't know what it is, do you, Mr Jones?" Dylan was said to have greeted the Stone during this time with the sarcastic "How's your paranoia meter?" The evening drifted into a candlelit jam session. Inspired by the potency of Dylan's stash, Jones played harmonica until his mouth bled then, heavily intoxicated, knocked over one of the candles and started a small inferno.

Parallel to the Stones' tour of America, LSD was in its final phase of ascendancy from laboratory to street. With users evangelising about the drug's extraordinary effects, the grapevine was electrified. Acid's explosion knew no bounds, and by the end of the year it was fast replacing marijuana as the drug of choice for the creatively aware. Revelling in his role as hip crusader Brian Jones was eager to turn others on at every opportunity. Hilton Valentine, guitarist with The Animals, who were touring the US at the same time, experienced his first LSD trip with Jones in New York during this period.

"The Stones came over to our hotel as we were going to go out to a club together," recalls Valentine. "Before we went, Brian said to me, 'Here, you should try this,' and I said, 'What is it?' And he said 'LSD.' He then showed me a sugar cube. So I said, 'What does it do?' and he said, 'It's just like smoking pot, but stronger.' So I thought I'd give it a go. So I dropped it and we went out in New York, tripping."

LSD's ability to radically rewrite the user's consciousness came with several issues, as John Steel, The Animals' drummer, recalls. "There was this division before acid and after acid. It was a completely different sixties to the early years where everyone was just finding their feet and having a lot of fun. Previously, it had just been an alcohol-fuelled thing with a bit of pot smoking thrown in. But when acid came, it actually divided groups, between those who did and those who didn't."

While still technically legal, LSD required contacts to liberate it from the laboratories to the street. When word of its recreational status started to spread pharmacists withdrew supplies, leaving the field open to less scrupulous sources. One legendary San Francisco rogue chemist produced 300,000 LSD tablets during 1965. The drug's growing popularity in the States was helped no end by the antics of author Ken Kesey and his band of associates, the Merry Pranksters. After his novel *One Flew Over The Cuckoo's Nest* received rave notices, Kesey piled a troupe of fellow acid freaks into an old school bus and headed off around the States, their brief to dose the entire nation with LSD's all-encompassing charms.

Given their artistic leanings, the Merry Pranksters held their own initiation ceremonies where LSD would be served up to those game enough to try it. These 'graduation' tests combined mind expansion with raucous music and obtuse theatrics. Despite an air of uncertainty, there were plenty of takers who turned up to engage in what was called 'The Acid Tests'. The Californian leg of the Stones' tour coincided with one of the Pranksters' initiation ceremonies, and party organisers handed out leaflets following the group's concert at San Jose Civic Auditorium on December 4. Somehow, one of the flyers – hysterically containing the demand 'Can You Pass The Acid Test?' – made its way to the Stones. Suitably intrigued and with the venue just a block away, Brian, Keith and Mick headed off to witness the Pranksters' shindig.

Also present were the neophyte Grateful Dead, Allen Ginsberg and New York counterculture iconoclasts The Fugs. Reportedly, both Brian and Keith imbibed some potent LSD mixed with orange Kool-Aid. According to Prankster Ken Babbs, Keith climbed on the stage during the Grateful Dead's set and attempted to take control of the microphone. Brian, similarly fried on LSD, became fascinated with Jerry Garcia's guitar playing. Mick, still apprehensive about the advertised life-changing effects of LSD, stalled on taking a dose, preferring to watch the real life psychedelia taking place.

While for the most part these acid experiences were as prescribed, LSD's unpredictability could easily overwhelm someone with a fragile grasp on reality, such as Brian. After the tour ended, the group remained in Los Angeles to record tracks at RCA studios, destined for their next album *Aftermath*. According to one source, Brian was having a particularly bad time on a trip and ran through the swanky Ambassador Hotel lobby screaming that the floors upstairs were crawling with snakes. Later that week, Brian fled from the studio, claiming that it was infested with insects that were slowly consuming the building.

Jones reportedly turned on many whether they liked it or not, and revelled in watching the unsuspecting down their newly spiked drink before veering off into the chemical stratosphere. Tony Bramwell, who worked for The Beatles' NEMS organisation, was privy to Brian's capers around London's clubland. "It was around this time that people started bullying you, saying that you've got to turn on and that you've seen nothing until you have taken a trip," he says. "There was always this fear that someone might spike you. Brian was such a nice guy before all that. He had a place in Beaufort Mews in Chelsea and you could always pop in, have a drink and a chat – listen to some music. Then he just became like a thug; totally out of control. Brian and Anita used to tumble around The Speakeasy Club, almost getting thrown out because they were so objectionable. But you couldn't throw a Rolling Stone out, so people had to keep saying to them 'calm down'."

By the close of 1965, it appeared as though British pop ruled the world. The Beatles investiture with MBEs at Buckingham Palace in October had provoked a reaction among retired army types who felt they were undeserving. This was a class of people who wrote letters to *The Times*, drank gin in golf clubs and wore ties on Saturdays. The rise of The Beatles and, more especially, The Rolling Stones represented a threat to a way of life they desperately wanted to preserve and – as events in the coming year would prove – they were unwilling to give it up without a fight.

CHAPTER 3
Chelsea

"Disks by the thousands spin in a widening orbit of discothèques, and elegant saloons have become gambling parlours. In a once sedate world of faded splendour, everything new, uninhibited and kinky is blooming at the top of London life... The Rolling Stones, whose music is most 'in' right now, reign as a new breed of royalty."

Time magazine, April 15, 1966

If 1965 hinted at the raft of social changes on the horizon, the following year processed them into full-blown Technicolor. Youth-driven cultural explosions were heard around the globe, but the powerhouse of the artistic movement was based in Britain. London was now the centre of the creative world, its attendant Pop Art culture appropriating the Union Jack as a fashion accessory.

This renewed passion for all things British soon trickled down to the masses. Joining the many disparate strands of this new optimism, England's victory in the World Cup in July 1966 certainly brightened the lives of those who felt alienated by the more creative advances occurring elsewhere. Labour Prime Minister Harold Wilson, elected in 1964, had made a point of fraternising with The Beatles, cleverly utilising pop culture for his own means, but the public at large were also engaged, whether it was wearing tacky imitations of their idols' apparel from Carnaby Street or buying the latest LPs from WH Smiths. For a while, at least, everyone joined in the fun.

'Swinging London' was projected globally, especially in the USA where country singer Roger Miller had scored with 'England Swings', a paean to the nation's euphoric revival. On a more serious level, the respected *Time* magazine made a more methodical effort to assess the vibrations that were electrifying the country, especially London. Dispatching a team of reporters from New York, an entire issue of the magazine was devoted to exploring what was driving the city's renaissance.

Time's gushing April 15, 1966 edition revealed London as an Aladdin's cave of rediscovered optimism, a place where race, class and even age issues had blurred to the point of collapse. Sexual freedom, seemingly exiled for centuries, had been ripped from its tomb. While *Time* detected that many in this renaissance were drawn from moneyed backgrounds, there was no denying that London's creative enclaves appeared far more accessible than in any other city. Gallery owner Robert Fraser, a character soon to loom large in the fortunes of the Stones, was quizzed on this new frisson electrifying the capital. "Right now," he said, "London has something that New York used to have: everybody wants to be there. There's no place else. Paris is calcified. There's an indefinable thing about London that makes people want to go there."

What *Time* failed to verbalise was that a symbiotic partner in this explosion was recreational drug use, especially LSD. During the first half of 1966 word of its extraordinary effects spread like wildfire, polarising the artistic community wherein those brave enough to imbibe wore their LSD initiation as a badge of honour, their glassy eyes and studious dialogue a clear indication that they were tuning into spectacular frequencies. For decades popping pills and smoking marijuana had become a ritualised part of the jazz world, naturally seeping into pop, but LSD challenged every atom of what had gone before. Keyboard virtuoso Zoot Money was one artist who was whisked off from R&B and into psychedelia. "It was a different acceleration," recalls Money on LSD's influence. "It was a totally different journey. It managed to loosen up uptight people. All the creative people of the time were enthusiastic about LSD as it offered a glimpse into what could be achieved."

"We thought we'd just discovered it all in the mid-sixties," recalls 'Gypsy' Dave Mills, close confidante of folk singer Donovan. "With mind changing substances and other ways of seeing things, we discovered new sensory experiences. It was as though we were living in a new time with a new thought and a new creativity. It was very special."

Having been inducted into the experience of taking the drug by Brian Jones, Hilton Valentine was another swift convert. "LSD just seeped through to all the bands that were around at the time," he says, 'It was all happening very quickly. It just opened up so many different areas in your mind. The idea was to try and capture it; to write, play or express it... that was the objective. Some people managed it, and yet some people didn't. It was an amazing time. Everything just went along with the music, art and fashions. By 1966, people couldn't wait to get out of the suits."

While acid prompted many to raise their musical game, the supremacy ofThe Beatles and the Stones remained unassailable. Music aside, sartorial change was occurring in both camps, with the Fab Four abandoning their matching suits, and the Stones glamming up, shifting from casual nonconformity to a dandified Edwardian look. Bordering on androgynous, the new approach was down in no small part to Jones and his girlfriend Anita Pallenberg's influence. Inspired by her innovative and fearless dress sense, Jones had been emancipated from his conservative mod threads, allowing the inert peacock within to spread its wings. With Brian leading the way in the Stones' fashion stakes, Mick and Keith weren't far behind in adopting a more feminine style. Make-up, previously the domain of the stage and film set, was now being used socially as a key male accoutrement. Jewellery, too, was worn regardless of gender.

With Carnaby Street now viewed as passé, rock's leading lights looked elsewhere to inform their wardrobes. Largely because of the Stones' patronage, Chelsea, in particular the King's Road, became the epicentre of the new direction, with stores such as Bizarre, Granny Takes A Trip and Dandie Fashions leading the way. High collars and military wear became something of a craze, the shop I Was Lord Kitchener's Valet just one of many catering for the extraordinary demand. Most popular with the groups during 1966 was the boutique Hung On You, situated just off the King's Road, which catered to all the styles and tastes of the era.

Always slightly to the left of London's crustier enclaves, Chelsea jealously guarded its independence; a place where different cultures and classes appeared to gel quite harmoniously in the same melting pot. Art, in all of its many and varied forms, had always been royally welcomed in SW3, and Mick, Keith and Brian were soon mingling with a new breed of brash, aristocratic dilettantes, all of them eager to engage in the stimulating energy that spun off the group. This appeal was reflected in magazines such as *Queen*, *London Life* and *Nova* which now featured pictures of The Rolling Stones in their society pages. Given that the Stones' popular metaphor straddled hedonism and danger, they became exciting party guests for those whose background and wealth had left them materially and emotionally sated. Eager to engage with these new and dangerous interlopers, young aristocrats with empty lives welcomed the Stones into their midst. "[It was] a strange mixture of aristocrats and gangsters, politicians, creative people, destructive people," recalls David Cammell, brother of filmmaker Donald, "all in a kind of exciting melange."

Jagger in particular was looking beyond nightclubs and discothèques to satisfy his mercurial tastes, presenting a conundrum which many found difficult to unravel. When interviewed, Mick came across as an erudite, thoughtful young man, which was often at odds with the image promoted by the popular press, which continued to pillory the Stones for what they imagined were their uncouth ways. In reality Mick found banter with fellow musicians boring and hackneyed; far more appealing were erudite conversations in the white stuccoed town houses of Chelsea sophisticates.

Mick, Keith and Brian each frequented Chelsea (Brian being the first to move there) and hob-knobbed with, among others, Guinness heir Tara Browne, oil baron's son Paul Getty and his girlfriend (and later wife) Talitha, noble European aristocrat Prince Stanislaus Klossowski de Rola (known to all as 'Stash'), photographer Michael Cooper, gallery owner Robert Fraser, interior designer Christopher Gibbs and artist cum film director Donald Cammell and his brother David. Marianne Faithfull and Paul McCartney, the latter now living in St John's Wood, were also component parts of a circle that enjoyed a shared sense of discovery. The Chelsea set offered the musicians new insights into art and intellect, while the Stones turned them on to music, fashion and streetwise attitude.

The Stones had more time to relax in 1966. Both they and The Beatles had cut down on touring – The Beatles gave it up completely that summer – to concentrate on recording. The result of this newly relaxed regime was more than evident on the Stones' album *Aftermath*. With the major advances The Beatles pioneered with *Rubber Soul* and The Beach Boys' *Pet Sounds*, the Stones' music was progressing in similar directions. The first indication of this was the February 1966 single '19th Nervous Breakdown', written predominately by Jagger, with lyrics that took a candid swipe at some of the personalities infiltrating the group's circle. Musically, it displayed an abrasive edge that hinted at darker, more introverted influences.

Released on April 15, *Aftermath* shot into the higher reaches of both the UK and American charts. The first Stones' album to be made up entirely of Jagger-Richards compositions, it pipped both The Beatles and The Beach Boys in delivering a sound largely removed from the public's perception of them. In a scene swamped with emerging creativity, *Aftermath* shook up the music community, setting a new benchmark for originality. Indeed, so taken were they with reports of the album's groundbreaking melange of sounds, The Beatles dispatched an aide to buy a copy while they were recording *Revolver*.

Aftermath was universally well received, with most reviewers praising its experimental, imaginative feel and drawing attention to its Englishness in the use of dulcimers and harpsichords. The cover, a stark, tinted image by Jerry Schatzberg, perfectly caught the group's disparate elements; Mick and Keith in a close huddle with Brian caught in mysterious half-portrait, eyes and mind evidently focused elsewhere. The few glitches in the production were mitigated by the strength of the compositions, the whole album serving to cement Jagger and Richards' reputation as songwriters as formidable as any the beat boom had thrown up.

Satisfied with their efforts, the Stones turned their attention to domestic matters. With London's swinging carousel revolving at all hours, there were times when even the most seasoned campaigner yearned for the pastoral comforts of the countryside. For those as active as the Stones, three years of constant touring had taken a considerable toll. While Brian Jones' health issues had been exacerbated by his all-consuming lifestyle, Mick had also been teetering close to a nervous breakdown, and was hospitalised at one point during 1966 for stress and exhaustion. Afforded a month off between tours in the spring of that year, frayed nerves were given a chance to repair with the desire to establish bases away from the city now something of a necessity. Charlie Watts and Bill Wyman led the way by buying large estates in the Home Counties, and during the early part of 1966 Keith, too, was ready to escape to greener pastures. "Although we made money, we were still living in rented apartments or hotels," declared Keith. "Consequently, we hadn't been able to appreciate the position we were in. By '66 we reached a point where another change was coming. ... We just needed to enjoy ourselves and take stock of what was happening."

Keith's property hunt led him down towards Chichester in West Sussex. Whether Richards knew it or not, the area had long been a retreat for those seeking pastoral and spiritual relaxation. Over the years, numerous artists had committed the quintessential beauty of the area to canvas, while writers such as the poet Hilaire Belloc had eulogised the understated beauty of the region. The close proximity to the sea was also a strong lure.

In search of a suitable retreat, Keith chanced upon an area just outside Chichester known as the Witterings, a peninsula with an array of charming villages. West Wittering was one such hamlet, its chocolate box environs appearing as if they had been passed over by time. Just outside the village lay Redlands, a beautiful 13th century thatched cottage situated at the end of a narrow road. Despite its modest presence from the driveway, a moat ran around the edges of the property with only a small bridge allowing entry towards the house. To its rear were fields that slowly dissolved towards the sea.

Although it is unlikely Richards knew it at the time, the house was one of the most important buildings in the county of West Sussex. Referenced in the Doomsday Book, it was rumoured that Anne Boleyn, the second wife of King Henry VIII, had once lodged at the property. For the best part of its history Redlands had been a farm dwelling, but despite some alternations over the years it retained a strong continuity with its past; the thatched roof and wooden beams all evidence of its remarkable vintage. Inside it was a similar story, with stone flagged tiles in the kitchen and rich oak panels covering the living and drawing room areas. Dominating the ground floor were two enormous fireplaces, their fashioned brickwork marking them out as the focal points. Upstairs would reveal a number of bedrooms that were perfect for housing a large contingent of guests. With a retained gardener and cleaner employed to tend to the property's needs, everything appeared perfect. At the beginning of 1966, Redlands' continuity with its agricultural past was about to end, farming couple Stanley and Joyce Fletcher deciding to put the house up for sale.

With Redlands for sale by auction in February, it would require some skilful bidding to secure tenancy of the house. Unfamiliar with auction protocol, Keith employed Stones' lawyer Timothy Hardacre to bid on his behalf. "Keith said, 'I'm interested in that house, and I don't know much about auctions. Could you come down and bid for me?'" recalls Hardacre. "So I went down to the Dolphin Hotel in Chichester. I spoke to the auctioneer and I said, 'I'm representing Keith Richards and I shall be bidding in his name.' So I kept on bidding and we got it for a very reasonable price... When Keith walked into the auction room I noticed a murmur of horror and disgust break out. And this was increased further when we all got in Keith's chauffeur-driven Bentley Continental and drove away, leaving these disgruntled people in Chichester."

Although some locals verbalised their disdain at having a Rolling Stone in their midst, Keith happily stumped up the £17,500 price tag. Following a short period while the previous residents took their leave, Keith was able to move in on April 16. With pet dog Ratbag as his most constant companion, the rural ambiance and rich infusion of country air was a welcome antidote to the suffocation that London, whether swinging or not, could frequently engender.

Mightily chuffed with his acquisition, Keith happily showed friends around Redlands' expansive lawns and rich arboretum. Most, it seems, were taken with the property and its attendant moat, where, as Keith was more than happy to point out, Saxon arrowheads had once been discovered.

Like The Beatles, the Stones had a monthly fan magazine devoted to them. While it would in no way challenge *The Beatles Book* for sales, it still served to keep Stones' fans up to speed on events that most newspapers would otherwise ignore. Given the strong likelihood that Richards' new property was of interest, Sue Mauntner, one of the publication's chief writers, paid a trip down to West Wittering to take a peek at Richards' country pile. The first witness report of Redlands under Keith's ownership, it paints a remarkable portrait of the musician enjoying the fruits of his hard-earned toils:

It was a beautifully sunny day when I drove down to Keith's fifteenth century house in Sussex. "Mr. Richards hasn't arrived yet," said the old gardener when I approached the drive.

Much to my surprise (and only because I was so nosy) I found the porch door open. So I took the liberty of entering. I was very interested and surprised to learn that that his books consisted of The Great War, Dictionary Of Slang, Guns, Great Land Battles, Drawings Of Rembrandt *and other books on England. I was even more surprised with his record collection. Among the Beatles, Otis Reading* [sic], *Dylan, Simon and Garfunkel, the Everlys, Temptations and Elvis were albums of Chopin's Nineteen Waltzes, Rossini and Segovia.*

The upstairs consisted of five bedrooms and a bathroom. I knew which was Keith's room, because the bed was unmade and there was a pair of shoes and a Dennis Wheatley book lying on the floor. All the rooms were unfurnished, and like the downstairs, it was all wooden beams and floors. One bedroom had half the floor missing, so I could immediately look down into the kitchen.

I came downstairs through the large dining room and into the kitchen to find some dirty dishes, a burnt sausage in the frying pan in the cooker, a rifle on the wall, a spur hanging on the other wall and a clock on the door, not to mention truncheon hanging from the ceiling (Keith had pinched it off a gendarme in Paris). Being a female, my immediate reaction was to put the kettle on for a cuppa.

As I was pouring my tea, Keith drove up in his Bentley Continental plus L Plates… Keith was very annoyed with the builders for leaving the house unlocked. "Whose boat is that?" I inquired. "Oh, that belonged to the owner, I bought it off him. You can paddle around the moat in it, but at the moment it's got a hole in the side."

With Keith retreating to West Sussex, Mick moved into a modern rented town house at 13a Bryanston Mews in the New Year of 1966. While most of the group looked beyond London for home bases, Jagger was evidently still enchanted with the capital. For someone as charged as Brian, the thought of relocation wasn't a priority. Sharing a modest Knightsbridge flat with Anita Pallenberg, he maintained an almost constant presence on London's swinging rotunda. If thoughts of retreat manifested itself, they were directed towards Morocco. Jones had already been schooled in the riches the country had to offer by dint of his fraternisation with London-based designer Christopher Gibbs. A noted forerunner of imaginative interior decoration, Gibbs mixed well-worn grandeur with vibrant treasures from Asia, the Middle East and Africa, particularly Morocco. Aware that much of Middle Eastern art and decor resonated strongly with the psychedelic experience, Gibbs was a much sought after expert when pop people turned their attention to decorating the interiors of their flats and houses.

Gibbs' shared a fanatical interest in Morocco with art dealer and gallery owner Robert Fraser. An old Etonian, Fraser was another character from the moneyed class who'd become attracted to the rat pack of musicians traversing Chelsea's party circuit, all of whom he welcomed warmly into his Duke Street gallery. Adding to his appeal, Fraser was passionate about exotic drug use, and was evidently happy to share his passions with others.

Gibbs and Fraser had already accompanied Jones and his former girlfriend, Linda Lawrence, to Morocco in August 1965. Seasoned to the region's customs, the pair shepherded Jones and his partner around the mosques, souks and other points of interest. Revelling in this smorgasbord of new experiences, Brian became enchanted by the indigenous music of the area as played by the Sufi musicians of northern Morocco. The ethereal vibrations from the pipe players would inspire him to record their exotic sounds in the future.

Pictures of Jones returning to London in quasi-Middle Eastern gear further signalled the Stones' departure from their earlier image. For the who'd loyally bought into the everyday semantics of 'It's All Over Now', 'The Last Time' or even 'Satisfaction', the turn into uncharted waters was a difficult pill for many to swallow, causing the Stones to lose space in the nation's teen publications.

Some were in a quandary as to where this new direction had originated. Critics weren't publicly correlating new sounds with the raft of substances flooding into the music scene, though for the musicians themselves, there was a genuine sense of naughtiness in coyly (or even overtly) name checking drug slang in their compositions. While The Beatles' cloaked songs such as 'Day Tripper' and 'Tomorrow Never Knows' in sufficient irony and metaphor to defer suspicion, others were less scrupulous. The Stones' 1965 collection *Out Of Our Heads* certainly suggested intoxication of some sort, and the single '19th Nervous Breakdown' contained the lyric: 'On our first trip I tried so hard to rearrange your mind'. In the US, Bob Dylan, The Byrds and The Velvet Underground were composing songs that contained thinly veiled references to their own submergence into narcotics. Quizzed on '19th Nervous Breakdown' by reporter Sue Mauntner, Jagger was typically coy. "People say that I'm always singing about pills and breakdowns therefore I must be an addict – this is ridiculous," he said. "Some people are so narrow-minded they won't admit to themselves that this really does happen to other people besides pop stars."

In reality, those in the press were fully aware what was happening, but were happy to turn a blind eye to drug use. Managers and agents fed the print media with chirpy photos and cheeky stories, and there was no immediate need to rock the boat. For most Fleet Street hacks, the pop groups were a much needed breath of fresh air after the dismal stories at the start of the decade: the Cuban Missile Crisis, the Profumo affair and the assassination of John F. Kennedy.

Don Short, the entertainment correspondent for the *Daily Mirror* during the sixties, was privy to this symbiotic relationship between pop musicians and the press. "In the early days, the press suddenly awakened to the fact that circulation could be handsomely boosted by pop stars," he recalls. "Suddenly they were very much in editor's minds as they sold newspapers. We as reporters certainly benefited from them greatly, and obviously we helped them in terms of the stories we were carrying from day to day."

This cosy relationship had run undisturbed for a good few years, but with events testing the boundaries of even the broadest minded of tabloid editors, by 1966 the tacit agreement regarding drug use and musicians was perilously close to breaking. The police, too, were starting to take an interest, and began monitoring the activities of the capital's musicians. Early in 1966, they were handed an own goal.

The folk-singer Donovan, a slight Glaswegian with a grin as permanent as his corduroy cap, was royally accepted into the pop fold for his impish smile and poetic nature. Much liked within music circles, he worked prodigiously; among the first of many young men with guitars who became omnipresent fixtures on the pop scene from the mid-sixties onwards.

Like Bob Dylan, Donovan moved from acoustic to electric, scoring a number two hit with the shimmering but fairly innocent sounding 'Sunshine Superman'. However, the flip-side 'The Trip', ostensibly a paean to the Hollywood nightclub of the same name, offered plenty of examples that suggested exotic substances were inspiring the young troubadour's creative impulses.

Such was Donovan's popularity that he was offered the chance to star in his own documentary courtesy of the producers of television's favourite pop show *Ready Steady Go*. Broadcast in early 1966 as *A Boy Called Donovan*, it featured Donovan's music as its soundtrack, and presented several sequences that depicted the musician and his largely itinerant band of kindred spirits in various states of relaxation. Towards the end of the film one of a seemingly interminable series of parties is broken up by the spectre of two revellers arriving dressed as policemen. Amid these comical antics some might have noticed that one member of Donovan's circle was smoking a marijuana reefer, an act that was almost bound to rattle sensitive antennas.

In tandem with the music's scene huge turnaround, London's drug squad was undergoing its own palace revolution. At its core was Detective Sergeant Norman Clement Pilcher, an officer who would become the scourge of the London-based rock musicians of the sixties. In his mid-thirties, Pilcher had a rarefied nose for his work that went well beyond his official duties. A family man from Kent, he was known to his colleagues as 'Nobby' and had worked his way up from desk duties at Chelsea Police Station to London's renowned Flying Squad. In early 1966, Pilcher transferred to the drug squad under the leadership of Victor Kelaher, an officer with strong links to overseas drug agencies. Pilcher brought to the squad a keen understanding of London's underworld, as well as a sizable list of informants. Witty and personable to his colleagues, he secured the confidence of his underlings with the phrase, "Leave it to your old dad". Working nothing short of 12-hour days for his weekly wage of £27, Pilcher enjoyed his status in the team, driving a souped-up Lotus Cortina around town. Adding to his authority, if the occasion demanded it he was licensed to use a gun.

With similar young and driven officers making up this modest team of around 20, they revolutionised the image of a drug squad whose target area was relatively small by today's standards. Nevertheless, with marijuana enjoying increased use in Britain, convictions were starting to rise. The influx of Afro-Caribbean immigrants into London following the cessation of the Second World War were partly to blame, as were jazz musicians who'd discovered it in the forties and fifties. Matters took a more serious turn in 1964 with an increase in non-medical use of amphetamines, especially among Mods. Their fondness for 'purple hearts' (a combination of amphetamine and barbiturate) led to the first post-war drug craze and in 1964 unauthorised possession of amphetamine was banned.

As a result of the hysterical press coverage all substances, regardless of strength, were indiscriminately lumped together. The government's 'Brain Committee' of 1964 largely informed the following year's Dangerous Drugs Act with sweeping recommendations, not least by heavily increasing the penalties for possession. Furthermore, the act led the way for police to later implement new powers for stop and search procedures. With little differentiation between substances, drug laws appeared to mimic the media's perception that all drug use was uniformly demonic.

It was an atmosphere that bestowed a great deal of confidence on the likes of DS Pilcher. It was reflected in the squad's dress sense; smart, modish and with more than a hint of gangster chic that was quite unlike the uniform of more traditional policing. Dubbed the 'Whispering Squad' by colleagues, Pilcher and his team took a broad approach to matters like surveillance, firmly believing that the end justified the means.

It was only a matter of time before the new drug squad focussed their attentions on the new breed of pop stars strutting around the capital. With the lines between press, informant and police well established, something was bound to break soon. Media stories about the growing epidemic of drug use among the young were rife and the squad was quick to realise that exemplary arrests – especially of celebrities – would be gold dust in their efforts to create a greater platform for their work. While busting everyday individuals for drugs might make it into the local press, arrests of high profile celebrities would guarantee considerable media coverage. The affront displayed on screen by Donovan was clearly an opportunity not to be wasted.

Fraternising across clubland and discothèques, Donovan lived in Edgware Road and his address was well known even beyond his own circle. Given that hordes of personalities, including members of The Beatles and Stones, frequented the property at all hours, it was a fairly easy address to locate. "The police had taken over a flat opposite us," recalls 'Gypsy' Dave Mills. "They were actually watching us all the time. We didn't know about it at the time, but that was the extent they were going to to try and bust people."

At 1:30 a.m. on June 11, almost five months to the day after his controversial documentary aired, Donovan's flat was targeted by Detective Pilcher and officers from the drug squad. Falling into bed after one of his regular parties, Donovan was tucked up with a female companion, 20-year-old Doreen Samuel. Still up, though, was the singer's friend and roadie, Gypsy Dave.

A knock at the door revealed a pretty woman in civilian clothes. Believing she was a party guest, Gypsy Dave beckoned her inside. Unbeknown to him, behind her were nine police officers, most of them dressed in smart suits. Pilcher led the charge as officers tore into the house. Woken by the chaos and confused by the smart set of invaders, Donovan leapt out of bed naked and jumped onto the back of one of them. Once restrained, the singer had a search warrant shoved in his face which he tried to knock out of the officer's hands. Reportedly, Donovan shouted at the officer, "I am too young to read a warrant. You can't nick me!"

Evidently, the squad were looking for more than just cannabis and, as Donovan went to the fridge to get a drink of milk, one of the officers shouted, "Quick, the LSD's in the milk!" As it happened there was no LSD on the premises but police found a large piece of hashish in Gypsy Dave's room. Knowing full well how much hashish they had between them, Donovan and Dave were surprised at the quantity of the find. According to Gypsy Mills, Pilcher showed them the lump and said: "I have you now, and any time I want to, I can just click my fingers and stick you in the nick. Just by bringing the evidence with me in me pocket, see? So you two just watch it, you hear me?"

Donovan, Gypsy Dave and Doreen Samuel were carted off to a police station where Pilcher handed the singer a less formal piece of paper to sign. "I am sorry about all this Don," he reportedly told him. "It's only my job. Can I have your autograph for my daughter?"

The following day, the three were charged with possession of cannabis and sent for trial on July 28 at Marylebone Magistrates Court. On the insistence of George Harrison and Paul McCartney, the services of Beatles' lawyer David Jacobs were made available. Ultimately, Donovan and Mills were spared jail, but both were fined a mammoth £250* and Samuel was put on probation for a year. Donovan was also on the receiving end of a stern admonishing from the magistrate that, like the ticking off the Stones had received following their petrol station incident, paid deference to his celebrity. "We would like you to bear in mind," the magistrate told Donovan, "that you have great influence on young people, and that in these circumstances, it behoves you to behave yourself." Later in the day, Donovan would reflect on events with the *Daily Mirror's* entertainment correspondent Don Short, telling the reporter, "The only shame I have is that I was the first to come a cropper of all the artists who could have been accused."

News of Donovan's arrest spread like wildfire around London's rock fraternity, bringing with it a degree of paranoia. The fact that Donovan

* About £3,600 in 2011.

had been caught with marijuana, while other parties were downing far greater quantities of harder drugs, caused a few musicians to take precautions. While many believed that Donovan's fate was sealed by his friends caught smoking dope on film, others felt it was only a matter of time before the whole scene would be blown apart. In August, Viv Prince, the madcap drummer formerly with The Pretty Things and a well-known face around clubland, was the next pop victim, being fined at Great Marlborough Street court for possession of amphetamine.

Those in the Stones who used drugs were fully aware of Donovan's arrest, although this didn't appear to inhibit their after-hours behaviour. The group's itinerary for the second half of 1966 certainly allowed them more time for partying. Recording, previously seen as nothing more than a formality, was now far preferable to the drudgery of live appearances but with the Stones' popularity in America showing no signs of flagging, a 14-date summer tour of the country was planned. While there, the group was able to witness the effect that drug culture was having on America's youth.

In New York the Stones were lionised by the city's socialites and Brian found Greenwich Village's independence from the rest of America much to his liking. "We've built up a kind of intellectual following among the hippies," he'd tell journalist Keith Altham on his return. "The Greenwich Village crowd all dig us." Jones mentioned that the drug scene was attracting heavy interest from the police. "There was a terrible scene out there just before I left," he revealed. "The police were stopping and searching everyone in sight, looking for drugs; it was frightening. Worse than a police state."

Another port of call was The Factory, Andy Warhol's Grand Central hang-out for artists and deviants. There, Jones socialised with Bob Dylan, filmmaker Kenneth Anger and members of The Velvet Underground including blonde ingénue Nico. Predictably, more parasitic characters populated the hangers-on, among them David Schneiderman, a 24-year-old Canadian temporarily based in Greenwich Village.

Born December 14, 1942, Schneiderman straddled many tributaries of the flourishing New York underground scene. He was a popular character around town, regarded as a 'good time guy' among the many who crossed his path. A child actor who'd later direct his talents towards

Shakespeare, he was intoxicated with the dangerous alliance struck between art and hallucinogenic drugs. According to his close friend Ed Ochs, Schneiderman's conversion to LSD was nothing less than life changing. "His brain reeked of it," recalls Ochs today. "His running commentary, his music, his ideas, his vision all reflected and simulated the LSD experience. David was definitely the 'Johnny Appleseed of LSD', spreading the eye-opening strands of enlightenment around the world that stimulated a generation of musical geniuses, not to mention artists, filmmakers, scientists, thinkers and dreamers. No doubt about it. I believe he had a direct connection to some of the early batches of pure Sandoz Lab acid* and was on a mission to turn on the planet. Nothing more, nothing less. I guess it could be said this was his greatest achievement and disaster rolled into one. I'm sure he never made a dime selling it; he gave it away."

Schneiderman's charisma harboured a dark side, however. He'd fled Canada following a string of drug and weaponry offences, his most notorious wheeze to dose a Toronto reservoir with LSD. Arriving in New York with a false passport and several revolving aliases, he managed to escape detection by immigration authorities by losing himself amid the anonymity of mid-sixties Greenwich Village where discussion of origin and provenance was considered wholly uncool among the hip community. His supply of LSD prised open many doors: when The Beatles were in town during August 1966, Schneiderman was reportedly on hand to meet John Lennon and George Harrison's needs, supplying them with a caché of LSD infused sugar cubes wrapped in tin foil.

High on the patronage of The Beatles, Schneiderman was easily able to penetrate the Stones' caravan when it rolled into town that same year. Like a psychedelic jack-in-the-box, he popped up to supply Brian Jones and Keith Richards with psychedelic sugar cubes whereupon Richards, evidently charmed by the Canadian's swift patter and encyclopaedic turn of phrase when it came to narcotic use, mentioned to this character

* Sandoz was the name of the Swiss laboratory where Dr Albert Hofmann first synthesised the drug now commonly known as LSD. In 1967, Eric Burdon & The Animals recorded the B-side 'A Girl Named Sandoz' in its honour.

David that if he was ever in London it would be good to get reacquainted. He'd probably made the same suggestion scores of times to numerous characters that momentarily took his interest. This time, he would live to regret it.

Back from the States, the last few months of 1966 afforded a gentle winding down for the Stones. Outside of a 12-date UK tour with support from Ike & Tina Turner, there was plenty of time for the group to settle into their new properties. Jagger moved to 50 Harley House, an ornate mansion-block in London's Marylebone area; Brian and Anita to a more expansive flat in Courtfield Road, south Kensington. Predictably, the couple's down time would be eventful, taking in another trip to Morocco in August with interior designer Christopher Gibbs. Despite Gibbs' genial and erudite presence, they engaged on a non-stop tirade concerning every minor detail of the trip. In one moment of madness, Brian's temper got the better of him, and he broke his wrist after throwing a punch at Anita that missed and hit a metal window frame. The injury meant he was never able to properly regain his ability on guitar.

Back in England during late 1966, the pair did an ill-advised photo shoot dressed up in Nazi SS uniforms. The photos were intended solely for a Danish magazine, but with the press eager to chance on anything that constituted a scandal, the pictures found a wider audience. The lapse in taste was exacerbated by Brian stamping on dismembered dolls. Much indignation followed and in typically combatant mode, Brian retaliated as best he could. "Why should we have to compromise with our image?" he asked *New Musical Express.* "You don't simply give up all you have ever believed in because you've reached a certain age. Our generation has grown up with us and they believe in the same things as we do. The recent pictures of me taken in Nazi uniform were a put down. Really I mean with all the long hair in a Nazi uniform, couldn't people see that it was a satirical thing? How can anyone be offended when I am on their side? I'm not a Nazi sympathiser."

The closest of Brian's male associates was Tara Browne, heir to a million pound Guinness fortune and a sartorial look-alike of Jones. Described as a "golden child of the sixties", at just 21 Browne kept impeccable company, and made his family home in Ireland's Wicklow Mountains available to anyone who needed respite, the Stones and their partners included. Browne was a passionate advocate of LSD and reliable company during acid-fuelled roller coaster rides. On December 18, Browne was driving across London in his Lotus Elan with his girlfriend, 19-year-old model Suki Poitier. High on LSD, he went straight through a red light close to Jones' flat in Kensington and, swerving to miss oncoming traffic, hit a parked van. While his girlfriend was spared major injury, Browne died instantly.

Distraught at his young friend's death, Brian Jones headed off on an extended holiday with Anita Pallenberg and Keith Richards. On Christmas Eve, the trio convened at the grand George Cinque Hotel in Paris where, to enliven the festive season, they dosed themselves up with amphetamines, cocaine and other substances during the day, and took powerful downers at night to bring them down.

"We spent the whole of Christmas on our knees," said Keith later. "We'd conned the hotel nurse into thinking we couldn't sleep so she'd given us all these downers that were very, very strong... We used to take two pills at a time and everybody would crash out, sleep and order another Christmas dinner."

On the same night that Tara Browne met his tragic end, another young life was on the brink. Chrissie Shrimpton's very public relationship with Mick Jagger was in freefall, the couple's relationship having descended into bitter acrimony. Despite the occasional lovey-dovey display for the press, Jagger was having more fun with others in his circle, notably Marianne Faithfull, whose marriage to John Dunbar was also in decline. By her own admission, she had already had flings with both Jones and Richards. Jagger, too, was becoming drawn to her innocent beauty and sharp intelligence.

In an attempt to rescue their faltering relationship Mick had booked a Caribbean cruise for him and Shrimpton over Christmas, but on the day of their departure he'd cancelled the holiday and went out to lunch with Faithfull instead. That night a grieving Shrimpton confronted Jagger in their Harley House flat. A furious row ensued, leaving Mick to exit into the unknown. In the ensuing days news leaked out that their relationship was over. Reporters, gagging for any salacious details, quickly homed in on Shrimpton for a quote. "We just grew out of each other," said Shrimpton at the time. "This was the only solution. We had been unofficially engaged for some time. We were very much in love. The strange thing is we argued the whole time. As time goes on, you begin to feel differently about life – and about each other. There was no explosive row or anything like that. We broke by mutual agreement. If anyone asked how I feel now – I don't. I feel nothing."

Whatever Shrimpton's state of mind when speaking to reporters, she attempted suicide in the flat she shared with Jagger. She survived the ordeal, spending several days in hospital. Six days later, Jagger was spotted dining alone in an Italian restaurant in London's Soho. Pressed for an explanation, Jagger replied that he and Chrissie had broken up by 'mutual agreement'. What the papers didn't know was that Shrimpton's belongings had been removed, allowing Faithfull to move in with him. Despite the press's speculative eyes and ears, the couple managed to keep their relationship to themselves for several weeks.

Marianne was a frequent attendee of the Stones recording sessions at Olympic Studios where the group were putting together *Between The Buttons*. In her autobiography, Faithfull asserts many of Jagger's more savage put-downs on the album, such as 'Yesterday Papers', 'All Sold Out' and 'Please Go Home' were directed at or inspired by his disintegrating relationship with Shrimpton. The album as a whole was redolent of the swinging world of bistros, discothèques and the Chelsea set in which the Stones moved now they were off the road. While disjointed in places, it remains an overlooked work in the Stones canon, perhaps because of its uncharacteristic nature embracing music hall, Dylan and fuzzed-out R&B. One song in particular, 'Something Happened To Me Yesterday', with its oblique reference to "something really trippy" hinted at the forces at work behind the scenes.

At year's end, business manager Allen Klein was bragging to the press that The Rolling Stones putative earnings for 1967 could easily top £20 million. This, he claimed, would be garnered from newly struck record royalties, touring and not least, their long-awaited film debut. The bold statement could be interpreted as a message from Klein to The Beatles who were reportedly at a crossroads in their career. Working at EMI's

Abbey Road Studios on their as yet untitled *Sgt. Pepper* project, their hibernation from the public eye led many to speculate that the group was well and truly finished. For those who monitored competitive issues, the Stones, by dint of their continued exposure, had it well and truly sewn up.

Klein's successful elevation of the Stones' royalty rates pointed towards a more structured year for the group. Nonetheless, there were still songs to be written for their as yet untitled next album, due for release early in 1967. Touring was also going to be scaled down, and despite a tour of Europe, nothing had been booked for the UK. Klein had evidently done his homework, and had noted the dwindling returns from Britain's cinemas and ballrooms. European venues were larger, with promoters happy to offer larger guarantees. Stateside, the possibilities were unlimited, with festivals and stadiums able to host enormous audiences.

The year started early for the Stones with a trip to New York to appear on *The Ed Sullivan Show*. As noted, Sullivan had been tetchy about the group since their boisterous first appearance in 1964 but with their public profile higher than ever before, Sullivan had consented to have them back on his programme a further three times in the interim. An enormous springboard to any new release, the Stones travelled to the States to appear exclusively on Sullivan's show, due for live broadcast on January 15, 1967.

A fair amount of goodwill accompanied the group's visit but difficulties were encountered during the recording of their new single 'Let's Spend The Night Together'. Manically sensitive when it came to viewers' expectations, Sullivan's team of producers assumed that the song's title implied a night between the sheets. Advised against starting another war of words, Jagger reluctantly agreed to alter the main lyric to 'Let's spend some time together'. The surviving broadcast reveals Mick's disgust as he mumbled through the compromise, although during the afternoon rehearsal, the original lyric was left intact.

Back on home turf, the Stones' next appearance came on January 22, on the top rated TV variety show, *Sunday Night At The London Palladium*. Since 1955, the programme had become as much a weekend institution as roast beef and Yorkshire pudding. The show had embraced the British pop explosion, and had even employed its own mop top Scouser, comedian Jimmy Tarbuck, to play host.

Its fairly conservative reputation apart, viewing figures of potentially 10 million made the show a useful tool for promoting the Stones' new double A-side 'Let's Spend The Night Together' backed with 'Ruby Tuesday' and album, *Between The Buttons*. The Stones' performance was suitably charged, but the group had no intention of standing on a revolving dais at the show's finale, waving customary goodbyes with the other artists. Indeed, they had good reason not to outstay their welcome since both Brian and Keith had spent the day tripping on LSD, and were over two hours late for rehearsals. The show's producer Albert Locke wasn't impressed either way, saying, "Who do the Stones think they are? Every artist that's ever played the Palladium has done it. They are insulting me and everyone else." Even though Andrew Oldham, visiting sound man Glyn Johns and comedian Dave Allen attempted to resolve matters, the group, Jagger especially, were adamant that they wouldn't appear on the roundabout. "Anyone would think that this show is sacred or something," Mick told reporters feeding from the mêlée. "That revolving stage isn't an altar. It's a drag."

Predictably, the Palladium saga made headlines at the bottom end of the newspaper evolutionary scale, re-establishing the Stones' image as uncooperative ne'er do wells. Perversely, the Palladium's producers would have the last laugh, with satirists Peter Cook and Dudley Moore appearing on the circular dais the following Sunday alongside papier-mâché effigies of the group. Column space aside, Oldham's attempts to quell hostilities at the Palladium did little to alleviate a growing rift that was developing between himself and Jagger. Considering Oldham's trademark manipulation of the press to be out of sync with the Stones' current status, Jagger decided to assume official spokesperson responsibilities, with seasoned public relations man Les Perrin drafted in to organise the fine detail.

Apart from some recording sessions at Olympic Studios in Barnes, nothing much was on the Stones' horizon until the opening of the European tour in late March. By dint of Anita working on a German film, *A Degree Of Murder*, Brian had managed to cop a soundtrack commission from the film's director Volker Schlöndorff. The first Stone to record outside of the group, Jones would revel in the freedom afforded to him.

Jagger, his break-up with Chrissie Shrimpton still a talking point, plotted an escape to Italy during late January. Marianne's appearance in the annual San Remo Song Festival would allow a chance for the couple to spend some quality time together but any hopes for anonymity were dashed when Riviera based press caught Mick being greeted by Marianne at Nice Airport. Now that paparazzi photographs were in circulation, the couple decided to come clean, Jagger stating, "I suppose we've got to come out into the open about it. I haven't talked about it before because there was Chrissie to think about, and didn't want to hurt anyone's feelings, but Chrissie seems happy now." Back in London Chrissie had evidently recovered and was already parading around town with her rebound beau, Small Faces singer Steve Marriott.

Once Marianne's duties in San Remo were over, she and Mick hired a yacht and took off along the Italian Riviera. Calling in at various beachfront discothèques and bars, the couple danced and partied long and hard. For a while they became enamoured with one particular establishment and, with their nocturnal lifestyle eating into their stamina, Marianne approached the club DJ and asked if he had anything that might sustain them through the night. Getting her to hold out her hand, the DJ poured a stream of white amphetamines into her palm. Perfectly legal in Italy, these little pills came with the legend 'Lippet' embossed on their side. To keep them all together, the DJ gave her a clear plastic phial.

The remainder of their trip was enlivened with sunshine and freshly discovered love. Four of the amphetamine pills Marianne had acquired ended up in the pocket of a green velvet jacket belonging to Jagger and, when the couple returned to the UK, they escaped the attention of customs officials at both French and British airports. The jacket was a favourite of Jagger's and he wore it a lot during early 1967, the contents of its pockets largely forgotten.

CHAPTER 4

West Wittering

"Teenagers the world over are weary of being pushed around by half-witted politicians who attempt to dominate their way of thinking and set a code for their living. They want to be free and have the right of expression; of thinking and living aloud without any petty restrictions. This doesn't mean they want to become alcoholics or drug takers or tread down on their parents. This is a protest against the system. I see a lot of trouble coming in the dawn."

Mick Jagger, 1967

Pop groups' turn into the left-field had not gone unnoticed by the press. Smiling groups of fresh-faced lads who sang and played guitars and drums had gradually given way to unsmiling young adults with attitude, and editors of popular national dailies were closely monitoring their activities. Many had enjoyed rags-to-riches fame, and they made for excellent and hugely readable stories. Favouring smiley, wholesome, unthreatening content over stark reality, most entertainment hacks were happy to ignore the groups' after hour's behaviour. Nonetheless, as celebrity culture gathered considerable momentum, there was a growing feeling that someone somewhere might decide to spill the beans.

The fragile détente had endured for three years, with the media happy to prolong the party as long as there was mileage in it. Furthermore, pop groups' press representatives and those who worked in the PR departments at their record companies were more than happy to farm stories and photographs out to embellish otherwise uneventful periods in the media calendar. However, by the end of 1966 this relationship had become exhausted, allowing a gulf to appear between the media and musicians who no longer saw themselves as docile symbols of an age that was fast disappearing.

Tony Calder was privy to this collapse. "As the sixties developed, the national newspapers which had taken rock and roll to its front pages became more and more interested in rock stars," he says. "So therefore they'd spent years being utilised by people like Andrew Oldham to build up their artists, now they were interested in trying to bring them down... The bands had been obviously using drugs since before they became famous in varying shapes and forms. However, journalists were now hanging out backstage trying to find out whether they were just smoking; whether they were doing a line of coke, what pills were they popping etc. So it was a marriage between what the newspapers thought society wanted to read, and also, part of their campaign to destroy the rock acts. It got heavier and heavier."

Somewhat predictably, it would be the *News Of The World,* the Sunday newspaper that took as its slogan 'All human life is here', that demolished this fragile agreement. Since 1843 the paper had capitalised on the lowest common denominator of public interest, with a heavy focus on sex, crime and sport. When these components merged with celebrity, sales increased considerably. By the mid-fifties, with a readership nudging towards nine million, the paper had become something of a weekly institution, enlivening the miserable reality of Sunday mornings with vicarious scandal and cheap titillation. Like many bottom-end journals, the paper royally welcomed the appearance of the British pop scene, and was happy to promote the new sense of optimism the groups brought with them.

In truth, the *News Of The World*'s relationship with the pop scene was no different from what had gone on with entertainers of the past. In the Music Hall era, the paper had included songsheets as a giveaway to its readers. In the fifties it would feature the teaching skills of guitarist Bert Weedon, his 'play in a day' technique sparking many to pick up the instrument. With the British pop acts set to take over the music world, the paper had sponsored a competition in 1963 whereby budding musicians would send in demo tapes for cash prizes and the chance of a recording contract.

However, the paper's institutional status came at a price, and behind the salacious newsprint huge power struggles were occurring within the upper echelons of the paper's editorial department. Their main rival, the equally colourful *Sunday People*, had drawn blood in early 1964 with an exposé concerning match fixing by footballers. The story generated enormous controversy, culminating in jail sentences for some of those involved. The *People*'s success prompted the *News Of The World* to establish its own investigative department, independent from the paper's editorial hub and staffed by a team of young instinctive reporters who scoured the country looking for suburban orgies, compromised clerics and teenage sex in all varieties.

Along with its self-appointed status as the nation's adjudicator on sexual behaviour, the paper appeared to be fixated with the activities of anyone under 21. In 1964, they'd gone into overdrive to expose the amphetamine craze that had become a component part of the mod lifestyle. With LSD gaining popularity, the paper had 'exposed' some of the psychedelic antics going on in London's UFO club. Situated in Tottenham Court Road, the club was as tangible an exposition of the LSD experience as could be achieved without actually ingesting the chemical. Presenting shows by psychedelic warlords such as The Pink Floyd, Soft Machine and Procol Harum, the audience merged seamlessly with the madness pouring off the stage. Alerted to the sort of wild abandon that LSD could evoke, *NOTW* reporters gatecrashed an evening at the UFO. The subsequent report of their experiences was accompanied by the unforgettable headline: 'I Saw Couples Injecting Reefers'.

Brian Jones unwittingly handed the Sunday papers a scandal of a more predictable nature during 1966. Forever in the slipstream of his roving affections, two paternity issues had surfaced which were picked up by both the *People* and the *News Of The World*. While the Stones' management had done their best to keep Jones' personal matters under wraps, the media's insatiable lust indicated that anything salacious regarding pop stars was seen as fair game.

With pop stars' use of narcotics bubbling under the surface, a decision was taken at the *News Of The World* to open one of their trademark investigations. Still wary of competition from the *Sunday People*, the paper's hierarchy instructed reporters that considerable kudos (and not least an extra swathe of readers) could be garnered by revealing pop stars' personal habits. Because LSD had just been made illegal in the UK, it could be argued that any such features were in the 'national interest' insofar as they exposed criminal behaviour. Furthermore, with many of these stars now internationally famous, the paper would have no problems in syndicating stories about them to a world intrigued by the antics of British pop artists.

With 'Swinging London' fairly easy to penetrate, it was not too difficult to investigate drug taking among musicians. Acquiring this sort of information might come at a price, but with chequebooks and wads of cash flapping around, a raft of personalities could be tapped to supply the sort of murky details that were required. Thus it was that on January 29, under the banner headline, 'Pop Stars: Facts That Will Shock You', the *News Of The World* introduced their findings with a typically moralistic preamble. Paying due deference to the extraordinary ascendancy of pop groups, the build-up was evidently constructed to knock them down later: "Ever since 'beat' groups arrived on the scene to lay the foundations for Britain's pop culture – one of the most astonishing phenomena of the century – rumours have circulated that many stars took drugs."

The bulk of this first instalment focused mainly on the antics of Donovan. By dint of his careless housekeeping, the singer's charge of marijuana possession required little detective work and scant possibility of legal retaliation. Over two pages, the paper revelled in its decoding of Donovan's new oeuvre of songs – many of them cloaked in drug metaphor. One of the singer's associates, Suzanne Lloyd, had evidently been persuaded to spill the beans on her own drug use, especially LSD. Recalling graphic hallucinations that appeared to have dropped out of a Hammer movie, her revelations had all the necessary components shock and outrage the paper's staid readership. Embedded deeper in the feature were references to Frank Zappa's Mothers of Invention and The Move whose songs were referenced as having drug-inspired lyrics. The feature concluded with a teaser for the following week's exposé. Billed as 'The Beat Groups Who Use LSD', readers were left wondering just how far the *News Of The World* would go to bring their targets to book.

To pull in as many Sunday morning voyeurs as possible, the first series of revelations were trailed by a TV advert the night before publication. In a further attempt to snare readership, the *News Of The World* provided newsagents with a garish poster featuring two boys who looked like pop musicians barking into microphones, topped off with a 'Pop Stars And Drugs' logo.

The first article out of the hat, other material was being lined up for the following week. While the Donovan feature was predominantly a rehash of existing information and required little in the way of covert infiltration, scouts had evidently been digging deeper for their next instalment. Though pop groups' after-hours activity was normally restricted to discothèques and night clubs, a house at 27 Roedean Crescent, on the edge of Richmond Park in Roehampton, had acquired something of a wild reputation. Its occupants were The Moody Blues, a five-piece R&B unit that had moved down to London from Birmingham to be closer to their commitments. Finding a flat in Knightsbridge too restricting, they'd taken on a lease of the property in January 1965.

The Moodies were not publicly associated with wayward behaviour but during off-duty hours they had been partying hard. Like most musicians living communally, they enjoyed carousing at all hours with like-minded industry colleagues. With various Stones, members of The Who and even a Beatle or two attending parties at the house, a veritable treasure trove of scandal was waiting for opportunist reporters.

Chris Welch, then a reporter for *Melody Maker*, was invited to one of The Moody Blues' shindigs well before the *News Of The World* blew the lid off events inside 27 Roedean Crescent. "I knew The Moody Blues pretty well because I had interviewed them a lot," recalls Welch today. "Their parties had become legendary, and I was invited to one. We were always going to parties then, but mainly in nightclubs. So it was quite unusual to be invited to a private house for a party, so that's what made it especially interesting. I drove over to Roehampton in my black Ford Consul after a hard day at the *Melody Maker*. I remember when I arrived it appeared quite a normal looking suburban villa. It was in a quiet street and wasn't anywhere near the main road. The first thing I saw was a giant bowl of punch which was near the staircase. Stevie Winwood of The Spencer Davis Group was there and he said, 'Whatever you do don't drink the punch!' Anyway, I did have a big glass which was ladled out by [Moody Blue] Denny Laine. Downstairs Paul McCartney was sitting on the floor strumming a guitar and I remember him saying, 'We want Cliff Richard!' He seemed quite merry sitting in the corner. Lulu was there as well, flitting around as was Herman [Peter Noone], Spencer Davis and [teen singer] Twinkle. That was the extraordinary thing, you just had to look up and down the stairs and all the people who were currently in the charts were roaming around this suburban house. After ignoring advice and drinking this punch, my head started spinning around. Next thing I knew I was being carried upstairs by Spencer Davis and Herman. I was then dumped on a bed. I remember being horribly sick out of the window and all over the garden. God knows what was in the drink? It might have been LSD for all I know. When I woke up the whole house was deserted apart from a roadie who gave me a lift to Barnes railway station."

Welch's recollection of the atmosphere at the house contrasts sharply with the dramatic exposé that appeared in the *News Of The World*'s next 'Pop Stars And Drugs' feature. Couched in salacious intrigue, the paper could barely contain itself with its findings, magnified – according to their informant – by the use of LSD. "On one night at Roehampton," ran the text, "the lead guitarist of a visiting group imagined himself to be Robin Hood." Quoted was one Phil Robinson, an employee of The Moody Blues, who recalled that, "There he was in Sherwood Forest with Allan a'Dale, Will Scarlett, and his bunch of merry outlaws... We didn't know it at the time of course, because he simply vanished in the gardens. It was when he came back he told us he had been Robin Hood, complete with bow and arrow."

Deeper within the article were plenty of other gaudy revelations to sate

Two years before the Redlands scandal broke, members of The Rolling Stones were in the dock at West Ham Magistrate's Court, London on July 22, 1965 – Mick, Brian Jones and Bill Wyman answering charges of insulting behaviour. (TED WEST/CENTRAL PRESS/GETTY IMAGES)

Mick squares up to the *News Of The World* allegations on the Eamonn Andrews chat show on February 5, 1967. Sitting alongside Jagger and Andrews are comedian Terry Scott, actor Hugh Lloyd, singer Susan Maughan and casting director Rose Tobias-Shaw. (LARRY ELLIS/EXPRESS/GETTY IMAGES)

Just hours before the raid on Redlands on February 12, 1967, Keith is pictured by Michael Cooper larking around outside his West Wittering cottage.
(MICHAEL COOPER/RAJ PREM COLLECTION)

The Redlands' party-goers partake of some sea air on West Wittering beach.

David "Acid King" Schneiderman and Keith Richards in a close huddle on West Wittering beach. (MICHAEL COOPER/RAJ PREM COLLECTION)

Keith and Robert Fraser's manservant Mohammed Jajaj at West Wittering.

While the other party goers preferred a van ride from the beach back to Redlands, Keith decided to retreat on foot. Evidently, the gravel outside Rose Cottage on the B1279 was much to his liking. (MICHAEL COOPER/RAJ PREM COLLECTION)

Right: David Schneiderman, AKA David Britton, AKA David Jove. The legendary "Acid King" his leather attaché case cum mobile dispensary on display. (ED OCHS)

Below: "If need be by force": published for the first time, the search warrant used by the Petty Sessional Division of Chichester on the night of the Redlands' raid: February 12, 1967.

REGINA -V- RICHARDS

EXHIBIT No /.

IN THE COUNTY OF WEST SUSSEX

PETTY SESSIONAL DIVISION OF CHICHESTER.

TO : Gordon Dineley, Stanley Cudmore, Michael Cotton, Pamela Baker, Rosemary Slade, Evelyn Fuller, Alfred Guy, Frederick Weller, Thomas Davies, John Challen, Donald Rambridge, Reginald Poat Raymond Harris, Reginald Mugford, Nathaniel Bingham, Derek Grieves, Leslie Stewart, Richard Smith, Ronald Pafford.

WHEREAS, I, the undersigned Justice of the Peace, am satisfied by Information on Oath laid this day by Gordon Dineley of the Police Station, Chichester in the said County, Chief Inspector of the West Sussex Police, that there is reasonable ground for suspecting that certain drugs to which Part 1 of the Dangerous Drugs Act, 1965, applies, are in contravention of the said Act, in the possession of KEITH RICHARDS in certain premises known as 'Redlands,' Redlands Lane, West Wittering in the said County.

YOU ARE THEREFORE HEREBY COMMANDED, at any time or times within one month from the date of this Warrant, to enter, if need by by force, the premises of the said Keith Richards known as "Redlands", Redlands Lane, West Wittering aforesaid, and to search the said premises and any persons found therein, and, if there is reasonable ground for suspecting that an offence against the Dangerous Drugs Act, 1965, has been committed in relation to any such drugs which may be found in the premises or in the possession of any persons found therein to seize and detain such drugs.

DATED this Twelfth day of February, 1967.

R.J. Bevis

Justice of the Peace for the County first aforesaid.

Mick and Keith greet the press at Redlands' front door prior to their first court appearance at Chichester, May 10, 1967. (PHOTOSHOT)

En route to Chichester Magistrates Court on May 10, Mick and Keith appear vaguely unconcerned with what lay ahead for them. (TED WEST/CENTRAL PRESS/GETTY IMAGES)

Mick and Keith leave Chichester Magistrates Court after pleading not guilty to charges emanating from the Redlands' raid, May 10.
(GRAHAM WOOD/GETTY IMAGES)

Opting to leave by the front entrance of Chichester Magistrates Court on May 10, Mick and Keith meet the full force of fans, press and police as they attempt to reach their chauffeur-driven car. (MIRRORPIX)

Found guilty and handcuffed to a warder, Mick is driven from Chichester Court to Lewes Prison to be held until sentencing was decided, June 27, 1967. (HULTON-DEUTSCH COLLECTION/CORBIS)

voyeuristic minds. Naming and shaming Who guitarist Pete Townshend for allegedly consuming LSD, there were further allegations made against three members of The Moody Blues and Cream drummer Ginger Baker. Townshend, who the paper would claim was regularly taking LSD, made no immediate response to the feature. Having announced in January 1966 on the BBC TV music and culture show *A Whole Scene Going* that he and members of The Who were "blocked all the time", Townshend had little room for manoeuvre.

In addition to the Roehampton parties, the *News Of The World* had been busy penetrating London's clubland for any available sleaze. To the average fan, tracking down these celebrity hang-outs required a broad compass; for reporters based in London it was a fairly straightforward task. While groups with a high profile couldn't walk into the average pub or discothèque, they could quite easily be spotted in London clubs such as the Ad Lib, Scotch of St James, Bag O' Nails, or Speakeasy. John Steel, drummer with The Animals, recalls rock's aristocracy all socialising under the same roof. "Everybody used to just cram into these clubs," he recalls, "especially if you'd come back from a gig or had a night off. I remember when we first got signed up in America, our PR manager from MGM, Frank Mancini, had come over to London on business. We took him down to the Scotch of St James and he was just absolutely gobsmacked. You had Keith Richards and Mick Jagger in one corner; you had The Who there; John Lennon and Paul McCartney were sitting behind a table. He just couldn't believe it. I remember him saying, 'If this was in New York the kids would tear the place apart brick by brick.'"

In between the few media engagements the Stones had in early 1967, Brian Jones was maintaining his presence in various clubs across London. His pockets full of substances and constantly on the look out for new and exciting adventures, Jones would occasionally call in at Blaises nightclub in Kensington. Housed in the basement of the long since demolished Imperial Hotel at 121 Queen's Gate, the club had become a popular meeting point for musicians disinclined to venture into the West End. Blaises had gained fame for hosting the first appearance of the newly arrived American guitarist Jimi Hendrix, his debut on December 21, 1966 drawing the likes of Pete Townshend, Eric Clapton and Jeff Beck to witness his virtuoso skills. For Brian Jones, the club was convenient; just a few blocks away from his Courtfield Garden flat, meaning he could stagger the five-minute walk back home if he needed to.

Trawling for any choice nuggets, *NOTW* reporters struck gold on a visit to Blaises during the last week of January. In among the gaggle of musicians, industry personnel and freeloaders was Jones. With Anita Pallenberg away on filming duties in Germany, he'd reverted to his customary access all areas persona, and was working his way around the club. Conspicuous by his blond mop and foppish dress sense, reporters cornered Jones and engaged him in some LSD talk and other drug related matters. What they received in return was exactly what they were after. There was just one problem. The reporters were either badly informed or, possibly, Jones prattled on about his 'leader of the Stones' status. Either way, they mistook him for Mick Jagger.

"I don't go much on it now that the cats have taken it up," Jones told them. "It'll just get a dirty name. I remember the first time I took it was on tour with Bo Diddley and Little Richard." Given that the Stones tour in question was back in September 1963, this was a bold admission – or a blatant lie – since LSD wasn't to make any noticeable imprint in the UK until at least 16 months later. Of course Brian or the reporters may have been confused: he was more likely discussing either amphetamines or marijuana. This was just one of many errors that made up the evening's discourse.

The *NOTW* reporters later witnessed the man they thought was Jagger swallowing around six Benzedrine tablets. "I just wouldn't keep awake at places like this without them," Jones added. As the conversation drew to a close, the hacks watched Jones flaunt a piece of hashish to a companion and two girls, and then invite them around to his flat "for a smoke".

The reporters may well have congratulated themselves as they scurried back to the *NOTW* offices. At the time, Mick Jagger was in Italy romancing Marianne Faithfull, as a cursory glance at the gossip pages would have revealed. Yet, such was the reporters' excitement at what was falling out of Jones' mouth they didn't bother to check the provenance of the quotes. Back at base, they transferred their findings to the accumulating dossier of information. Jagger's name was also linked to the psychedelic shenanigans attached to events at The Moody Blues' property, the paper claiming that he had attended several of the "Roehampton Raves".

On Sunday, February 5, the second part in the series of articles hit the newsstands. For The Moody Blues, the revelation that their gatherings had become public knowledge came as something of a major surprise. As a result, the group were quick to fire their road manager Phil Robertson, the main source of information about their parties. To qualify their suspicions, a couple of The Moody Blues' associates staked out the *NOTW* offices on the day when the informer was supposed to receive his payment. For reasons best left to Robertson, he never showed up and, as far as anyone knew, the money remained uncollected.

Mick Jagger and Marianne Faithfull were equally shocked by the *News Of The World* that Sunday morning. The couple had just returned from their holiday on the Italian Riviera the previous day and, as usual, they'd had the morning papers delivered to their flat. Like most celebrities in the public eye, they were eager to scan the pages for any titbits that might concern them or others in their circle.

Jagger and Faithfull were conscious that their holiday in Italy was newsworthy, especially in the sleaze-heavy Sunday press. Jagger evidently saw the front page of the *News Of The World* with its trailer teasing readers towards the 'Pop Stars And Drugs' revelations inside. Opening its pages, Mick was staggered to see a large photograph of himself with an accompanying caption stating that he'd "admitted to our investigators that he had taken LSD".

While Mick was certainly no stranger to drugs, he hadn't at that point taken LSD, nor had he spoken about his other, more modest, drug use to anyone outside his immediate circle. On further inspection, he and Marianne detected Brian's idiosyncratic argot leaping out of the newsprint.

At roughly the same time, Allen Klein and Andrew Oldham were also reading the *News Of The World*. Aware that if the allegation went unchallenged it could cause serious problems with travel plans, especially to the US, they agreed that a robust response was called for. Mick's absence in Italy was easily verifiable, thus settling the issue in Jagger's favour and causing massive embarrassment to the paper. Furthermore, it would stymie any further revelations the paper intended to print. With a call to his lawyers on the afternoon of the publication, Jagger was primed to take on the might of the *News Of The World*.

That night, the Stones had been booked to appear on Eamonn Andrews' late-night TV chat show, performing 'She Smiled Sweetly', from *Between The Buttons.* In between the music, Jagger had been lined up for a short chat with the amiable Irish host and his fellow guests, comedian Terry Scott, actor Hugh Lloyd and singer Susan Maughan, who'd arrived on the programme with her pet poodle, Bobby. Despite Andrews' trademark geniality, it was a difficult encounter, the guests rounding on Jagger regarding the Stones' recent appearance on the London Palladium show. Comedian Terry Scott, who claimed to be present at the recording, scored a cheap shot by saying that he had to hoover up after the Stones had left their dressing room.

Predictably, Andrews steered the conversation towards the *News Of The World* feature. Still incensed by the revelation, Mick used the opportunity to announce that he was suing the newspaper. "I want to make it quite clear," Jagger told Andrews, "that this picture of me is misleading and untrue. The matter is now in the hands of my lawyers."

Jagger's uncompromising response clearly killed the conversation, leaving Andrews to steer the debate towards safer avenues. At the offices of the *NOTW*, staff waiting for Jagger's response swiftly realised their spectacular gaff. Their first reaction was to temporarily suspend any further 'Pop Stars And Drugs' features. Their shoddy journalism might soon be the subject of a potentially substantial libel action, and with compensation to Jagger potentially running into six figures, there was much to fight for on both sides.

Rolling Stones' lawyer Timothy Hardacre recalled Jagger's outrage at the slur and the reaction of the tabloid once legal papers were served. "Mick told me the allegation was totally untrue," says Hardacre today. "I knew enough about him to know that he hadn't been involved. The libel action caused huge fury with the newspaper. I remember the editor ringing me up and saying, 'I'll make sure that your clients never get mentioned in my newspaper again!' Obviously the paper was pretty upset because I think if we had gone ahead with our action we were on pretty good grounds. They didn't have direct evidence and they'd have to prove what they were alleging was correct... So they were worried about that because the damages could have been huge and would have made them look stupid. And so one thing led to another."

With the *News Of The World*'s back up against the wall, a plan to thwart Jagger's libel action was required. To untangle what was one ungodly mess, two young reporters, Mike Gabbert and Trevor Kempson, were charged with finding something that would compromise the libel suit. Both writers were possessed of an avaricious nose for a good story. Gabbert was on a roll following a transfer from the *Sunday People*. In 1964 he'd been instrumental in exposing the football racketeering saga, which had resulted in several players being jailed. Kempson was similarly brazen and legendary for his brassy, foot-in-the-door investigative style. Something of a minor celebrity around Fleet Street, Kempson's career had received a boost when as a cub reporter in Reading he'd revealed the whereabouts of some of those involved in the Great Train Robbery. In early 1963, he revealed plenty of sordid detail from the Profumo affair, much of it acquired with considerable subterfuge.

"There was no doubt that it was a pride and personal thing," Kempson told writer Terry Rawlings in 1998. "The paper was embarrassed at not recognising Jagger from Jones and they knew that they had been right about their report in the first place. If only they had got someone that knew which Stone was which, there wouldn't have been a lawsuit to face. They wanted to get the Stones badly, and the best way to get them was to get someone on the inside, which was easy."

Kempson and Gabbert duly set about finding any weak links in the Stones' circle. Informants were promised considerable sums for information and approaches were made on several levels.

Unaware of what was taking place, Mick and Marianne continued their lives as best they could. Although paranoia was rife among those living on the front line of drug use, some strange, inexplicable events did indeed occur following the delivery of the libel suit on February 7. The couple noticed a rather antiquated van parked outside their Harley

House apartment, yet unlike the delivery vehicles that came and went every minute of the day, this ageing blue and white van remained outside their building on London's Marylebone Road. Keith, who'd been staying in his *pied-à-terre* flat in St John's Wood, noticed a similarly mysterious van outside his property. While Mick and Keith initially failed to connect anything untoward with these vehicles, they certainly noticed some strange irregularities on their telephones; one minute echoing their voices, the other, transmitting an irregular clicking sound. These peculiar noises could also be heard on Richards' phone down at Redlands. With sensitivities already aroused by the *NOTW*'s feature, everyone had due reason for a serious bout of paranoia.

Confirming this worry, news filtered in that Mick and Keith's phones were being interfered with. A telecommunications engineer known to the Stones' management as 'Sunny' had occasionally been employed to assist with the group's phone requirements that were either too complex or too laborious for the nationalised GPO service. A fan of the group, Sunny informed the group's management that Mick and Keith's telephones in London, and also down in Sussex, were being monitored surreptitiously.

Privy to this disturbing information was Tony Calder. "Sunny said 'You got to be careful boys. Take me seriously.' And we didn't. Nobody really thought that you've had your phone tapped, this was England mate!"

With this and heat honing in from other directions, Jagger spent the first part of the week beginning February 6 at his lawyer's officers, substantiating the libel he was going to serve on the *News Of The World*. The rest of the week he busied himself with Rolling Stones business around town. Contractually, the Stones owed Decca a new album, and with The Beatles hard at work on their eagerly awaited *Sgt. Pepper* LP, a record had to be ready to catch the associated interest the Stones would garner following a new Beatles' release.

On Thursday, February 9, Mick, Bill and Charlie convened at Olympic Studios in Barnes to begin recording tracks for the Stones' next album. Brian was absent in Germany with Anita, attending soundtrack duties for the film *A Degree of Murder*, as was Keith, most likely in an attempt to evade the heat circulating around London.

Despite the absence of Jones and Richards, those present at Olympic still managed to record songs including one with the working titles of 'She Comes In Colours' and 'Lady Fair', which eventually became 'She's A Rainbow'. While Glyn Johns assisted Oldham in the control booth, the Stones trio was augmented by keyboard virtuoso Nicky Hopkins with multi-talented (and later Led Zeppelin bass player) John Paul Jones helping out with the string arrangement.

The following night, Mick and Marianne joined in on a star-studded affair at EMI's Abbey Road studios in St John's Wood. While recording sessions (even for The Beatles) were a somewhat tedious affair, this night proved to be a momentous exception. The Beatles were recording the orchestral build-up for the closing *Sgt. Pepper* track, 'A Day In The Life', and had declared 'open house' for their large retinue of friends and colleagues. Lennon and McCartney's impressionistic composition required a suitably free-form climax to a song that would assume legendary status. With Beatles and Stones close friend, the recently deceased Tara Browne, enshrined in the lyrics as the man who "blew his mind out in a car", Mick and Keith (freshly arrived back from Germany), Donovan and numerous luminaries from 'Swinging London' convened in the cavernous Studio One to watch proceedings. The Beatles hired a 72-piece orchestra to best capture the trippy, fragmented climaxes in the song, and the studio was transformed into an ersatz night-club-cum freak-out for the evening.

With a clutch of 16mm cameras handed out among those present, the ad hoc psychedelia was captured on film, with Mick and Marianne in the thick of the action. As evidenced by the splintered footage, at one point Mick was seen discussing events with John Lennon; Jagger's purple, open-neck shirt covered by his omnipresent green velvet jacket, which he would remove as the evening wore on. Marianne, welded closely to Jagger's side for the entirety of the evening, appeared for the most part in a fairly convivial mode. Keith was also caught on film; having stepped off the plane from Munich just moments before he was seen rubbing his weary eyes while chatting with Lennon.

Despite the late hour spent with The Beatles, Mick and the Stones *sans* Brian would continue with their own recording efforts the following day, spending the best part of Saturday evening laying down tracks at Olympic. Keith, still fatigued from his trip back from Germany, spent a short time with the group at the studio. When Brian and Anita returned from their film work in Germany, they called in to the studio then left to enjoy the weekend as best they could.

The initial idea to hold a gathering at Keith's Redlands home the coming weekend came from Robert Fraser. This was quite in character for him, as Christopher Gibbs recalls. "Robert was the person who'd say, 'Right we're doing this, and you're coming'. He would have orchestrated things." Richards was more than happy to play host, especially with so much paranoia manifesting itself around the Stones organisation in London. He was happier spending time in the country where he could assume a greater anonymity than in town. As was his style, he'd even entertained the odd day-tripper or starstruck teenager anxious to have a peek around his property. The press, too, were intrigued by Richards' charming residence. When column space called for a piece on the property, he was fairly accommodating to media requests: the week prior to the Redlands' gathering, he'd been featured in *New Musical Express*, photographed sitting irreverently on a discarded toilet in Redlands' garden with his faithful dog, Ratbag, on his lap.

Keith was also aware that his relationship with Mick clearly needed shoring up. Their songwriting partnership was integral to the Stones' musical future but Richards' immersion into LSD had driven a temporary wedge between them. Though to all intents and purposes Jagger in his finery looked every bit the acid head, he'd yet to try out the world's newest chemical craze, and the weekend offered an opportunity to remedy this.

The familiar chant of 'you're not hip 'till you trip' was flying around London's hip elite, and for Keith Richards and Brian Jones LSD was an exciting opportunity to play Russian roulette with their consciousness. Jagger, however, was wary. Like Paul McCartney, he had monitored closely LSD's debilitating effect of 'ego loss' on his peers, and he was still cool towards the prospect of an undetermined chemical neutering the driving component in his psyche. After a party the previous month at which Keith and Brian had freaked out after taking some particularly strong acid, Mick commented to close associate, film director Donald Cammell: "This is all getting out of hand. I don't know where it's all going to end."

Despite LSD's canonisation among rock's more adventurous mind travellers, few were intelligently monitoring the actual effects of the chemical. Nonetheless, from the available data it was generally considered that a safe environment in which to take the drug was paramount, especially for neophyte users. Dr. Timothy Leary, already by 1967 the world's foremost proponent of LSD use, had helped put together a user's guide to traversing acid's unpredictable corridors. Helped by fellow psychedelic notables Richard Alpert and Ralph Metzner, Leary would rework the *Tibetan Book Of The Dead* into *The Psychedelic Experience,* in layman's terms the equivalent of an LSD Haynes manual. With copies surreptitiously imported by the likes of the *International Times* bookshop, the volume had fallen into the hands of the pop elite. Repeated frequently in its text was the edict of 'Set and Setting'; LSD's cautious mantra to ensure a safe environment to expand one's mind.

Despite the book's propensity to wallow in flaky metaphor and allegory, this instruction was largely good advice. Many had been badly burnt in psychedelic clubs and 'happenings' under the influence of the drug; some had been hospitalised or even killed themselves. With seasoned trippers calling for caution among first-time users, many were finding pastoral landscapes more appropriate environments in which to peel back their consciousness. For Jagger's initiation into the drug, this advice found no better host than the embracing woods and protective moat that surrounded Richards' West Wittering pile.

To re-tune Mick's consciousness, it was decided that the gathering at Redlands would be ideal to induct Jagger into the joys of LSD. A supply of reliable acid would be paramount to the party's success, making the reappearance of a character Keith met fleetingly the previous year hugely fortuitous. Visiting one of London's hip joints the week before the gathering, Keith re-encountered David Schneiderman, the drug dealer from New York. Schneiderman had arrived in London following a hugely circuitous route. Late in 1966, immigration officials had tracked him down to Greenwich Village and detained him. With numerous charges awaiting him back in Canada, Schneiderman feigned madness and was committed into a state institution. With security notably more lax than in police custody, he escaped, and with the benefit of numerous passports and aliases that spanned 'Jordan', 'Edwards' and 'Britton', he'd made his way over to Europe and finally Britain, where he claimed he had relatives. Schneiderman hit town in January and at a time when London was a citadel for exotic drug use, the Canadian's unique chemistry set, dispensed from a monogrammed attaché case, gave him enormous collateral to enter any gathering.

Even before bumping into Richards again, Schneiderman had impressed Chelsea's prime 'psychedelicatessen' Robert Fraser with his thesaurus of drug lingo and wide array of narcotics. Fraser duly dubbed the Canadian the 'Acid King', an accolade guaranteed to embellish his credentials among those on the front line of chemical exploration. Slightly less intoxicated by Schneiderman's arrival was Christopher Gibbs who'd witnessed the Canadian's presence around town before the Redlands' party.

Christopher Gibbs: "He was at every party one went to for about 10 days, and there was this charming, smiling young man handing out 'candy' to all and sundry. He was very charming, personable and friendly. There didn't seem to be anything horrible about him. If anything he was just a bit crazy. He was an acid evangelist, and his mission was to turn on the world, talking about spiking the water system and stuff like that."

In a scene awash with the weird and bizarre, Schneiderman's unique presence elevated him above the pack. With a beatific smile, gleaming teeth and a mop of auburn hair, he appeared totally non-threatening to the sensitive crowd he was charming. His patter, too, was as stratospheric as the drugs he carried. There was method to this madness as his friend Ed Ochs would later recall: "To make it more difficult for outsiders to crash his scene – and easier for him to crash theirs – he spoke his own language, a confusing, amusing, seemingly random blend of UFOlogy, Scientology, Crowleyisms, I-Ching anagrams, street talk, and a home-grown code he dubbed '21st century curbstone jargon'."

Schneiderman's quick acceptance around town was helped no end by the large quantity of 'Californian Sunshine' he brought with him.

A massively strong variant of LSD, these orange coloured pills were manufactured by the high priest of acid composition himself, Stanley Owsley. A rogue chemist then operating out of San Francisco, Owsley's brand of acid had already made huge inroads into the world's psychedelic culture. Such was his prodigious output, he'd reportedly produced somewhere in the region of half a kilogram of the substance, enough to construct around five million tablets of LSD. The vibrancy of Owsley's acid had swiftly been communicated across the globe, imbibers promptly declaring its potency as 'electric'. Indeed, so intoxicated were they with these reports, The Beatles reportedly sent a film crew over to the Monterey Pop Festival in California (held June 1967) to surreptitiously acquire several phials of the drug.

As preparations for the Redlands' bash gained momentum, Fraser, his own chemistry set rivalling Schneiderman's, mentioned the party in the week leading up to the gathering. Thus alerted, Schneiderman made a swift beeline to charm Keith into allowing him to attend. By dint of the Canadian's electric pharmacy (and presumably no other reason) the invitation was forthcoming.

Others from Mick and Keith's circles were also invited. Gibbs, whose good vibrations and impeccable taste ensured he was a safe pair of hands to trip with, was a natural choice. Much like Gibbs, Fraser had an eye for the unusual, effusive charm and vast experience of drug use, and would mould seamlessly into the deep piles at Redlands without ruffling anyone's sensitivities. Fraser had been an important cog in turning many onto LSD, and his Mayfair flat at 23 Mount Street was a virtual clearing house for substances. While it's never been confirmed, John Lennon's Beatles' song 'Doctor Robert' (from *Revolver*) reeks of the sort of ambiance Fraser embodied. Helping everyone he could was certainly his trademark.

Fraser's tastes went way beyond smoking dope or tripping on LSD, however. While largely frowned upon in hippie circles, heroin had started to make inroads on the fringes of London's underground movement. Still available on prescription by sympathetic doctors, obtaining the drug was relatively easy if one had the right credentials. Fraser had secured the services of one of the bolder characters in the Stones circle, one Tony 'Spanish' Sanchez who was currently the main link in maintaining

Fraser's heroin habit of crushing pharmaceutical heroin tablets and snorting them, a less intrusive way of imbibing the drug than using a needle. Through Sanchez, Fraser had acquired 24 heroin tablets on the Thursday prior to the Redlands party and, as usual for him, kept them in an ornate pillbox with an ivory lid.

Also among the guests was photographer Michael Cooper, a close friend of Fraser, who'd just received a commission from The Beatles to shoot their *Sgt. Pepper* album cover. Despite the intimacy of his portraits, Cooper was discreet, with a tacit loyalty that endeared him to all he met. "Even in very tense situations," Marianne Faithfull later recalled of Cooper, "Michael could take pictures without disturbing an atom."

A less celebrated invitee was ephemeral flower child Nicky Kramer. A fixture on SW3 invites, redheaded 'Kramer', as he was best known, was deemed acceptable company, although as befits the time, no one remembered ever inviting him down to West Wittering. "Nicky Kramer was very thin and frail," Gibbs recalls. "Very delicate, pale with high cheekbones; sort of sweet and dreamy. He was just a flower child wandering about. He was just a groupie type of person. I don't think he was particularly close to anybody that weekend."

A more practical invitee was Mohammed Jajaj, Fraser's north African manservant. Originally a student in London, he'd come across Fraser socially, and they had become friends and later (reportedly) lovers. With Fraser's growing obsession with all things Moroccan, Jajaj had become his personal assistant. With the likelihood of Fraser being heavily intoxicated for the duration of the weekend, Jajaj was best placed to drive his employer down to West Sussex.

Her romance with Mick in its first spring, Marianne Faithfull was the only female to be invited, her poetic and adventurous disposition making her the emotional centre of the gathering. With the prospect of mixing LSD with visits to ancient monuments and sacred sites around the Redlands locale, she was excited by what lay ahead. Despite being at the centre of a scene awash with acid, Marianne, like Mick, had not as yet imbibed. Reports of the drug transporting its users into a fairyland of indeterminate beauty would have been more than enough to ignite her inquisitive nature.

There were others destined for Redlands who in the end failed to appear. Dealer Tony Sanchez was said to be one. Brian and Anita, despite their propensity to battle out their emotions in public, were expected, especially as LSD was a centrepiece of their activities. Evidently, Keith was due to shepherd the couple down to Redlands but on arriving at their flat he found the pair engaged in another of their unpleasant rows. Unwilling to bring their unsettling presence to what was intended to be a convivial gathering, Keith decided to leave them to their own devices and travel down to Sussex alone.

Another less definable entity in the weekend activities was Keith's part-time chauffeur, a Belgian by the name of 'Patrick'. Among other duties, he'd been acting as Richards' driver, a vital requirement given Keith's provisional learner status. While details of the Belgian have proved impossible to trace, it appears likely that he was the weak link in the Stones' employee chain, and was acting as informant to the *News Of The World*. It is also likely that the Belgian drove Keith down to Redlands that weekend, although what became of him afterwards is unclear.

Invitees and interlopers united as one, the procession to West Wittering left London around 9:30 p.m. on the Saturday night, the journey taking 90 minutes. The most unlikely vehicle in the caravan was Fraser's cream coloured van, driven by Mohammed. Normally used for transporting Fraser's artwork across London, it had been commandeered for the weekend in case larger transportation for the trippy crowd was required. While Keith and Mick had their own chauffeur-driven vehicles, Schneiderman made his own way in a Mini.

Infused by the damp February mist, Redlands took on a wholly fantastical appearance in the moonlight. The temperature was slightly above normal for a winter's evening, and all appeared just perfect for the touch of mystery that lay ahead. With Schneiderman's LSD to look forward to the next day, a sense of adventure permeated the atmosphere. "It was meant to be a lovely weekend taking acid with my dearest friends," Marianne would say later.

After settling into the house the party tucked into a late night supper of bacon and eggs cooked by Mohammed, and stayed up talking until around 5 a.m. Happily tired, all but Keith repaired upstairs. The one double and three single bedrooms were all occupied so Richards was content to sleep in an armchair in his living room. Before they retired Schneiderman informed everyone that the following day's LSD experience would be optimised by conserving their energies. Under his precise butlership, the 'Californian Sunshine' would be dispensed to each guest as they awoke, washed down with a cup of tea.

With the sun rising at 7:32 a.m. on the Sunday morning, little effort was made in rousing anyone from their slumber. Schneiderman was the first up, followed shortly by Mohammed. Aware of the late hour everyone had retired to bed, the Canadian waited until around 11 a.m. to serve his lysergic breakfast. This he did, visiting each of the four bedrooms on the upstairs floor in turn. He accompanied his dispensing with a patois that was wholly in keeping with his persona. "This is the Tao of lysergic diethylamide," he whispered as he handed out the drug. "Let it speak to you. Let it tell you how to navigate the cosmos." Evidently Mohammed was spared a dose. As befits LSD protocol for tripping *en masse*, it added an air of security to have at least one member of the party straight to 'babysit' events.

The freshly dosed ensemble made their way down the winding stairwell into Redlands' expansive lounge. With its inordinate space making a mockery of the property's outward bijou charm, the group settled into the drawing room in varying states of elevation. With the acid making swift inroads, reality would barely enjoy a foothold that day. Such was the potency of the drug, first-time users Mick and Marianne were physically sick as the drug kicked in. After this dramatic prologue, things soon settled down, allowing a collective harmony to hover around those present.

While everyone was engaged in their own mind games, Schneiderman prepared a further concoction for anyone not fully blasted by the onset of the LSD. "I remember him with his little suitcase full of all sorts of things," recalls Gibbs. "He had this drug called Dimethyltryptamine or DMT, which was a sort of 20-minute roller coaster hallucinogenic. He was dripping it onto mentholated cigarettes during the morning and passing them around."

Cooper was also privy to the contents of Schneiderman's attaché case and the other, more unusual items it contained. The photographer later revealed that at some point during the day he'd rifled through the case in search of some marijuana. Inside, Cooper claimed he found "a whole collection of different passports in different names and different nationalities on them." Richards, too, had been shown Schneiderman's caché of documents, while the Canadian explained how he was out to turn on the world, and had equipped himself with around "a dozen" passports to ease his way around immigration desks.

Cooper also recalled Schneiderman's interest in areas a world away from the gentle vibrations his substances were designed to produce. "He talked to me about guns and weapons in the same sort of way that most guys talk about chicks."

Schneiderman's bizarre ramblings aside, the signs augured well for the weekend's ultimate objective: to tune Jagger into the same frequency as Richards. With the weather unusually warm for a mid-February morning, it appeared as though the spirits were with them. Enchanted by the rich, mysterious woodlands that surrounded Redlands, Marianne briefly escaped the house to commune with the trees. When she returned, much to the delight of her fellow trippers she brought with her pieces of natural ephemera – branches, leaves and such. Keith, too, would spend an hour or so wandering around Redlands' lawns while his house guests kept close to the cottage.

To take advantage of the limited daylight hours available to them, a decision was made to visit the beach that ran along the edge of West Wittering village. Cooper began taking a few impromptu photographs of the ensemble prior to leaving. His white sheepskin coat pulled up over his head, Keith found the rocking chair in Redlands' garden much to his liking, rocking himself to the point where the chair toppled over, an event Cooper recorded for posterity. The group then climbed into Fraser's van and with Mohammed at the wheel they left Redlands under the watchful eye of Keith's gardener 'Jumping' Jack Dyer, to whom Keith proffered a 'thumbs-up' sign. Dyer would later recall how happy everyone appeared. Schneiderman decided to make his own way in his Mini.

Once at the beach, the party revelled in the dramatic landscape that slowly dissolved into the sea, edged by rupturing dunes. With shallow lagoons traced out at low tide and a line of iron groynes with metal tops like miniature umbrellas, the area was as fantastical as anything Schneiderman's acid could muster. Cooper's omnipresent camera captured numerous images of the happy troupe, out playing as though it were a Sunday school outing. Gibbs' tall, willowy figure was the subject of a couple of Cooper's impromptu snaps; black, knee-length coat turned up at the neck and large square-tinted sunglasses hovering over his nose, he looked every part the stoned Martian stumbling through the shingle and driftwood. Ever the explorer, Gibbs had brought with him a pair of binoculars to better observe the landscape. Not surprisingly, the party's host was a major focus for Cooper's lens. At one point, a grinning Mohammed was captured holding two reefers while Keith larked around in the background.

Among the range of snaps, Cooper unwittingly captured an iconic image of Richards and Schneiderman in a close huddle, their smiles and shared laughter betraying the euphoria of the moment. The trip to the beach was short-lived though, lasting between 20 and 30 minutes according to Richards. Towards the end of the outing, someone noticed that Schneiderman had mysteriously driven away.

When the tribe resumed their places in the van for the short journey back to Redlands, deciding he didn't fancy the cramped atmosphere, Richards opted to walk back. Cooper, ever on hand to record events, snapped him stopping momentarily to light a cigarette outside a small grocery named Birdham Stores. Further along Cooper captured a totally zonked out Richards rolling around on the gravel drive outside a quaint little property called Rose Cottage.

Back at the house, Keith found his guests in no mood to relax. To try and engage their frazzled senses, he retrieved the small sailing dingy that he'd bought from Redlands' previous owners and with a little help it was lifted from its storage in the garage and dropped into the moat. There followed 45 minutes of vain attempts to steer the vessel around the water before a snap decision was made to get back into the van and head off in whatever direction the wind took them. With Mohammed again at the wheel, the van left Redlands for the second time that day –

this time with Schneiderman riding along with everyone else. At some point during this aimless ramble, someone remembered that the home of surrealist artist Edward James was situated nearby. With fantastical tales of James' outlandish artwork and goofy sculptures filling the van's interior, the gang tried desperately to find the house. After driving up and down numerous country lanes, they eventually found the property at West Dean, about six miles outside Chichester. They arrived just after 5 p.m., but despite Gibbs personally knowing the property's custodians, they were refused entry as the house had just closed to the public.

The sun was setting as the party retraced their steps, arriving in Redlands Lane at around 5:30 p.m. The van's headlamps sliced through the early evening mist, illuminating the small, dense woodland that enveloped the house, giving it a spectral, wraithlike appearance. About 15 minutes later, the happy-go-lucky group were settled in the living room, Schneiderman's acid beginning its slow retreat from their minds.

It was at this point that the party was enlivened by a late, unexpected arrival. George Harrison and his wife Pattie turned up in their customised Mini Cooper. While any of the Beatles would have made excellent house guests, Harrison's spiritual understanding of LSD was a welcome addition to the gathering and his presence was the icing on the cake. George and Pattie had been invited down during the 'A Day In The Life' recording session at EMI just a few days before. The Beatles' latest single, 'Penny Lane', was set for release the following week, its joint A-side 'Strawberry Fields Forever' a shimmering product of John Lennon's acid-drenched imagination.

Also travelling down independently at some point during the afternoon was Beatles' aide Tony Bramwell. A friend of Harrison's since their Liverpool school days, Bramwell was employed by Brian Epstein to attend to various group needs. Bramwell's recollections were not as beatific as the others, principally down to his own dislike of drugs, and he found the visit to Redlands a fairly pointless exercise. "It was just one of those things that occurred," he says. "It didn't appear as though anyone had arranged anything, it was just a stoned gathering. I just hated all those people who hung around the Stones. They were just awful. I didn't stay for the night, I was just there for the afternoon.

I quickly skipped out of there and went off to visit a girlfriend in nearby Selsey."

Outside darkness had fallen and temperatures were just below freezing, but those inside Redlands were enjoying the warmth from the freshly lit fire in the living room. Keith retired upstairs for a bath and a change of clothing which occupied him for the best part of 45 minutes. Marianne was also slightly soiled from her adventures, and she took the opportunity to have a soak in the tub in the bathroom adjacent to the room she was sharing with Mick. Lounging in the warm, soothing water, she watched as the detritus of her afternoon's larking about floated among the soap suds around her.

Her instincts having overridden prior planning, Marianne hadn't thought to bring a change of clothes for the weekend, and had left her lace blouse, black velvet trousers and black half-coat on the back of a chair in the bedroom. Once finished with her bath, she walked back to the bedroom and wrapped herself in the large fur rug that had covered the double bed. Made up from animal pelts on one side with a tawny coloured cover on the other, the rug was more than sufficient to cover her five-foot five-inch frame.

Dressed in the rug, Marianne ambled down the stairs towards Redlands' living room, the big fur-skin easily covering her body. Elsewhere, others had prepared themselves for whatever the evening had to offer. Jagger, keen as always to maintain a sense of order around his profile, had utilised some lipstick and other cosmetics before relaxing on the lounge sofa. In the spirit of the gathering, Gibbs paid homage to the exotic flavours in the room by dressing for the evening in what he describes as "a Pakistani pyjama suit". According to Marianne, an "overwhelming sensation of warmth and safety" permeated the house. The time was around 6:30 p.m. With two of the three downstairs windows having their curtains drawn, the outside world might have been a thousand miles away.

On a chaise lounge, Marianne had draped herself over Mick's lap, her legs resting on the floor while Mick gently massaged her back and stared aimlessly around the room. To Marianne, it seemed the acid had levelled Mick out, reducing his normally charged persona to a cool, calm and gentle presence. Sat at the far end of the chaise lounge was Nicky Kramer.

Like Marianne, he'd brought no change of clothes, and had borrowed one of Keith's silk kimonos for the evening. Like Jagger, he'd also put on some make-up. Kramer maintained a muted, silent demeanour for much of the evening, an abstraction that would weigh heavily against him in the following weeks.

Sitting alone, Fraser appeared more engaged. The potency of Schneiderman's LSD having visited every atom of his psyche, he'd levelled off some of its effects by swallowing some of the heroin jacks he'd brought down with him. Richards was sitting in an overstuffed chair, quietly enjoying the final stages of the acid comedown.

With everyone engaged in their own receding hallucinations, earthly distractions were of little or no interest. Adding to the unworldly imagery, a small strobe light – a popular accessory for acid fuelled gatherings – blinked away to no prescribed rhythm in a corner of the room. To the left of the fireplace, a large TV set was switched on, acting as nothing more than a backdrop. With only a documentary on Christian iconography or a programme about brass instruments to choose from, someone decided to turn the volume down and let the imagery play itself out, the mass of monochrome pixels dancing irregularly across the screen adding a further dimension to the imprecise ambiance of the evening. Someone had suggested watching the BBC1 screening of *Pete Kelly's Blues*, a 1955 film starring Janet Leigh and Jack Webb, but like most things proposed that day, the idea floated off into the ether. From elsewhere in the room loud music emanated from Keith's state-of-the-art hi-fi system, its enormous speakers placed at the opposite end of the room from the turntable, The Who's most recent album *A Quick One* vying with Bob Dylan's *Blonde On Blonde*. Of no apparent significance until later would be track one from Dylan's classic double-album, the hugely ambiguous 'Rainy Day Women #12 & 35', its thinly veiled invocation of "everybody must get stoned" serving as a suitable backdrop to the evening.

At around 7 p.m., much to everyone's delight, Fraser's *aide-de-camp* served a traditional Moroccan dish of heavily spiced couscous. To add to the ambiance, Mohammed had changed into Moroccan national costume. For this treat, the group wandered a few feet from the living room into a dining area. As Gibbs later recalled, the atmosphere exuded a warm domesticity. "It was a nice friendly gathering of people who, by and large, knew each other, liked each other, and were very much at one with one another."

Half an hour later, the highly fragrant meal had been consumed, leaving everyone to return to the main room. Much in the spirit of these gatherings, Schneiderman decided to roll out some joints to level off any sensitivities bruised by acid's marathon effects. His ubiquitous attaché case contained numerous strains of marijuana and other potions to dazzle or placate the senses. Most likely on his advice, various sweets were lying around in case anyone needed a 'sugar rush' if a downer happened. Gibbs clearly remembers them, recalling that Schneiderman referred to them as 'candy a go-go'. Richards, too, has since recalled the presence of confectionery, and confirmed their stabilising properties.

Given that the joint rolling required a level base to construct them successfully, Schneiderman leant over a stone table, measuring some five-foot by two, situated close to the fire, which was perfect to build the makeshift reefers. With flecks of stray dope already embedded in its stone top, it had obviously been used before for this particular task. On the table lay a pipe bowl and metal tin containing loose incense, a necessary aide to infuse the air with a pleasant, slightly exotic, smell. During the evening, some of this incense was burnt on a grate by the fire. Elsewhere around the house, joss sticks were lit to infuse the air with a less invasive aroma than that of marijuana.

At around 7:55 p.m. George and Pattie made a snap decision to leave the party. Harrison later went on record as saying that he was bored and, as his diary for the following week makes clear, it was apparent that he had other, much more pressing duties to attend to. The Harrisons said their goodbyes and headed off in the Mini Cooper back to their bungalow in Esher, Surrey.

Whether Harrison knew it or not, as he left a large number of people were gathering at the end of Redlands' drive, collecting autographs the last thing on their minds.

CHAPTER 5

Redlands

"No one would have believed in the last years of the nineteenth century that this world was being watched keenly and closely by intelligences greater than man's and yet as mortal as his own; that as men busied themselves about their various concerns they were scrutinised and studied, perhaps almost as narrowly as a man with a microscope might scrutinise the transient creatures that swarm and multiply in a drop of water."

HG Wells, *The War Of The Worlds*

Unbeknown to those enjoying the ebbing hallucinations inside Redlands Cottage, strenuous efforts to derail Mick Jagger's libel action against the *News Of The World* had been gathering momentum elsewhere during the previous 24 hours. It now appears that the fuse that exploded the time bomb within the Stones' camp was lit by a phone call to the *News Of The World* at 10 p.m. the previous evening. With the paper traditionally working late on Saturday night in case any last-minute news stories broke, the call – reportedly from an informant – was put through to the paper's news desk. One of the reporters on duty that night was Robert Warren. He recalled developments that night to the BBC in 2007.

Robert Warren: "It was enormously fortunate when on Saturday evening I was in the office at the time, in the newsroom. The phone went on the news desk, and I saw the deputy news editor looking quite excited. I listened in, and it appeared to be an informant telling us that The Rolling Stones were having a drugs party in Sussex. What happened that night was that we spoke to the informant at some length, and arranged to meet him in St James Park the following morning. One of our senior investigating reporters kept that meeting. [He] was satisfied that the information handed over was pretty convincing."

The senior reporter was evidently Trevor Kempson. His informant has never been convincingly identified, although Keith Richards in his 2010 biography *Life* believed that 'Patrick', his Belgian chauffeur, had swallowed the *News Of The World* bait. Others have suggested that Stones driver Tom Keylock may have been involved in the subterfuge, and while Keylock had a high-ranking relation in the London police force, he had yet to work solely for Richards. While there is no exact confirmation on who spilled the beans, what is abundantly clear is that the informant had detailed knowledge of events at Redlands, and how many guests would be present. With this information to hand, a decision was made to pass the details over to Scotland Yard in the hope that they would take appropriate action. Before this was done though, the *NOTW*'s editor had to be contacted to authorise the decision.

The paper's editor-in-chief, 56-year-old Stafford Somerfield, was seasoned enough to realise that in passing this information on to the police the paper could avoid an inordinate amount of embarrassment over Jagger's libel case. Somerfield, reportedly contacted at 3 a.m. on the Sunday morning, gave his blessing.

Later that day, with all the information collated, a senior executive at the paper transferred the intelligence to Scotland Yard. According to reporter Robert Warren, the Yard rebuffed the approach, deeming it a parochial matter for the authorities in Chichester. However, *International Times* contributor Steve Abrams was later told by the officer who received the tip-off, Chief Inspector John Lynch, that he wanted nothing to do with the set-up, believing the implications could be hugely counter-productive.

Steve Abrams: "He said that he was not expected to stamp out cannabis, but to keep its use under control. If he arrested Mick Jagger every lad in the country would want to try some pot. He was, after all, head of the drug squad, not head of the 'Lynch' mob."

Undeterred by Scotland Yard's rebuff, someone at the *News Of The World* relayed the information to West Sussex police in Chichester. On duty that weekend was Detective Sergeant Stanley Cudmore, an officer who maintained links with London's CID. A traditionalist policeman, Cudmore would insist on nothing other than total adherence to police rules, imploring those under him to "do it right". In recently uncovered documents, it was reported that Cudmore received the information regarding the activities at Redlands at around 3:30 p.m. on the Sunday afternoon. Whereas Chief Inspector Lynch was seasoned enough to weigh up the consequences that might result from the paper's tip off, Cudmore was the sort of policeman who felt obliged to act.

The source, according to Cudmore's superior Chief Inspector Gordon Dineley, was "from someone other than a police officer". Later and under oath, Dineley would say that he was "not prepared to say if that person was connected with a well-known newspaper", which appeared more of an admission than a straight rebuttal. With Dineley mobilised into action, a lot of activity was evidently happening in Chichester police's otherwise sedate offices that afternoon.

Despite not having the resources that Scotland Yard could call on, the decision was made to launch a raid on Redlands that evening, after discussions at every level of West Sussex police officialdom. Interestingly, while Keith Richards' presence at Redlands was known to the local police, it was not considered a priority for the area's dedicated narcotics team. John Rodway, while not actually on the raid, had just joined the West Sussex drug squad, and was present at Chichester police station that weekend.

"The Stones were not what the drug squad were interested in," recalls Rodway today. "The drug squad were interested in the sort of people who imported drugs; selling drugs; passing off drugs into the clubs, into schools. While Keith Richards might have had access to a lot of drugs, he certainly wasn't pushing them out on street corners, or going to dance halls and giving them away."

Nonetheless, with the information received compelling enough to justify a raid, action – of some sort – had to be seen to take place. If they had chosen to ignore the tip-off, there could have been an almighty backlash on many levels, especially if the *News Of The World* decided to enquire just why they'd passed on it. Someone might suggest that unlike the public at large, pop stars were immune from prosecution, that the police turned a blind eye to their unsavoury habits. The Chief Constable of West Sussex was acutely aware of the compromising situation.

Though police numbers in 1967 were higher than present levels, it was a weekend and extra constables were recruited from neighbouring areas along the south coast. Police on the beat were informed of the night's action on Redlands when they checked back with base by public phone. While it might appear comical today, the only realistic way of keeping up to speed on events in the days before mobile phones was by using a bright red public telephone kiosk. As a formality, police on the beat were issued with four-penny coins at the start of their shift, with instructions to call back to base at intervals during their patrols to receive orders.

Not that either the *News Of The World* or Scotland Yard were aware at the time, but the Redlands party dovetailed with a major crackdown on crime by West Sussex police. The previous Monday, the Chief Constable of West Sussex, Mr Thomas Williams, had spoken to the local press regarding his "deep concern on drugs". With crime figures in the county for the past year on a steep rise, Williams called for society to take a new approach to what he saw as an epidemic.

"I have not the slightest hope of giving a precise solution," Williams told a local news conference. "Some people tell me it reflects the deterioration in the moral standards of the public... I sometimes ask myself if society contains sufficient safeguards for people to have a fair chance of being resistant to the contagion of less moral neighbours and workmates."

Late the following Sunday afternoon, while Richards and his friends were returning from their acid-fuelled stroll along the beach, a preparatory briefing session was taking place at Chichester Police Station in anticipation of the raid that evening. Redlands Cottage was well known to police based west of Chichester, so it didn't require any major reconnaissance. Contrary to popular belief, officers were not under orders to arrest anyone that night. Obviously, if the situation deteriorated, then there would have been grounds, but no one anticipated any major resistance. If suspicious items were found, then they would be taken away and examined. If they turned out to be illegal, then formal charges would ensue. Furthermore, nowhere in the police brief was there any mention to search the vehicles belonging to those inside. While on other raids it was a formality to check cars for any illegal substances, the plan was to concentrate on activities inside the house.

Believing that The Rolling Stones' enormous popularity could draw huge numbers, 18 officers were collected for the job of visiting Richards' property that evening. With the necessary signing of a warrant by a local Justice of the Peace, Colonel RG Bevis, collected from his home address that afternoon, the last of the day's contingency plans were finalised. Mindful of the sensitivity of the operation, officers were instructed to temporarily remove each person present from the hub of the gathering so that they could be searched in private.

Among the team were two specialised forensic officers whose role would be to identify and record any items collected. Given that the informants had mentioned the possible presence of at least two females at Redlands, and with the likelihood of intimate searching having to take place, two women officers also made up the quota of police that night.

At the head of this task force was Chief Inspector Dineley. While it was not normally a prerequisite to have someone of his rank leading a domestic raid, his superior, Chief Constable Thomas Williams, was fully aware of the potentially huge media that could result from the action. Not wanting to put a rank and file sergeant in the firing line, Williams felt that someone of Dineley's experience needed to be present if indeed the media were alerted. Given that the information had come from the *News Of The World*, Williams insisted that several officers be stationed outside, just in case any opportunist hacks attempted to gatecrash proceedings or snatch photos through the windows. Taking no chances with any vagaries on narcotics law, Dineley came equipped with a hard copy of the 1965 Dangerous Drugs Act.

With everything in place, at 7:30 p.m., the team drove the six-mile journey from Chichester to West Wittering in an Austin Cambridge, a 1966 cream-coloured mini-van and an Austin A40, a rather unsophisticated convoy even by 1967 standards. Adding credence to the belief that arrests weren't expected that night, no Black Marias were employed for the raid, although several were available back at Chichester if required.

Arriving at Redlands Lane at around 7:50 p.m., the cortège made a slow procession along the narrow road leading to Keith's house. With a public walkway running alongside Redlands' borders, the police vehicles would have little trouble finding parking space. Just before 8 p.m., the modest roar of a souped-up Mini preparing to exit Redlands Lane would have startled the officers. Whether they knew it or not, at the wheel was one of The Beatles, heading back to his Esher home with his wife.

The timing of George Harrison's departure from Redlands has been a source of much speculation over the years. Many, including Harrison himself, believed that the police were waiting for the Beatle to leave before they could move in on the party. With information on the occupants at Redlands evidently included in the police's intelligence, it has been heavily speculated (but never confirmed) that Harrison's presence during a raid could have incurred considerable embarrassment.

Even with their recent sojourn into psychedelia, The Beatles were still regarded as sacrosanct by the British nation, decorated by royalty and the toast of the Treasury when it came to incoming revenue. Being afforded virtual diplomat status on their globe trekking, busting a Beatle for drugs could have had a potentially disastrous effect. While pillorying the Stones had become a national pastime for the press (and by extension some sections of the establishment), the arrest of one of the Fab Four in such questionable circumstances could have had serious ramifications both on public and political opinion. While in early 1967, all four Beatles were frequently taking drugs, to a world unawares they were still the lovable clean foursome.

However, according to police sources, no one was aware that Harrison was present that night. In fact, the majority of raiding officers would have had difficulty in determining just who Harrison was among the other guests. Nonetheless, the *News Of The World* would later allude to the fact that the Beatle and his wife had been present – and that they left just before the police arrived.

Whether by design or otherwise, with Harrison now on his way, the police began their advance along Redlands' drive. Evidently, their knowledge of the house had made them aware that the bumpy, uneven track was wholly unsuitable for a convoy of vehicles. Abandoning their cars, the posse walked over the small bridge that crossed Redlands' moat, and then along a footpath that led to the front door situated to the left of the property.

For over 40 years, the identity of the officers that made the 200-yard walk up the drive has been shrouded in secrecy. However, recently discovered papers list the police personnel that converged on Richards' property that Sunday night. Their ranks range from Gordon Dineley's Chief Inspector status, down to Police Constable Alfred Guy, the village bobby for the nearby hamlet of Birdham, its population just a few hundred. Alongside Gordon Dineley and Stanley Cudmore were Michael Cotton, Pamela Baker, Rosemary Slade, Evelyn Fuller, Alfred Guy, Frederick Weller, Thomas Davies, John Challen, Donald Rambridge, Raymond Harris, Reginald Mugford, Nathanial Bingham, Derek Grieves, Leslie Stewart, Richard Smith and Ronald Pafford.

The list reveals a batch of indigenous Sussex surnames; your everyday policemen and women, drawn from modest south coast enclaves surrounding Chichester. For most of them pounding a depressing, out-of-season beat in places such as Littlehampton, Selsey and Bognor Regis on a winter's Sunday night offered little in the way of excitement; but whether they knew it or not, all were about to become a part of an event that would subsequently shape the cultural direction of the 20th century.

With Dineley leading the advance, Redlands came into view. Almost uniformly in witness statements later compiled, police noted "the loud strains of pop music" on their approach. These reports also indicated that two out of the three downstairs windows that faced the drive had their curtains drawn.

On the other side of Redlands' stone walls, the volume from Richards' hi-fi was so overwhelming that no one had heard the sound of the impending raid. Fatigue had begun to eat into the addled senses of those inside, and it probably wouldn't have raised so much as an eyebrow even if they'd heard any advancing footsteps. At just past 8:00 p.m. with the muted TV imagery from the film *Pete Kelly's Blues* competing with the sounds from the record player, LSD's indeterminate Neverland was evidently being maintained.

At 8:05 p.m., what appeared to those inside to be the face of a middle-aged woman pressed itself against the sole window whose curtains weren't drawn. Schneiderman was the first to spot her and he alerted Richards who, believing it to be an intrepid fan, wasn't unduly bothered, only slightly irritated by the intrusion. An unfortunate by-product of his local celebrity was the occasional unsolicited drop-in by over eager admirers, not least because word on the fan network was that Keith was fairly receptive to such visits though they rarely, if ever, occurred after nightfall.

What bemused Keith more was that the face at the window appeared to be more of a "little old lady" than a teenage fan. Hoping that by ignoring her she would go away, everyone did just that, but after a few minutes she began tapping on the glass. Again she was ignored.

Five minutes later a thunderous banging on the front door left no one in any doubt that this wasn't a fan after an autograph. As a wave of unease cut through the atmosphere, a languidly stoned Fraser dismissed the loud knocking with a curt and haughty retort. "Don't bother," he billowed. "Gentlemen ring up first. Must be tradesmen." Faithfull, too, offered a wonderfully child-like response. "If we don't make any noise," she whispered, "if we're all really quiet, they'll go away." It certainly seems that those inside remained fairly unmoved by what was occurring outside. As the observer at the window would later declare, "There was no panic or anything like that."

Eventually Schneiderman turned to Richards and offered to see who it was. Without replying, Richards took on the mantle of householder and walked over, unlocked the door and found himself confronted by the stout figure of Chief Inspector Gordon Dineley. In his large white overcoat and braided cap, he cut an imposing presence in the darkness. At Dineley's side was Cudmore, the detective who'd first taken the call from the *News Of The World*. Given the five-minute time lapse in responding, the Chief Inspector had considered forcing down the door to gain entry.

While it was pitch black outside, the squad of 18 police would have been an incredulous sight for Richards' dazzled senses. Indeed, in his disoriented state he had some difficulty in figuring out what was happening. He'd later reflect that they appeared to him to be more like a troupe of goblins from Tolkien's *The Hobbit* than anything as mundane as police officers.

As realisation slowly replaced bewilderment, Dineley engaged Richards with the preliminaries to the raid. "Are you the occupier and owner of the premises?" he asked.

Slightly bemused by the officious request, Keith replied with a chuckle: "Well, I live here."

Holding up a sheet of white A4 paper, Dineley explained the reason for his and his colleagues' presence. "I am Police Chief Inspector Dineley of the West Sussex Constabulary, and I have a warrant to search these premises and the persons in them, under the Dangerous Drugs Act of 1965."

Handing Richards the warrant, Dineley then invited him to read its contents. This Keith did, attempting to decode the legal text headed with a decal of the crown. Embedded in the warrant was the unequivocal line declaring that the police were "to enter, if needs be by force, the premises of the said Keith Richards". In addition to the legal requirements were the names of the police personnel primed to cross Redlands' threshold. Following his reading of the 30-line document, Richards acquiescently responded to Dineley, saying: "All right, I have read it."

With that, Dineley and his team moved into the house. Rumoured to have been mentioned that night, but not confirmed in police documents, Richards allegedly said to his house guests: "Look, there's lots of little ladies and gentlemen outside. They're coming in. They have this funny piece of paper, all sorts of legal rubbish." The police constables were dressed in traditional uniform, while detectives wore plain clothes. The "old lady" seen earlier at the window was, in fact, Detective Constable Evelyn Florence Fuller, drawn from Bognor Regis police station for the night. "As I entered the house," she later recalled. "I noticed an unusual smell. It was not the smell of burning wood. It was similar to that of incense." Detective Constable Thomas Davies too, would take note of "a very strong, sweet, smell" inside the house. Leading the team into the Redlands drawing room, Dineley repeated to the occupants what he'd said to Richards earlier, that the property was to be searched for drugs.

Close behind Dineley was Cudmore. He too caught a "rather strong, sweet smell" on entering the premises and, later, in all the other rooms of the property. He recalled in detail the scene, especially the deportment of Jagger and Faithfull. "Jagger and a woman were sitting on a couch some distance away from the fire," Cudmore later noted. "This woman had wrapped round her a light coloured fur skin rug which from time to time she let fall, showing her nude body. Sitting on her left was Jagger, and I was of the opinion that he was wearing makeup."

The police jostling for space with Redlands' nine residents made for a fairly crowded scene. While drawers, cupboards and various receptacles were being searched, a state of confusion fell over those present. "No one was expected that night," recalled Gibbs. "Then all of a sudden, these people in blue came flooding in. It was a rather dream-like experience."

Adding to this strange drama fast unfolding, the record player was still blaring out from the two huge speakers. With conversation above the sound system virtually impossible, Dineley asked Richards to turn it off. "No," replied the defiant musician. "We won't turn it off, but we'll turn it down." The muted television set remained on.

Leaving sufficient personnel to cover the downstairs sweep of the house, DC Fuller and Sergeant John Challen began a search of the upstairs rooms. Fuller's exploration led her first to the room that Jagger was sharing with Faithfull. Aware that the details of her search might be scrutinised in court, Fuller's inventory was extraordinarily detailed. "There were pink ostrich feathers lying on the bed," she'd later report. "On a chair in the bedroom were items of clothing; a pair of black velvet trousers, a white bra, a white lace Edwardian blouse, a black cloth half coat, a black sombrero-type hat and a pair of mauve-coloured ladies boots, one of which was lying on the bed, the other on the floor. I also noticed a large chest of drawers on the top of which were a number of books on witchcraft; one book was called *Games To Play*." Fuller also noted that on the floor was a large holdall which contained "two or three dagger-type weapons".

While Fuller was making an inventory of Mick and Marianne's possessions, Challen searched Richards' bedroom. Finding a "pudding basin containing three cigarette ends" by the bed, he extracted the contents and placed them in a plastic bag. Once finished inspecting Keith's bedroom, he joined Fuller in Marianne and Mick's room. With Fuller noting the fine detail, Challen examined the pockets of the clothes in the room. Inside Jagger's green velvet jacket he found four white tablets in a clear plastic phial in the left-inside pocket, the amphetamine pills from the couple's Italian holiday which had remained in Jagger's jacket ever since.

Returning downstairs, Challen inquired who owned the green jacket. When Mick replied in the affirmative, the detective asked that he accompany him upstairs to discuss his findings. To witness his questioning of Jagger, Challen asked forensics specialist Constable Richard Smith to accompany them back to the bedroom. The following conversation, written shortly after the raid, is taken from Challen's notes.

"Do these tablets belong to you?" Challen asked.

"Yes, my doctor prescribed them," replied Jagger.

"Who is your doctor?" continued Challen.

"I think it is Dr Dixon-Firth," said Jagger. "But I can't remember if it was him." [Although he was being economical with the truth concerning the drug's origins, Dr Raymond Dixon-Firth was indeed Jagger's current GP.]

"Where does he come from?" pressed the sergeant.

"I am not sure of his address," replied Jagger. "It might be Wilton Crescent, Knightsbridge." [Jagger was correct; the full address of Dixon-Firth's practice was 20 Wilton Crescent, London.]

"What are they for?"

"To stay awake and work," Jagger confirmed.

While the drugs found that night had come from Marianne, Mick had reportedly consulted with his doctor concerning the use of amphetamine-based drugs on a previous occasion. Furthermore, Jagger's chivalrous attitude would not have let on they were acquired by Faithfull.

Interrogation over, Challen duly cautioned Jagger and handed the pills over to Smith. Mick then requested permission to make a phone call. On being granted this, he made the call from the bedroom. Although it is likely that he was contacting a member of the Stones' entourage rather than a lawyer, there is no exact record of whom he called that night. Nonetheless, even through the haze of the LSD, Jagger's concern would have been considerable.

After finishing his search of the upstairs quarters, Detective Fuller returned to the drawing room. With her brief to concentrate on the female occupants, she requested that Faithfull accompany her back upstairs to be searched. Given Marianne's modest costume, this was clearly a hilarious suggestion. Nonetheless, Faithfull offered no resistance. According to Fuller, Marianne appeared "to be in a very merry mood, and naked apart from a fur rug wrapped around her". The policewoman also noted that Faithfull made a hugely seductive dance up the staircase, allowing the rug to slip from her body as she traipsed upwards.

Reaching the landing, Faithfull led the policewoman back into the room where Jagger had been questioned. He was still on the telephone and Sergeant Challen was still present when Faithfull entered the room with the female detective behind her. Seeing Mick's face riddled with anxiety, Faithfull later summarised the unwelcome intrusion that had derailed Jagger's first foray into psychedelics. "Poor bugger," she later recalled, "his first trip, a lovely day, and now this." A strange, stilted ambiance hovered over the room as Marianne decided to bring a touch of impromptu theatre to the proceedings. "She let the rug fall, showing herself completely naked," recalled Fuller. "She then said, apparently to Jagger: 'Look, they want to search me!'" Mick gave out a large guffaw and, with Challen looking on somewhat aghast, Fuller took Faithfull into the bathroom across the landing.

A brief and presumably intimate search completed, Fuller accompanied her young charge back into the bedroom to identify her clothing, allowing the detective the opportunity to search them in her presence. This done and with a carefree look of vague unconcern, she then asked Fuller, "Can I go now?" When the detective replied in the affirmative, Faithfull wandered back downstairs in the direction of the lounge, the rug still wrapped around her. At one point during her theatrical descent, Marianne heard one of the police remark, "See her unusual behaviour? She's likely under the influence of cannabis [sic]." Later in notes, policewoman Fuller observed that Marianne "seemed unconcerned about what was going on around her".

Seeing as officers were checking every crevice of the house, it was a formality that the other inhabitants would be searched. Gibbs, dressed somewhat ostentatiously in his Pakistani pyjama suit, was frisked by one of the officers. Despite any suggestion to the contrary, the police presented themselves in a totally professional manner. "They were perfectly polite," recalls Gibbs. With his erudite argot and amenable presence, the antiques dealer reported that his arresting officer "didn't do anything discourteous".

While Gibbs was being searched, Sergeant Donald Rambridge prepared to check over Fraser. During the initial sortie of the house, the gallery owner had taken something of a temporary refuge, placing himself behind the couch in the drawing room. Knowing full well the power of exhibiting his gentlemanly credentials, old Etonian, ex-army Fraser remonstrated with Rambridge's frisking of his person, remarking: "Do you really think it necessary?" Responding to Fraser's clearly aristocratic tone, Rambridge retorted deferentially: "Sir, this is mere formality." Fraser then reluctantly agreed, telling the sergeant: "Of course. If that's what you want to do, you do it."

Fraser had other reasons for layering on his "old boy" persona. Evidently, at some point during the opening salvos of the raid, he had emptied his heroin stash from his ornate engraved box into his right-hand trouser pocket. Rambridge, however, soon came across the two dozen tablets. Clearly intrigued by the quantity, the officer asked Fraser what they were. "I am diabetic and these are prescribed by my doctor," he replied.

Asking if he had a card to verify his condition, Fraser stalled, mentioning that although he didn't have it on his person, it might be in the room he'd slept in overnight. With Rambridge leading Fraser upstairs, a cursory search found no trace of any card. Undeterred, Rambridge decided to check with his superior, Cudmore on how best to proceed.

On returning downstairs with Fraser, Rambridge called Cudmore over to look at the large stash he'd found.

"This man tells me that these tablets are prescribed for him by his doctor because he is a diabetic," Rambridge told Cudmore.

"Is that so?" replied the seasoned detective, clearly not impressed with Fraser's attempt at a bluff. "These look like heroin tablets to me."

"No," Fraser shot back, once again drawing on his impeccable deportment and delivery. "They are definitely not."

"Have you a card?" asked Cudmore, requesting more authenticity than just Fraser's words.

"No," replied Fraser. "I have looked but I can't find it."

Despite his protestations, Fraser was cautioned by Cudmore and told that if the substances turned out to be illegal, he would be charged with possession. Sensing that his reputation might be called into question in denying his arrestee essential medication, Cudmore instructed the junior sergeant to take two of the tablets for analysis and then to "give the remainder back to him". Rambridge handed Fraser the majority of the pills before placing two in a transparent plastic bag for testing. As a formality, he confirmed to Fraser that the pills would be sent for analysis.

Fraser's trauma did not end there. A cursory glance behind the drawing room door by PC Raymond Harris revealed a dark jacket belonging to Fraser that contained eight green capsules of undetermined origin. Again, Fraser attempted to diffuse any illegality, claiming they had been prescribed by his doctor for a stomach complaint. Like Jagger before him, Fraser was asked who his doctor was. "It's one of three," he replied haughtily, "Dr. Greenberg, Dr. Epples or Dr. Gray."

With no address of the trio of doctors other than London determined, two of the green capsules were also retained for analysis, with the remainder given back to Fraser. "You will find them alright," said Fraser, somewhat hopefully.

Following the individual searches, the drawing room was thoroughly examined for any evidence that suggested drug use. Aware that they would be taking numerous items with them that night, police had brought in an "exhibits officer" to detail and catalogue the items seized, a task undertaken by PC Richard Smith. During the evening he'd commandeered a table in Redlands' living room, and as items from officers were passed to him, he placed them in plastic bags to which he attached handwritten stickers.

At 8:40 p.m., Sergeant Rambridge searched Richards' dining room. In a Welsh dresser, he found a box containing joss sticks. Elsewhere detectives removed a pipe bowl "without a stem" that was on the table to the left of the living room fireplace. Just in case any residue contained cannabis resin, several scrapings were made from the stone table's top.

In addition to the searches of the living and dining rooms, Richards' kitchen was also checked for substances. Scattered around was a large collection of condiments such as mustard, mayonnaise, hotel soap and shampoo in plastic sachets, each collected by Keith from hotels on his interminable travels around the world. Hard as it might be to conceive in the 21st century, such packaging was totally unfamiliar in the UK where in the sixties everything came out of a glass bottle.

While not noted in witness or evidential statements, the detectives assumed that the packets might contain illicit substances, and tore some of them open, leaving a gooey, multicoloured mess around the kitchen. The detectives were certainly diligent, checking every other part of the house, opening cupboards, emptying drawers, searching anywhere for any trace of drugs or associated paraphernalia. It's probable that the confectionery scattered around was given a cursory inspection, although police records bear no witness to this. Other items allegedly requiring further inspection were tubes of suntan lotion and Richards' consignment of Earl Grey tea. While all this has become the stuff of legend since the raid, it must be stressed that there was no reference to them in police notes taken at the time.

With their attentions focusing on the drawing room, officers allegedly found it unavoidable not to trample over Richards' collection of ornate Moroccan cushions and throws and he later recalled verbally admonishing the officers for the lack of respect they paid towards his furniture; with so many officers in the room, there was evidently little he could do to curtail their movements.

Last to be searched was the mysterious figure of 'Acid King' David Schneiderman. As the raid took place, his feral instincts took him to the far end of the living room. His suntan somewhat at odds with the winter pallor of the other guests, he was meticulously searched by Detective Constable Thomas Davies. With his attaché case certain to be loaded to the gunwales with various illegal drugs, things didn't look good for the Canadian. Davies' search on Schneiderman was thorough and productive. In his right-hand breast pocket, two pieces of a brown substance weighing 66 grains were discovered. In another jacket pocket, an envelope was discovered that contained a powdery substance with one of his pseudonyms, 'Donald Britton', written on it. Elsewhere, the detective found a cigarette tin that contained three pieces of a brown substance; a decorated wooden pipe and stem with traces of a substance; a fairly large ball of a brown substance; a blue and white phial containing white pills; an orange coloured pill; and numerous other items.

At some point, Davies searched Schneiderman's attaché case which, according to Davies' notes, had been placed in the dining room of the house away from the other guests. All he recorded finding inside was a packet containing 'Perfumed Incense'. Schneiderman's celebrated caché of drugs remained undetected. Not recorded in police notes, but recalled by some of those present, was the fact that when Davies went to open the leather case, Schneiderman pleaded: "Please don't open that case. It's full of exposed film." At this, it's claimed that the DC hesitated at searching the contents and politely closed it up.

While this story has been retold by many of the guests there that night, it doesn't appear believable given the circumstances and thoroughness of the raid. John Rodway was a colleague of Davies in 1967, and he recalls the officer's thorough, if somewhat blunt approach to his work. "Knowing Tom Davies as I did," says Rodway, "he would have undone it and shook it out on the floor and then said, 'Sorry'. Tom was never the sort of detective who would do what he was told. He was very black and white and if someone said, 'Don't open it, it's got unexposed film in it', the first thing he would do was open it."

Whatever the claims from those inside Redlands, Schneiderman's rumoured gargantuan quantity of LSD, cocaine, DMT and other substances went undetected that night. Equally, his caché of passports was not discovered or noted in police statements.

Adding further intrigue, Davies' notes reveal Schneiderman's eagerness to acquiesce under questioning, to the point where he studiously noted the time of his own movements and pertinently that of the other guests throughout the day and evening. While the Acid King's surname was in some doubt, the DC would record his name phonetically as 'Sniderman'. Nonetheless, the pharmacopoeia of material found on the Canadian's person would ensure that he was cautioned, and the substances (numbering 16 items) were taken away for analysis. While the brown material suggested hashish of various strains, it was the raft of powders and the 'orange pill' that would require intensive scrutiny. With the likelihood that these were hard drugs, Schneiderman had every reason to worry.

Remarkably, Michael Cooper had managed to avoid a formal search. He'd leapt to his feet the moment the police entered Redlands, and snuck up one of the stairwells. Just before events wrapped up, one of the officers engaged in a search of the upstairs quarters came across the photographer wandering down a hallway. Cooper told him he had just arrived at the gathering, the officer reportedly believed Cooper's story and he escaped being searched.

At 9:05 p.m., around an hour after their arrival, the police began to wind up their work. In closing, Detective Cudmore in the presence of his superior Chief Inspector Dineley, read Richards the formalities, saying: "Should the results of our laboratory tests show that dangerous drugs have been used on this premises and are not related to any individual, you will be held responsible."

"I see. They pin it all on me,' replied Keith, clearly aware that although no cannabis had been found on him personally, he would still be responsible for allowing it to be smoked in his home. Although the evidence was circumstantial, the penalties could vary from between three to six months in prison or a fine if presented in a magistrates court but if the offender opted to be tried at a higher level, the sentence and fine could be considerably higher if a guilty verdict was passed.

The raid concluded, the police retreated from Redlands at 9:15 p.m. Also making its way out of the house was a collection of clear plastic bags. Back at Chichester police headquarters, the contents would be itemised in two pages of notes. Schneiderman's caché of substances required its own inventory, but the 29 other items retrieved from the house ranged from 'debris' and 'a candlestick' to 'deposit from hearth rug', 'soap' and 'butt ends (marked B&H)'. These and other substances less definable were sent away for detailed analysis at the Forensic Science Laboratory at New Scotland Yard.

As the door finally closed on the exiting police, someone went over to the record player and turned the volume back up on Bob Dylan's *Blonde On Blonde* album. Fittingly the strains of 'Rainy Day Woman #12 & 35' was adjudged a suitably appropriate finale to the strange pantomime that had just taken place. With the police walking down Redlands' drive laden down with evidence, everyone inside the house burst into a huge, unrestrained bout of laughter, the sound of Dylan's rowdy tune echoing in the air.

"Well they'll stone you and say that it's the end
Then they'll stone you and then they'll come back again
They'll stone you when you're riding in your car
They'll stone you when you're playing your guitar
Yes, but I would not feel so all alone
Everybody must get stoned!"

With everyone engaged in a hysterical chant, the phone rang. Keith picked up the receiver. On the other end was Brian, calling from his Kensington flat. His fight with Anita having now expired through fatigue and having completed his scheduled session for the *A Degree Of Murder* soundtrack, the pair had decided that it might be fun to travel over to West Wittering to join in the fun. Keith, at that point in a whirl over what had just transpired, could only mutter, "Don't bother man. We've just been busted."

Elsewhere, news of the raid was travelling fast. The severe content of Jagger's phone call was swiftly relayed across the Stones' management network. At 3 a.m. on the Monday morning the group's lawyer, Timothy Hardacre, was awoken by Tony Calder, saying: "There's trouble, you're needed." With a need to assess what had exactly happened, a meeting was arranged with Jagger and Richards back in London the next day.

Inside Redlands' living room, the group reviewed the evening's rather mixed events. There were a few laughs when recalling the embarrassed looks as Marianne waltzed theatrically down the stairs. Since Schneiderman's major stash had escaped examination, and with no one actually arrested, there was an optimistic feeling that maybe everything else would be ignored.

In fact, only Fraser was unduly concerned about what had been taken away. Knowing that his tablets were not the diabetic pills he'd told police, he urgently needed to confer with his dealer, Tony Sanchez. With the Spaniard's labyrinthine tentacles penetrating every atom of London's underworld, Sanchez was the only viable resort in such a desperate time. Schooled to a junkie's sense of survival, Fraser knew that with the right contacts, a backdated prescription from a dubious practitioner might succeed in short circuiting a possible charge. In 1967, heroin was available legally to registered users and if prescribed by an accommodating doctor, legitimate paperwork could absolve prosecution. If that was not available, there were other, even more questionable routes to follow. Fraser instructed Mohammed to prepare for the 70-mile drive back to London, a sense of great urgency accompanying the van's trip through West Sussex's country lanes.

Also signifying his intention to leave was Schneiderman. With police confiscating his not insignificant haul for forensic inspection, he was understandably keen to get away. While only Fraser rivalled Schneiderman in terms of the amount of drugs found on his person, a possible arrest could trigger all manner of issues, not least his pending extradition back to North America. Shortly after Fraser's exit, Schneiderman headed off in his Mini – his destination as mysterious as his arrival. From recently discovered documents, it appears that Schneiderman waited 48 hours before absconding through France to Spain, his revolving aliases aiding the speed of his exit. In any case, most of the substances in his possession on the night of the raid would have required a lengthy process of analysis. As a result of this, he would have had ample time to abscond before British border controls were alerted. The Canadian's disappearance into the ether would become the subject of fevered debate in the coming weeks; the ultra paranoid individuals he left behind wondering just who he really was and what role had he played in the raid?

Back at West Wittering, a mixture of incredulity and fatigue swamped Redlands' occupants. No one bothered to retire to bed that night, preferring the warm collective safety of each other's company in the living room. With the final residue of Schneiderman's 'California Sunshine' fading from their systems, everyone dozed off where they sat.

CHAPTER 6

Marrakech

"You sit at home and you think you are safe because you are not in South Africa or some other police state. But when suddenly the police move in it's very disturbing and you begin to wonder just how much freedom you really have."

Mick Jagger, March 1967

The sun rose at 7:19 a.m. the morning of Monday, February 13, the slightly bruised occupants of Redlands Cottage opting to make an early escape. Uncertainty hung heavily in the air, and it was generally agreed that everyone would feel safer in the anonymity of London. With curtains drawn and no trace of any vehicles, the property took on a look of desertion. Only the familiar figure of Jack Dyer remained, tending as always to the needs of the expansive garden.

In tandem with the exodus from West Wittering, eyes were trained on the day's papers for any reports of the raid. With Vietnam dominating the headlines, there was no mention of the previous night's activities in any of the morning papers, or even in the provincial evening newspaper covering West Sussex, the *Evening Argus*. However, just in case the press decided to run with the story, Keith wrote to his parents informing them of what had occurred. Letter writing had become Richards' favoured mode of communication since he discovered his phone was being monitored. The Redlands' raid having processed his paranoia into a reality, it was going to be a while before he felt confident to make a call again.

As the day progressed, no communiqué from the police arrived. Nonetheless, Mick's urgent phone call had necessitated a conference with Andrew Oldham and Tony Calder to discuss events, and how best to challenge any possible action. The meeting took place late in the afternoon at Oldham's office in central London, and though details of the discussion have never been revealed, it's clear that the Stones' manager was seriously spooked by what had happened.

Robert Fraser had even more cause for concern. Where the majority of the substances found could be classed as soft drugs, his heroin possession elevated issues considerably. Once back in London, Fraser contacted his dealer Tony Sanchez, urging him to come over to his Mayfair flat where he filled him in with the details of what had occurred. Desperate to extricate everyone from the mess, Fraser quizzed Sanchez on any possible routes to best defer prosecution.

Sanchez assured Fraser, and later reportedly Jagger and Richards, that various corrupt police insiders could be tapped to substitute the seized evidence with less noxious substances. According to Sanchez, the price for that sort of interference would be somewhere in the region of £7,000, equivalent to around £100,000 in today's money.

According to Sanchez, Jagger and Richards reportedly stumped up £5,000 in cash, leaving Fraser to pull together the remainder. The deal was struck in a Kilburn pub the following Tuesday, a plastic bag containing the money allegedly handed over to his contact who would hopefully scupper the forensic examination. All remained quiet and by the following Saturday there was still no mention of the bust in the press or any formal notification from police. This brought a quiet expectation, if not more than a nervous hope, that Sanchez's bribe may well have been successful. As coordinator of the affair, Fraser fled to Amsterdam on an elongated drugs binge. Not expected back in London until the following weekend, he too was hoping that Sanchez's bung would hit its target. For Mick and Keith, events at Redlands were momentarily put

on hold as they reconvened at Olympic Studios to continue wo
Stones as yet untitled next album.

The weekend of February 18 and 19 was desperately cold for Britain, with temperatures dropping to their customary low winter level. Any hopes that the police's threatened prosecution may have been shelved were dashed with the arrival of the Sunday papers. While the *News Of The World* had momentarily suspended their 'Pop Stars And Drugs' series of features the weekend of the Redlands bust, they were back with a renewed vengeance. Spilled over its front page, the paper was brandishing the story of the raid, detailing in lurid context the events that occurred. With a banner headline, 'Drugs Squad Raid Pop Stars Party', it was clear that the report could only have come from someone close to events. Although the story teasingly referred to "three nationally known names" being present at the gathering, the paper stopped short of naming them.

Dramatically, the *News Of The World* reported that LSD had been found on one person at the gathering – an assertion that was not subsequently proved in court. The paper also claimed that police had received information that a "foreign national" (i.e. David Schneiderman) was currently at large, and that a close watch was being maintained at airports and docks in case he attempted to leave the country. Most telling was the revelation that just minutes before the raid took place, a "pop star and his wife" unwittingly escaped the net by driving away before the police swooped. This nugget of information revealed that despite claims to the contrary, George Harrison and his wife's presence that night had been noted by persons unknown.

Harrison would record his own feelings on what transpired for a Granada Television documentary in 1987: "The funny thing about it was that they said in the newspapers later, 'another international pop star and his wife escaped moments before the net closed in.' I left there and it was about 7 p.m. So all it did was show me that they were waiting there until I left because they were climbing the ladder and they didn't want to get to the Fabs yet."

Despite the careful anonymity employed by the *News Of The World*, others were in the loop as regards to the finer details of the

Redlands' affair. *The Sunday Telegraph*, not previously known for observing the machinations of the pop world, dug considerably deeper with its report. Published the same day as the *NOTW*'s exposé, the *Sunday Telegraph*'s crime reporter Peter Gladstone Smith went as far as to reveal Mick, Keith and Marianne Faithfull's presence at Redlands that night. Much of Gladstone Smith's detail was correct, in particular his mentioning the visit to the coast the troupe made the morning of the raid where, according to him, "They had formed exuberant beach parties and had taken snapshots of each other near the mouth of Chichester Harbour." With this information in circulation, it suggested that surveillance on the partygoers – from whatever provenance – had extended well before the raid.

On the evening that these reports appeared, Faithfull found herself fulfilling a long-standing engagement as a guest on *The Eamonn Andrews Show*, somewhat ironically the same programme that Jagger had announced his intention to sue the *News Of The World*. With details of the Redlands' story in the public domain, Andrews steered clear of engaging Faithfull in any talk about narcotics. Nonetheless, a discussion regarding drugs did take place with fellow guest Lord Boothby but the renegade peer's dialogue was deemed so provocative that it was edited out prior to broadcast. With Marianne's name in circulation regarding the raid, newspaper photographers were waiting outside the studios to record her exit.

Taking a lead from the *News Of The World* and *Sunday Telegraph*, news of the raid was spread across most of the daily papers the next day. With such enormous media interest, West Sussex police appeared tentative in responding to questions. Nonetheless, a spokesman revealed that, "It may be several more days before we know the results of the tests on the samples." Scavenging for any titbits, reporters roamed West Wittering's country lanes, collaring Richards' gardener Jack Dyer and the property's housekeeper for statements. Both noted that they found nothing untoward the morning following the raid, other than that the guest bedrooms had not been slept in.

Quizzed for a comment from the protagonists of the affair, the Stones' management offered a cautious response, saying only that lawyers had advised Jagger and Richards not to talk. With still no formal charges having been brought, on the afternoon of Monday, February 20, the two Stones met with Allen Klein and their legal team at the Hilton Hotel in London's Park Lane. Also present was QC Victor Durand. A lively advocate of the underdog, Durand was a celebrity of the English Bar; his most famous coup having been to successfully defend the notorious Kray Brothers against protection racket charges in 1965.

"I instructed Victor Durand QC, the leading criminal silk in the business to meet with everyone," recalls Stones' solicitor Timothy Hardacre. "We had a conference with Mick, Keith and Durand to discuss the whole thing. Victor Durand said at the meeting, that a raid like that with the sort of personnel involved would take a long time to set up."

It was obvious that Jagger's suit against the *News Of The World* would have to be momentarily shelved. To pursue a libel case with a drug charge pending would – despite Mick's proven innocence – be unsustainable. Of course, this was just what the paper had hoped for.

The meeting also served to elevate Klein's profile. The absence of Oldham, on business elsewhere, was duly noted. By default, Klein would now have a greater leverage in his dealings with Jagger and Richards. His street-level instinct made him aware of the consequences if the case came to court, the worst-case scenario being prison sentences, which could easily see the Stones' dollar-earning empire dissolved in an instant. Nonetheless, with only a few reefer butts, scrapings from a stone table and Jagger's four amphetamine tablets taken as hard evidence, it was decided to deny any potential charges rather than admit them at the first hurdle. With the Rolling Stones' overseas touring commitments requiring transparent visas, there was no other way to proceed.

Fraser's return from Amsterdam prompted those involved to debate furiously on how the bust had come to pass. Given that details of the party were known only to a small coterie, there was plenty of head scratching regarding how police tuned into the gathering in the first place. Durand's comments that the police action would have had a considerable gestation period provoked a fair amount of suspicion. With Jagger, Richards, Fraser and Schneiderman all cautioned, the spotlight of possible guilt momentarily swung elsewhere. While any suggestions that Gibbs, Cooper, George and Pattie Harrison or even Fraser's manservant were informers were considered ludicrous, it left just the one unknown entity, Nicky Kramer, who had floated into the gathering almost unannounced.

Kramer's willowy presence and impervious demeanour on the night of the party prompted deep suspicions, and with no obvious target to label as a snitch, heightened paranoia suggested that Kramer may well have been working for the other side. When fingers started to point, other characters in Mick and Keith's circle were hatching a more brutal approach to establishing who the guilty party was. One figure not beyond utilising physical means was David Litvinoff. Known as 'Litz' to those on speaking terms with him, the Jewish émigré was a close confident to MP Tom Driberg, Lord Robert Boothby and other loose cannons among the aristocracy. Fashionably gay and passionate about London's mercurial art scene, Litvinoff proved scintillating company for the Chelsea set. Adding to his popular enigma, Litvinoff straddled London's underworld network, bringing a razor's edge to the dinner party. A later 'advisor' on the film *Performance*, Litvinoff's dodgy persona was further embellished by a deep wound across his face, allegedly the result of an altercation with Ronnie Kray.

With talk in the air concerning Kramer being the alleged informant, Litvinoff decided to sort out the issue in true gangster fashion. Collaring the hapless Kramer at his Chelsea flat, Litvinoff employed some of the Krays' trademark methods of extracting truths, beating Kramer up and, when nothing was forthcoming, hanging him out of the window by his ankles. While this may have appeared overtly dramatic, Litvinoff was merely repeating his own experience of being dangled out of a fifth floor flat on Kensington High Street by an associate of the Krays. A witness to this shocking display was Christopher Gibbs. "I can remember this horrible performance of David Litvinoff roughing up Nicky Kramer and trying to get him to confess to being the informant," he says. "It was very unpleasant, awful and bullying. I'm sure [Nicky] had nothing whatsoever to do with spilling any beans."

Despite the brutal extraction methods, Kramer maintained his innocence and suspicions were lifted. From that point onwards, it was of little surprise that the fey figure of Nicky Kramer would swiftly disappear, rarely to be seen again.

Thoughts next turned to Schneiderman. Having been cautioned with Keith and Mick, he'd initially been absolved from any collusion but the ease in which he had left the country was now starting to come under close scrutiny. With controversial snippets of Schneiderman's dialogue being revisited, talk of his alleged library of aliases and passports caused sensitive alarm bells to ring. Of equal concern was the slick way he'd been able to ingratiate his way into the group around the same time of the *News Of The World* investigations, and the fact that the police ignored his attaché case of substances. While no one had previously cared about his smooth patter and seemingly rootless existence, his slick assimilation into their inner circle was now under heavy suspicion.

While reports are sketchy, the so-called 'Acid King' evidently ditched the 'Schneiderman' moniker once out of the UK. Given that it was the name he was arrested under at Redlands, it made total sense. Under another alias, David Jove, he remained largely undetected, hopping over to Spain and Ibiza, and then on to Israel, along the way falling effortlessly in with whatever party scene happened to be occurring. He'd eventually make his way back to New York City, where he was briefly detained by police on offences predating his movements in England. Once again, his convincing patter extricated him from any sustained incarceration. While reportedly still engaged in his acid evangelising, he'd keep his involvement with the Stones and the Redlands' affair well under wraps.

With the press awaiting further news concerning the raid, Mick and Marianne made altogether different headlines by arriving eight minutes late for a performance of *Madame Butterfly* at London's Royal Opera House on Thursday, February 23. With royal guest of honour Princess Margaret having already taken her seat in the auditorium, by 1967 standards the couple's late arrival was seen as something of an affront, and news of the supposed insult garnered several front-page columns. However, none of the press articles saw fit to reference any of the accusations pending involving Jagger.

Nonetheless, with the saga very much active, Chichester police made a more expansive press statement regarding the raid: "On the evening of February 12, 1967, police officers entered a house in the Chichester district with a search warrant issued under the Dangerous Drugs Act. A number of names were taken and certain articles and substances were brought away. These were later taken to the Metropolitan Police laboratory for examination, and as a result of that examination, a report has been received by the Chief Constable who will, in the light of the report, seek legal advice on the subject before any further action is taken." Given West Sussex Chief Constable Mr Thomas Williams' prior comment regarding his "deep concern on drugs", the possibility of any clemency appeared slim.

This dismal landscape invading their every step, a decision was made by the Redlands coterie to escape Britain for a complete change of scenery. Speaking with Victor Bockris in 1992, Richards' revealed the sense of urgency: "Although the bust happened in February we weren't charged then… We weren't even arrested. For a while it was hoped that the lawyers could get the whole thing dropped. In the meantime everybody thought the best idea was to get the fuck out of England so nothing else could happen. We decided to go to Morocco."

Just the thought of Morocco's amorphous landscape was enough to salve bruised and paranoid sensitivities. Sensing more practical reasons to get away, Allen Klein agreed to the idea as well. On Saturday, February 25, a more relieved than happy caravan containing Keith, Brian and Anita flew out to Paris, bedding down at the George Cinque hotel. Joining them was model and (then) consort of filmmaker Donald Cammell, Deborah Dixon. With Jagger, Gibbs, Cooper and Fraser flying direct to Tangier, Richards' idea was for his troupe to drive through France and Spain in an attempt to slowly wind down. Keith's Blue Bentley – named the 'Blue Lena' after actress Lena Horne – would undertake the 1,200-odd miles trip, with roadie cum chauffeur Tom Keylock at the wheel. As per requirements, the car's rear seats would assume the appearance of a mobile Bedouin tent, with cushions, furs and other homely accoutrements. Travelling through the ever-changing scenery, the woes of the last few weeks were momentarily lifted on the drove through France. Along the way spirits were raised with the news that 'Ruby Tuesday', the Stones' latest single, had topped the charts in America.

Any renewed sense of bonhomie was soon lost by the mercurial moods that hovered over Brian. With the Bentley's confined space exacerbating his argumentative side, Jones got the needle over Anita's desire to move fully into films, a medium in which she felt very much at home. Jones had witnessed Pallenberg's spellbinding presence on screen while composing soundtrack music for *A Degree of Murder,* but his chauvinism was such that he was deeply resentful of her assuming any degree of success. Adding to this disquiet, Jones had been picking up covert smiles and knowing glances between Anita and Keith. With these very complex energies vibrating around the car, anxiety levels increased mile by mile.

Charged on a variety of substances and other more personal traumas, Jones' asthma returned with a vengeance as the caravan approached Toulouse. Rushed to The Centre Hospitalier d'Albi in the nearby town of Tarn, doctors suspected Brian had pneumonia and recommended immediate hospitalisation. This emergency was enough to derail the trip momentarily but after four days of hanging around, a decision was made to leave Brian in the care of the hospital, with the proviso that he would catch up later. Blood having been discovered in Jones' lungs, there was little he could do but accept the situation.

As the Bentley made its way down towards the Spanish border, the space vacated by Jones' incapacity afforded a new kinship between Keith and Anita. Richards' trauma over the Redlands and Pallenberg's troublesome relationship with Brian acted as an emollient, bringing the two together amid the fur rugs and soft cushions. The back seat shenanigans were evidently too much for the car's other passenger, Deborah Dixon, who jumped ship at the first opportunity and returned to her lover, Donald Cammell, in Paris. Approaching Valencia on Spain's west coast, Keith and Anita, along with driver Tom Keylock, checked into a hotel to break up the journey and share a romantic dinner but complications set in when the restaurant refused to accept Keith's credit card. Without any ready pesetas, they were hauled off to the local police station, quizzed throughout the night and eventually released after being allowed to make a call to Keylock who brought their passports to the police station.

Back at the hotel, they were handed a telegram from Brian. He'd revived sufficiently to communicate with the outside world, and called the Stones' office in London, only to learn that Keith and Anita had docked into Valencia for the night. Ready to be discharged from hospital, Brian, in typically demanding tones, ordered them back to Toulouse to pick him up. Not wanting to sully the good vibes they'd struck, Brian's message was ignored and the pair headed south towards Marbella. Somewhere along the way they consummated their newfound relationship.

Released from hospital and with no transport available, Brian decided to fly back to London to consult his doctor about his asthma. The Stones' office had told him of Keith and Anita's whereabouts so Brian cabled Anita, asking her to accompany him on his flight to London. She flew back to Toulouse to ferry Jones over to London for treatment, leaving Keith and Keylock to undertake the final leg of the trip to Morocco by themselves. After a brief stopover in Gibraltar, Keith finally convened with the rest of the party who'd flown over to Tangier on March 5, and once his hospital appointment was out of the way, Brian and Anita flew to Tangier to join them all. Accompanying them was Marianne, who'd been rehearsing in London's West End for her role in Chekhov's *Three Sisters*, and was also eager to get away. Tripping on LSD during the flight, they too made a stopover in Gibraltar, an otherwise pleasant visit sullied by Jones' bizarre attempt to engage the tribe of monkeys that inhabited Gibraltar's Rock in the soundtrack music he'd recorded for *A Degree Of Murder.* However, the Barbary Macaques were not impressed with Jones' blues infused psychedelia, and several went into an uncontrollable fit.

Relaxing in the splendour of Tangier's Hotel El Minzah, the fugitives could finally relax. Built in 1930 on the orders of English aristocrat The Marquis of Bute, the hotel had a colonial look that embraced regal splendour with the rich atmosphere of the district. While the signs were good for a peaceful retreat, Brian's frighteningly acute senses swiftly detected the strong chemistry that was developing between Keith and Anita. To kill the anxiety, he indulged in as many substances he could get his hands on. Christopher Gibbs, who had done most to inform the group of the region's magic, quickly detected what was taking place, and found accommodation elsewhere.

The Stones' presence at the El Minzah attracted others, among them 51-year-old performance artist Brion Gysin. A left-field dilettante spanning poetry, art and sound, Gysin had previously shepherded the likes of Timothy Leary and William Burroughs around town. He took a room in the hotel, and subsequently committed to paper his thoughts on the group's stay:

"The action starts almost at once. Brian and I drop acid. Anita sulks and drops sleepers. (She) goes off to sleep in the suite she shares with Brian. Keith has plugged in and is sending some great throbbing sounds winging after her and on out into the moonlight over the desert.... Robert (Fraser) puts on a great old Elmore James record out of his collection. Gets Mick doing little magic dances for him. For the first time, I see Mick really is magic. So, as the acid comes up on me, Brian recedes into Big Picture (sic). Looks like a tiny celluloid Kewpie doll, banked all around by a choir of identical little girl dolls looking just like him, chanting his hymns... Room service arrives with great trays of food in which we toboggan around on the floor. I am sorry to say. Food? Who needs it? How very gross."

After a few days of splendour at the El Minzah, the party moved deeper into Morocco, travelling the 300 miles to Marrakech. Whereas Tangier was receptive to tourists, Marrakech appeared to have escaped any move towards modernity. "We enjoyed being transported," recalled Keith on the madcap pantomime that revealed itself in Marrakech. "You could be *Sinbad The Sailor, One Thousand And One Nights.* We loved it."

With finance no obstacle, the party booked into Marrakech's sumptuous Hotel Es Saadi whose palatial suites, exotic pool and collection of independent villas proved the ideal environment from which to venture out and experience the town's rich magic. Fearful of sharing space with other holiday-makers, the group took over the entire eighth floor of the hotel for their stay.

Among the other guests was high society photographer and artist Cecil Beaton, for whom Jagger had sat for a portrait the previous year.

During the Stones' meteoric rise, Beaton had been waxing lyrical about Jagger, and the portrait, entitled *The Singer*, was briefly exhibited in London. Beaton, clearly at home in the exotic bonhomie of the hotel, kept an exhaustively detailed diary of his adventures, and his report on events during the evening of March 7, 1967 is a wonderfully rich portrait of the state of The Rolling Stones at that time.

"On the Tuesday evening, I came down to dinner very late, and to my surprise, sitting in the hotel lobby, discovered Mick Jagger and a sleepy band of gypsies. Robert Fraser, one of their company, wearing a huge, black felt hat, was crouching by the swimming pool. It was a strange group. The three Stones: Brian Jones and his girlfriend Anita Pallenberg – dirty white face, dirty blackened eyes, dirty canary drops of hair, barbaric jewellery. Keith Richard (sic) in eighteenth century suit, long black velvet coat and the tightest pants; and, of course, Mick Jagger.... (Mick) is very gentle and with perfect manners. He has much appreciation and his small albino-fringed eyes notice everything. He has an analytical slant and compares everything he is seeing here with earlier impressions in other countries. I didn't want to give the impression that I was only into Mick, but it happened that we sat next to one another as he drank a Vodka Collins and smoked with his pointed finger held high. His skin is chicken-breast white and of a fine quality. He has an inborn elegance."

Later that night the party, with Beaton in tow, trooped off from the hotel for a late night meal in Marrakech. He shared the ride with Mick, Brian and Anita in Keith's Bentley.

"We got into two cars. The car was filled with pop art cushions, scarlet fur rugs and sex magazines. Immediately the most tremendous volume of pop music boomed in the region of the back of my neck. Mick and Brian responded rhythmically and the girl lent forward and screamed in whispers that she had just played a murderess in a film that was to be shown at the Cannes Film Festival."

Arriving at the restaurant, Beaton spoke with Jagger, noting his reserved qualities and erudite manner that contrasted with his popular image. Exiled from the stifling rigidity of Britain, the singer and the artist compared notes on a variety of subjects; Jagger mentioning his own contretemps with the law at Redlands, and that he believed Britain was turning into a "police state". Not surprisingly the subject soon veered towards drugs.

"He (Jagger) asked: 'Have you ever taken LSD? Oh I should. It would mean so much to you; you'd never forget the colours. For a painter it is a great experience. One's brain works not on four cylinders but on four thousand. You see everything aglow. You see yourself beautiful and ugly, and other people as if for the first time. Oh yes you should take it in the country, surrounded by those flowers. You'd have no bad effects. It's only people who hate themselves who suffer.'"

Beaton asked Jagger how the authorities were coping with LSD.

"'Oh no,' (replied Mick) 'They can't stamp it out. It's like the atom bomb. Once it's been discovered it can never be forgotten. It's like the atom bomb, and it's too easy to make.'"

The meal ran late into the night, the party finally returning to their hotel at around 3 a.m. The following morning, Beaton was present to capture Jagger's re-emergence.

"At eleven o'clock, he (Jagger) appeared at the swimming pool. I could not believe it was the same person walking towards us. The very strong sun, reflected from the white ground, made his face look a white, podgy, shapeless mess; eyes very small, nose very pink, hair sandy dark. His figure, his hands and arms were incredibly feminine…

"Brian, at the pool, appears in white pants with a huge black square applied at the back. It was very smart in spite of the fact that the seams are giving way. But with such marvellously flat, tight, compact figures as they have, with no buttocks or stomach, almost anything looks good on them."

Sensing a break in the continuity, Beaton seized an opportunity to take a photograph of Jagger in swimming trunks. With nothing else to hold his attention, Mick consented to a few photographs being taken in front of the foliage that surrounded the hotel. The resulting images capture a dangerously waif-like Jagger, hands on hips, leering at Beaton evidently shooting from ground level. With Mick's modest costume leaving little to the imagination, Beaton later noted his effortless presence when a lens was trained on him.

"*The lips were of a fantastic roundness, the body almost hairless and yet, surprisingly, I made him look like a Tarzen by Piero di Cosimo* (15th century renaissance painter). *He is sexy, yet completely sexless. He could nearly be a eunuch. As a model he is a natural.*"

After photographing Jagger by the pool, Beaton persuaded him to move indoors where he encouraged him to remove his trunks so he could take a photo of his rear *au natural.* This apparently occurred, and while too sensitive to be revealed in its original form, Beaton would later commit a study of this to canvas. Mick then showed the fashion conscious Beaton the group's extensive wardrobe.

"Mick showed me the rows of brocade coats. Everything is shoddy, poorly made, the seams burst. Keith himself had sewn his trousers, lavender and dull rose, with a band of badly stitched leather dividing the two colours."

For the shoot with Beaton, Jagger selected a dark polka-dot shirt with long collar to best offset his facial characteristics. The striking monochromatic shot showed a haunted and sullen Mick, peering out through some of the hotel's indoor foliage. To add further intrigue, Beaton got Jagger to hold his hands reverentially to his face as if in prayer. With only a drip of light illuminating Mick's profile, Beaton successfully captured the singer's slightly unworldly presence.

When not being courted by Beaton, the Stones entourage began to enjoy Marrakech's vibrant, rich and aromatic atmosphere – a million miles away from moribund Britain – visiting its street markets and buying all manner of jewellery and clothing. Among the rogues gallery of characters, they'd strike up a friendship with a lively carpet seller named Achmed with a smile as permanent as the sun whose sideline was selling potent home-grown marijuana, for which he relieved the party of a large wad of cash.

Despite the evident relief at being detached from events elsewhere, the vibrations spinning between Keith and Anita were undermining Brian's ego. Noticing this, Fraser suggested that Jones remove himself from the main hotel to one of the villas in the grounds of Hotel Es Saadi. Gysin, who'd followed the party down to Marrakech and who was in tune with Jones' chemical odyssey, was dispatched to keep him company.

On one particular day, a decision was made to troop out for an acid-drenched ramble in the desert. Before they left they stopped off to collect Jones from his villa but found him dishevelled to the point he couldn't even get out of bed. Not wanting to spoil the day, they headed off into the desert without him, the Atlas Mountains acting as a powerful backdrop to their hallucinations.

The trip into the desert was cut short when a thunderstorm took them all by surprise. Heading back to the safety of their hotel, Anita decided to pay a courtesy call on Brian at his villa and on arriving found him in bed with two tattooed Berber prostitutes. Brian wanted her to indulge in a threesome with the whores while he watched but she felt cheapened by the suggestion, turned her back and walked away. This act struck a sharp nerve in Jones and he turned on her, assaulting her viciously. She escaped, running to Keith's room. Seeing her bruised face and body, Richards was outraged.

"By then I'd given up on Brian," he recalled years later. "I was disgusted with the way he treated Anita Pallenberg and the way he behaved. I knew there wasn't any possibility of any long-term friendship lasting between Brian, me and Mick. But then Anita had had enough. Besides we were really into each other."

Jones' behaviour prompted talk of leaving as quickly as possible. Capturing the moment when the alchemy turned sour was Brion Gysin. In his idiosyncratic argot, he detailed the change in the osmosis:

"Around the hotel swimming pool, I saw something that I can only call mythological. Mick is screaming about his hotel bill, getting ready for takeoff. The cynics among us are snickering because it looks like love at first sight. At the deep end, Anita is swinging in a canvas seat. Keith is in the pool, dunking up and down in the deep water, looming up at her. When I go to pass between them, I see that I can't. I can't make it. There's something there, a barrier. I can see it... I don't like the looks of this one bit, so I check out of the hotel immediately and move in with a friend who has a house in the medina, the old Arab quarter."

There were other reasons why a swift evacuation was necessary. Tom Keylock had discovered that several newspaper reporters had got wind of the Moroccan caper, and had arrived in Marrakech. While most of the group were careful not to flaunt their personal habits, Keylock knew that Brian's lack of tact might be easy meat for the press. Knowing that Gysin had a topographic knowledge of the area, he asked the artist to sideline Jones for as long as possible. "We do have one weak link," Keylock told Gysin. "You know who it is, Brian. Brian talks his bloody head off to reporters. Tells 'em everything."

At Keylock's suggestion, Gysin took Jones on a protracted meander around Marrakech. Meanwhile, unbeknown to them, the rest of the party made their escape. Innocent to what was occurring, Gysin escorted Jones around the bazaars, eavesdropping on the host of colourful characters that congregated around such landmarks as Djemaa al-Fna in Marrakech's Central Plaza. Otherwise known as the 'Square Of The Dead', Brian revelled in the mad carnival playing itself out in front of him. With pungent marijuana smoked openly, he indulged happily, enchanted by the pipe players.

At some point during the afternoon, Brian was handed a large ornate hookah pipe adorned with matted hair, old teeth and bones which he bullied the owners to sell him. A considerable amount of cash was exchanged, after which Jones headed back to the hotel to show off his new acquisition. When he got there, he found out to his dismay that everyone had checked out. He phoned Gysin. "Come! Come quickly," he sobbed. "They've all gone and left me. Cleared out. I don't know where they've gone? No message. The hotel won't tell me where they've gone. I'm here all alone, help me. Come at once!"

Consumed by a betrayal magnified by the side-effects of his drug taking, Brian collapsed in the hotel lobby, then was taken to a room recently vacated by his friends. Sedated, he slept for two days in a chemically induced state then, still nursing the hurt he felt by the rejection, flew to Paris to spend time ruminating in Donald Cammell's flat. After a dismal few days, Jones headed back to London, arriving on March 8. Adding to his woes, Brian's hookah pipe was confiscated as he passed through customs at Heathrow Airport. The pipe eventually made its way to London's drug squad headquarters where it was displayed close to the desk of Sgt. Norman Pilcher.

While Brian was asleep in Marrakech, Keith and Anita had transferred briefly to an apartment elsewhere in the town before fleeing to Malaga via Tangier and then on to Barcelona. From Spain, they flew back to London, leaving Keylock to drive the Bentley home. Marianne Faithfull left Morocco earlier to continue her West End rehearsals, while the other members of the party made their way back to London. Mick, still evidently consumed by the flavours of the Middle East, visited Casablanca before returning to Britain.

Back in London, Anita cleared her possessions out of Brian's Kensington apartment and moved into Keith's St John's Wood flat. A distraught Brian tracked them down and confronted her. With tears shed on both sides, she informed him that he was impossible to live with and that she was leaving him for good; an ultimatum that the ostracised Stone found difficult to believe. Jones reflected bitterly on what he saw as a total betrayal by his two closest associates, upping his drug intake to exceed even his past excesses. While hoping Anita would return to him, he took up with Suki Poitier, the former girlfriend of his deceased friend, Tara Browne.

Mick flew back to London on March 17, into the welcoming arms of Marianne who was waiting at the airport. Hours later, West Sussex Police notified lawyers representing Jagger, Richards and Fraser that summons were to be served on them relating to the raid on Redlands. This sounded the death knell on a variety of expectations, not least that Sanchez' attempt to pervert the course of justice had failed miserably and as a result £7,000 had vanished without a hope in hell's chance of recovery. In an era when police corruption was rife, it had simply been filched.

As was customary, news of the impending summonses were circulated to the press. The police were tight-lipped on the exact wording, citing only "alleged offences", but with the *News Of The World* having already reported "illegal possession of drugs" in its February 19 edition, there was little doubt what the charges were actually for.

While Jagger and Richards' names dominated column space, police mysteriously declined to identify the two other persons cautioned that night at Redlands. Robert Fraser's name might have been known to the capital's art circuit, but the name of David Schneiderman meant nothing other than to a few in the London rave set he'd infiltrated. Schneiderman's absence from the summonses might have been explained by the police already discovering that he'd absconded overseas, but the fact that his name was withheld served only to heighten suspicions that he had been complicit in some way with the raid.

Mick and Keith's lawyer Timothy Hardacre received the hard copy summons on March 20 for them to appear at Chichester Magistrates Court on Wednesday, May 10, to answer the charges. While the Moroccan experience had raised spirits somewhat, news that they would now have to stand trial deflated all renewed optimism. Indeed, the only winners were the media who were already gearing up for one of the most newsworthy court cases of the decade, especially as it appeared the accused were going to enter "not guilty" pleas.

With the May date hanging ominously in the air and the tension surrounding Keith and Brian, Stones business, in its various forms, had to continue. Songs needed to be written and recorded for the next album, expected later in the year. In addition a booked European tour was fast approaching, and rehearsals were needed to sharpen up the group's live act (they hadn't played on stage since the previous October). With the uncertainly over the outcome of the trial, no one was holding their breath as to whether there would be further tours.

The European sojourn was littered with controversy from the offset. Arriving in Malmo, Sweden on March 24, the group and entourage were subjected to a strip-search by officials. The London *Evening News* reported: "Swedish customs officers have searched the Rolling Stones from head to toe for drugs. The pop group, arriving from Copenhagen, said they were delayed nearly an hour as officers inspected sixteen pieces of luggage. 'They were looking for pot,' said Mick Jagger, 'and they went through every bit of clothes we had, even our underclothes.'"

Other borders in Europe were equally unforgiving, handing the accompanying British press a field-day in building up their portfolio of scandal. On April 10, after flying from Zurich to Paris, the group underwent another thorough search by French customs. Painkillers and cold remedies were minutely inspected, undeveloped film was removed from cameras, and the group's stage equipment was dismantled and subjected to a comprehensive inspection. "Everything we had was stripped and examined," road manager Tom Keylock told reporters. "It was obvious they had been reading a lot of press reports about drugs and had taken things a bit too seriously." On leaving Paris' Le Bourget Airport, an altercation between Mick, Keith and an over-zealous immigration officer was broken up by Keylock.

Mick apparently snapped when asked by reporters if the group's name was being circulated between customs via Interpol's alleged 'Red List' of offenders. "Of course there's a list," Mick told a press conference. "And of course they are after me. In the last two months there have been four occasions when, on landing in London, I have been taken to a private room and searched, obviously for drugs... I feel as if I am being treated as a witch. And I have no broomstick handy."

There was trouble inside the venues, too. In Sweden, police with dogs chased fans who attempted to climb up on stage during the group's performance. In Vienna, a smoke bomb was ignited as the Stones took to the stage. The concert was stopped midway through, leading to large-scale chaos and 143 people being arrested. The worst violence occurred in Warsaw, Poland on April 13, the Stones being one of the first western rock bands to play behind the Iron Curtain, where rioting fans at the Palace of Culture concert were met by police with tear gas.

For a group attempting to infuse their music with a new sophistication, these scenes were as disheartening as they were irksome. Additionally, with LSD and other substances having brought on a degree of hitherto absent introspection, Jagger in particular was starting to find it difficult to come to terms with the reason why he was on stage in the first place: if Stones' concerts were nothing more than an excuse for fans to riot, there was clearly a need to take stock.

A chaotic catalogue of catastrophe behind them, the Stones'

European tour closed after a hysterical concert in Athens on April 17. At the beginning of May an uneasy truce prevailed between Brian and Anita at the annual Cannes film festival when, by dint of their respective duties on the film *A Degree Of Murder,* they were required to help promote it. Jones and Pallenberg caught the same plane, Keith making his own way by car to the French Riviera but staying well off Brian's radar. While the promotion duties were certainly awkward, Brian and Anita nonetheless put on a brave show for the paparazzi, and were pictured all smiles and glad rags on the perfunctory stops of the Cannes festival rotunda. Keith left France independently on the morning of Tuesday, May 9. He arrived back in London and shot straight over to meet Mick and their legal team to discuss the following day's court appearance in Chichester.

Anxious not to be tainted by negative publicity associated with the two Stones, Robert Fraser opted for the services of a separate barrister, William Denny QC, for his defence. This mutually agreed decision with Jagger and Richards' legal team had the benefit of distancing them from Fraser's more serious charge of heroin possession. Since a unified decision was taken to deny the charges against them, all had to physically appear to enter "not guilty" pleas. Tom Keylock drove Mick and Keith down to West Wittering on the evening of Tuesday, May 9. Fraser was offered room space at Redlands but, still haunted by the raid, he decided to stay in London and travel down to Chichester early the next morning.

Mick and Keith awoke early to prepare for their first day in court. They were dressed fairly conventionally; Jagger in green jacket, shirt and grey tie, Richards in navy-blue jacket and pink tie. With media, both local and national, waiting outside Redlands, the pair left for Chichester Magistrates' Court a little after 9 a.m. Six miles away in Chichester, others too were preparing. Word had spread on the fan network and a crowd of over 100 gathered to catch a glimpse of their idols. Local schools barred any pupil from skipping lessons, but many defied their teachers and joined the hardcore supporters outside the court, some of whom had travelled down overnight from London to be present.

Aware that the celebrity of Jagger and Richards would draw a large gathering, police conferred with the Stones' PR man, Les Perrin, to ensure that the pair were delivered into court with as little fuss as possible. In order to facilitate this, arrangements were made for police to meet Mick and Keith on a Chichester slip road, and for them to be ferried into court via an unobtrusive grey Morris Minor.

The dupe was successful, and once inside the sterile courthouse they were afforded an unwelcome reminder of the world they'd left behind. Fraser arrived from London to little fanfare, and the trio sat in an anteroom with other defendants awaiting their own cases to be called. Among those heard before Mick and Keith's appearance that day was that of a Chichester poacher fined £15 for trespassing and killing rabbits without a licence.

Listening to these minor infractions, Mick and Keith were of the belief that they would receive nothing more than a sharp admonishment: "It was like being back at school," Keith recalled later. "I don't think even at that point we expected any more than a cuff on the side of the head or a ruler across the knuckles."

With the 40 spaces in the public gallery occupied by press and hardcore fans, officials monitored events throughout the building via walkie-talkie. Expecting a stampede at the rear of the courthouse from over-eager fans, police blocked off the entrance by forming a human barricade.

At just after 10 a.m., Jagger, Richards and Fraser were ushered into court. Given the inordinate amount of personnel present, the trio had to sit in the area normally reserved for the jury. With everyone in situ, the magistrates took their places on the bench, a trio of laymen led by chairman Basil Shipman, a celebrated member of the Chichester hierarchy and part of a family famous locally for manufacturing meat paste products. To open proceedings, the charges were formally read out; Jagger for possession of four amphetamine derivative tablets, Richards for allowing his house in West Wittering to be used for the smoking of cannabis, and Fraser, charged with heroin and amphetamine possession.

Charges were also read out against the elusive David Schneiderman. According to the court prosecutor, he'd been found with "very large quantities of cannabis resin" on his person, specifically 229 grains. However, with Schneiderman off the radar, the magistrates decided that since he wasn't present he should be given a cloak of anonymity

– and the press was ordered not to reveal his name. While this was in accordance with procedure (given his failure to answer the summons), it served only to fuel already deep-rooted suspicions concerning his role in events.

The prosecution was then invited to present its case. They were evidently taking no chances, calling on nine police witnesses (two of them forensic experts) to give evidence. This was the first occasion that both sides had seen each other since that February night.

The charges of possession against Jagger and Fraser required little collaborative evidence other than the forensics' report detailing the nature of the substances found on them. Richards' offence of allowing his house to be used for the smoking of cannabis was more complex. To assist them in this, police and prosecution lawyers had constructed a comprehensive resume of what they had witnessed at Redlands that night. This was duly read out, much to the delight of the press gathered in the gallery.

Following preliminary statements, a lunchtime adjournment was called. Contrary to the meticulous planning regarding their arrival earlier in the day, Mick and Keith left the court building by the front entrance, evidently at the behest of Les Perrin who was by their side. It seems they were not averse to satisfying the requests from the press for a photo opportunity, perhaps in order to embarrass the authorities. Either way, it was in defiance of the earlier agreement.

Caught amidst a phalanx of press and curious onlookers, Mick and Keith prompted a brief period of chaos, with over 400 bodies desperate for a glimpse of them. Perrin and Allen Klein – freshly arrived from New York – walked protectively behind as Jagger and Richards moved down the steps towards their chauffeur-driven Bentley. Despite a police cordon, some ambitious fans broke through police lines to reach the pair, and according to local press reports, there was also some booing from disapproving Chichester residents.

The chaotic exit was subsequently viewed as a considerable affront to the meticulous planning conceived by police and court officials, leading to an enquiry by the authorities, who viewed with contempt the resulting photographs of the Stones' being manhandled. Ignorant of this affront to protocol, Mick, Keith and their legal team repaired to a nearby hotel for lunch before being driven back to the court.

Back before the bench, the trio of Jagger, Richards and Fraser listened as their legal representative, Geoffrey Leach, cross-examined some of the police who were present at the raid. Chief Inspector Dineley was the first to be called. Anxious to draw a connection with the exposé already published in the media, Leach asked him who furnished police with the information regarding the party. Dineley appeared unable to answer the question, saying only that a tip-off had been received by his colleague Sergeant Stanley Cudmore from "somebody else". When Cudmore was called to the witness stand, Leach dug in deeper as to the provenance of the information.

Geoffrey Leach: "Was that person connected with a well-known newspaper?"

Cudmore: "I am not prepared to answer that, sir."

In closing, Leach told the court that his clients denied "most strongly, the allegations" and furthermore, would challenge the interpretation of events by the prosecution and "on the evidence in its possession". Fraser's representative, William Denny QC, said that his client would welcome the earliest opportunity to answer the allegations made against him.

The trio's "not guilty" pleas ensured that the case would be heard at a higher court than Chichester Magistrates. Bail of £100 was demanded for Jagger, Richards and Fraser, and the case was formally adjourned to a date at the end of June.

The business of the day concluded, there was still the not inconsiderable matter of leaving the building safely. The crowd outside the court had now swollen to even larger proportions, and unlike their lunchtime appearance, there was no option other than to leave via the rear entrance. With a decoy car employed, Mick and Keith managed to avoid the crowds and shot away in the direction of Redlands.

While this was safely accomplished, police elsewhere were ramping up the campaign against The Rolling Stones with a surprise attack on another flank. Whether pre-determined or through an act of unnerving synchronicity, as Mick and Keith's court appearance became the subject of intense media scrutiny, Brian Jones found himself the target of

Norman Pilcher and his squad of detectives. Jones and his close friend and Stones associate, Prince Stanislaus Klossowski de Rola (aka Stash) had gone on to Paris after the Cannes Film Festival and arrived home the night before.

In an interview given to Peter Markham for *Ugly Things* magazine in 2011, de Rola recalled the dubious circumstances surrounding the bust. "All that fateful May morning the phone had rung off the hook. Brian and I had taken turns in answering it and invariably it was journalists – some of them known to both of us – who asked, 'Have you been busted?' *That was before the actual raid*!"

At 4 p.m. precisely, 12 police officers led by Pilcher entered Jones' flat at Courtfield Road. After a thorough search of the premises, they detected a quantity of marijuana, along with traces of methedrine and cocaine. On being shown the drugs, Jones admitted the cannabis was his but denied any knowledge of the other substances. "No man," he'd tell Pilcher. "That's not mine at all. I'm not a junkie." Given Pilcher's questionable reputation, it was possible that the substances had made their way into the flat by other means, but it was also more than plausible that any of the numerous characters who stopped by Jones' flat at all hours of the day and night could have left traces of their habits behind.

In a scene redolent of the Redlands' raid, an enormous collection of Jones' household items were taken away. Of the 29 items confiscated, 17 were found to contain cannabis-based substances. More worrying for Jones was a part-empty phial labelled methedrine, and traces of other crystalline substances that could bring charges of a more serious nature than mere cannabis possession.

Jones and de Rola were taken to Chelsea Police Station to be formally charged. Remarkably, press photographers and television news crews were waiting to catch their arrival, strongly suggesting that others were already in the loop regarding the raid. The following morning, the pair appeared at West London Magistrates Court where, following a three-minute hearing, they were remanded on bail until June 2. Back at the flat Jones dashed off a telegram to his parents in Cheltenham. "Please don't worry," he cabled. "Don't jump to hasty conclusions and don't judge me too harshly."

At the preliminary hearing on June 2 Jones and de Rola elected to have their charges transferred to a higher court before a jury. Bail was set at £250 each. Jones was advised by Allen Klein to steer well clear of any permanent residence until the whole episode had died down and, as a result, the beleaguered musician took to staying in a succession of hotels or the homes of friends.

All of this court activity was covered enthusiastically by the print media in a succession of lurid headlines that created the widespread impression that The Rolling Stones were degenerate and unapologetic drug users who held the law of the land in utter contempt. The timing of the court appearance and the raid on Brian's flat was clearly designed to create this belief and turn public opinion against them. In some circles, however, disquiet was being expressed. One such voice was Dick Taverne, MP for Lincoln and a Home Office minister. Like certain others, he was concerned at the amount of pre-trial information in circulation regarding Mick, Keith and Brian. "One cannot anticipate the outcome of what these proceedings will be," he told a conference of justice clerks' secretaries in Wales. "But whatever happens elsewhere, can one really say there will be no prejudice in the minds of the public against these defendants, even if they are acquitted?"

"I think there was quite a lot of adverse feelings in certain quarters that these were a lot of rather subversive musicians and not a part of the proper establishment," recalls Lord Taverne today. "One of the issues that we proposed was that if the defendant wished, they could ask to have the committal proceedings held in private. A lot of cases had arisen at that point where there was massive adverse publicity before the trial actually started."

Another minister perturbed at events was MP Tom Driberg. At 62, Driberg was a proud Communist, a closet homosexual and later outed as a double agent. He was a prominent loose cannon on the Labour left, and had a variety of reasons to lend his support to the group, not least his fascination for Mick Jagger whom he was rumoured to have propositioned at the Gay Hussar restaurant in Soho. An occultist, he'd counted himself a personal friend of Aleister Crowley before the Great Beast's death in 1947. During the sixties, he'd become a confidante of the Kray twins. Deftly mobile when it came to socialising, Driberg had met Jagger at a dinner party, and was energised by the liberal atmosphere promoted by the likes of the Stones.

In November 1965, Driberg raised an Early Day Motion in Parliament in response to a Glasgow magistrate's call for the Stones to be banned from Scotland. Citing "irrelevant, snobbish and insulting personal comments" made by the magistrate, Driberg hoped for a measure of support in Parliament. While he received only one signatory to his motion, he'd made his point. With news of Jagger, Richards and Jones' impending court trials gathering momentum, Driberg, like Taverne, felt uneasy about the media's prurient interest in their cases and called for a news blackout before events transferred to court.

To escape the pressures Jones made a snap decision to attend the Monterey Pop Festival in northern California during the weekend of June 16–18. At this early manifestation of the hippie culture, Brian basked in the glow of thousands of festivalgoers, many of whom were in awe of the blond rock god wandering in their midst. Fraternising with the likes of Jimi Hendrix, whom he introduced on stage, Eric Burdon, The Who and Velvet Underground singer/actress Nico, Jones was confronted with a vast array of drugs circulating around the site, and among other things took a dose of STP, a composition of LSD and amphetamine that elongated the psychedelic experience to around 72 hours. With stories of even seasoned trippers being hospitalised by the drug, Jones was stripped to his very core.

Back in England, Brian's physical and mental health was at such a low ebb that he was placed under the care of a Harley Street psychiatrist who recommended a visit to London rehabilitation centre, The Priory at Roehampton, where he was sedated for two days. On awakening he asked if he could attend the Stones' ongoing recording sessions at Olympic Studios in nearby Barnes. Permission granted, Jones gobbled a multitude of drugs and was barely coherent when he arrived. Sadly, his dishevelment was captured for dubious posterity in a film clip directed by Peter Whitehead for the Stones' next single. When he returned to The Priory later that night, his condition was considered so grave that he underwent the sedation process all over again.

Just six months into 1967, a seismic year in terms of cultural impact, The Rolling Stones were looking defeated. With no concerts booked lest court activity determine otherwise, the group ambled on as best it could. Mick and Marianne went back to Morocco while Keith and Anita kept a low profile. Brian, his demons never far away, bounced precariously between clinic and nightclub. Andrew Oldham, also imploding on a cocktail of paranoia and excessive drug use, was shaken by the impending trials. Fearful that he was next to be harassed, he opted to remove himself.

Andrew Oldham: "I had a slight problem in that the police were trying to bust me. I knew that I would not be faced with little girls sitting outside the jail going 'Free Andy'. Had I been busted I would be – sadly for the first time in my life – referred to as a businessman; a businessman who has fallen on squalid times. And I would have had my visa and ability to work for The Rolling Stones, or The Small Faces or Immediate Records or anything, taken away from me. And therefore my usefulness in employment would have been taken away. So I did the most sensible thing and got on a plane and went to America in about May of 1967."

Any chance of engaging in the so-called 'Summer of Love' was going to be problematic for all concerned, though Mick, Keith and Marianne and several other "beautiful people" attended The Beatles' recording of 'All You Need Is Love' at Abbey Road during the evening of June 25. The proceedings were being filmed as part of *Our World*, a special BBC programme marking the first global satellite link-up with an expected worldwide audience of over 400 million. Amid the carnival atmosphere in Studio One, joyously charged with incense and song, Mick was captured briefly, clapping and singing along to the infectious chorus that became one of the summer's main anthems.

Two days later he and Keith were expected at court in Chichester where a singular lack of love awaited them.

CHAPTER 7

Chichester (Day 1)

"I will gather and carefully make my friends
Of the men of the Sussex Weald;
They watch the stars from silent folds,
They stiffly plough the field.
By them and the God of the South Country
My poor soul shall be healed."

From Hilaire Belloc's *The South Country*

Just six miles from Redlands, the city of Chichester has always cast an imposing shadow over the patchwork of villages that pepper its borders. With its towering 16th century cathedral symbolic of its authority, Chichester's position as the capital of West Sussex has never been questioned. Though its infrastructure was carved out by Roman invaders, solid British C of E Christianity has always found a receptive welcome in its lush environs; a litany of churches reflecting the godfearing nature of its inhabitants and making Chichester the natural location for the seat of the West Sussex judiciary.

As the 20th century took hold, the indigenous population coveted their parochial justice system as much as they prided themselves on their manicured lawns and hedgerows. Like most conurbations the size of

Chichester, petty crime was a predictable, if irritating occurrence. While post-war policing could quietly inflict the occasional rap across the knuckles, more series offences were dealt with at the local Magistrates Court.

In 1967, cases that required a harsher sentence than magistrates were permitted to deliver were heard at an interim court known as the Quarter Sessions. Deriving their name from an aged statute of 1388, these hearings were ordered, as their name suggested, to be held every three months to tidy up crimes not serious enough to require the attention of the next rung of judicial authority, the Crown Courts. With Jagger, Richards and Fraser opting to be tried before a jury back in May, the so-called 'Midsummer' hearing of the Quarter Sessions was their next port of call.

The (then) structure of the court employed a bench composed of three members of the public known as Justice's of the Peace, all upstanding citizens who derived their income from means other than the law. Just to make sure that they didn't get too carried away with the powers appointed to them, a presiding chairman equipped with legal expertise was appointed to guide the decision of these volunteer laymen. If those accused felt that they wanted to be judged by their peers, a jury could be sequestered. Ultimately though, sentencing was left to those behind the bench who would administer a judgement they felt was commensurate with the crime.

While the court did not have the power to sit on serious offences like murder or manslaughter, they were given a free hand on more parochial matters, drug possession among them. While occasional amphetamine and cannabis offences were heard in Chichester, they were usually treated as minor and dealt with by the Magistrates Court unless, as in the Stones' case, they opted for a jury trial. Drug use may have been on the increase, but court time in Chichester was more concerned with driving offences, poaching and the occasional public display of drunkenness.

While Quarter Sessions reduced valuable Crown Court time, their unbalanced structure and frequently outlandish judgements had led to serious reservations as to how legally reliable they were. Indeed, so questionable were some of the sentences handed down, the whole system was withdrawn in 1971 when the Courts Act set about modernising the judicial system.

In 1967, however, it was the formality for drug-related charges to be tried in this fashion. Aware that they would be passing judgement on two of the world's most famous pop stars, the authorities in Chichester were evidently nonplussed on how to deal with the magnitude of what lay before them. While normally sitting in judgement on a collection of Chichester's underbelly, this unwieldy collision with the entertainment world was unquestionably the most extraordinary moment in the lives of these amateur lawmakers. A global spotlight potentially bore down on their every move, and much anticipation had built up since the cases were referred.

Since there was little chance that Mick and Keith would be judged as ordinary young men, a decision was taken to employ lawyers from the top of London's legal community to fight their corner. Selected to lead the defence team was the eminent barrister Michael Havers, QC. Son of eminent High Court Judge Sir Cecil Havers, Havers junior had followed his father into a legal career with high aspirations, both legal and political. Following service in the Royal Navy, he continued his legal training at Cambridge. In 1964, and at just 41, Havers was named as Queen's Counsel, the youngest barrister ever to receive the accolade. While his career would eventually take him to the highest seat of the British judiciary, representing Mick Jagger and Keith Richards was the most unusual case in his professional life thus far. The father of two teenage boys, Philip and Nigel, Havers was not unfamiliar with the pop scene, if just a little curious at how it had enchanted so much of the world's youth.

Watching the television news on the night of the initial Magistrates Court hearing in May, Havers jokingly mused to his family on who would be game enough to represent the musicians when they transferred to the higher court. Nigel Havers recalls the strange turn of events that evening. "When the story first broke and hit the news, I remember my father saying, 'I hope they don't ask me to defend them'. Later that night the phone went, and he came and told us, 'I'm defending The Rolling Stones.'"

The following day, Michael Havers' office was alight with the news. Several of his colleagues implored him not to touch the case, which left him in something of a quandary. Nigel recalls the scenario. "Because he was getting so much opposition from his contemporaries, my father went to visit my grandfather. He asked him, 'Should I take this case on? Because I am on a loser aren't I?' To which my grandfather replied: 'You must do it, and you must win!'"

After agreeing to represent them, Havers was keen to make some sense of Jagger and Richards' unusual world. The first step was to invite them over to meet him at his office at 5 King's Walk in the Temple area of London. The sight of Mick and Keith wandering through the stuffy corridors of Temple Bar was strange enough, but Havers warmed to his two young clients immediately. "My father was really impressed with both Mick and Keith," Nigel recalls. "He was so impressed with how absolutely intelligent they were; really alert and smart. He said that they didn't suffer fools at all."

In fact, the only demand made of Havers during that first meeting was for a glass of Scotch. Since he was bereft of alcohol, Havers had to borrow a bottle from a neighbouring chamber. From then on, he ensured that a drinks cabinet was always available when his celebrated clients visited.

Conviviality aside, there was still the business of how best to approach the trial. While Havers was well up to speed on the reputation of London's court procedures, like many of his contemporaries he viewed the independence afforded to Quarter Sessions with considerable suspicion. Because these courts were presided over largely by amateurs, it usually fell to the presiding chairman to arbitrate, and with the strong likelihood of him being elderly there was a distinct possibility that he would be unsympathetic to the likes of Mick and Keith.

Sadly, the embodiment of Havers' darkest fears came with the news that Judge Leslie Kenneth Allen Block would be sitting in judgement at the trial. At 61, his background was as far away from the Stones' unorthodox lifestyle as was conceivable. Just six months into his duties at Chichester, Block was a steely, traditionalist member of the establishment, with heavy connections to both the military and London's legal network. Born on August 9, 1903, he'd initially set his sights on a life in the navy but following the prescribed route via National Service and Royal Naval College, he diverted into law. The advent of war in 1939 derailed his legal ambitions, but his prowess at directing operations saw him ascend the naval ladder. By the end of hostilities in 1945 he held the rank of Commander, his efforts having secured a Distinguished Service Cross.

Out of the service, Block reverted to his legal work, initially as an assistant judge in the Corporation of London, with special responsibilities for the Mayor of London. These duties occasionally took him to the Old Bailey where he gained a modest celebrity among his peers, once famously stopping a trial there because the temperature inside the court had become too hot.

On retirement Block switched his attention to farming and estate management. Having married into West Sussex stock, he combined these rural activities with some legal work from his 10-roomed, Tudor-style property, Shiprods in Henfield. Though still being a member of esteemed London clubs such as the MCC and Garrick, Block assimilated himself easily into the West Sussex agricultural community, and was a popular face at the calendar of events in the district, cricket being a particular passion. In addition, his part-time role as Chairman at Chichester Quarter Sessions required only a few days of his time each year.

While it was a long way from the wig and gown of the Old Bailey, Block clearly relished his position within Chichester's judiciary. Aware of the interest surrounding the Redlands case, the challenge would no doubt have reignited his thirst for the limelight. While pop culture was nothing less than total anathema to him, Block was seasoned enough to realise that The Rolling Stones' association with non-conformity would place him in the role of batting for the establishment.

Block was well known to those who made their livelihood from maintaining the law. In 1967, John Rodway was a young police officer based at Chichester Police station. He recalls Block's reputation. "Judge Block was no bumbling old fool, he was a very astute man. As far as we were concerned, Judge Block was known as 'the hanging judge'. He was very much a policeman's judge. In his view a policeman did not tell lies. If you were a police officer and you were going in front of Judge Block, you had to be right with what you were saying, because he didn't suffer fools gladly, very much so. Equally, he had a belief in the rule of law, and if a police officer had done something right, he would support that officer."

Briefings between Jagger, Richards and their legal team continued up to the day before the trial started on June 27. In between the formal sessions there was some awkward socialising, and during one break, Havers took the pair for lunch at his London club, ironically the same as Block's, The Garrick in Covent Garden. Nigel Havers takes up the story: "The whole bar went silent as they came in. As they walked towards the bar, everyone just took a few steps back. It was like the scene from *Lawrence Of Arabia* when Peter O'Toole walks into the officers' mess with his Arab companion – both terribly filthy, and the Arab downs a glass of lemonade. I think it was dad's way of cocking a snoop at the old guard."

Despite these rare moments of repose, there was still the business of competently representing the two Stones in court. While the chances of a custodial sentence on the pair were considered relatively slim, there was a possibility that it could happen if the court decided to make an example of them. The group's vast finances could easily absorb a fine, but the threat of prison was certainly disturbing in view of the tendency for celebrities in the dock to suffer prejudice. Havers and his team had been advising Mick and Keith on how best to convince the court of their innocence, and equally, to neuter the tide of guilt already expressed by the media. Shortly before his death, Havers spoke to writer AE Hotchner about a briefing session he had with Jagger on the issue of giving evidence.

Michael Havers: "[Mick] spoke in two tongues, a quite proper London accent and a Cockney put-on, which he used interchangeably. I told him to restrict himself to his London accent on the witness stand… I did tell Mick that once in the courtroom he would have to disregard everyone but me, never to guess at an answer but to say that he didn't know or that he forgot, because if you guess, I told him, you'll guess wrong."

Briefings continued up until the day before the trial. Following a final meeting with lawyers in London, Jagger and Richards travelled down to Redlands that evening in order to be as fresh as possible for their first day in court. With them was Robert Fraser. While he'd baulked on staying at the property the night before the magistrates' hearing in May, he'd evidently decided that with the media intent on capturing Jagger and Richards' every movement, he had to be there to present a unified front.

Whether they got much sleep that night is open to speculation. The sun rose over Redlands the following morning at 4:45 a.m. to a cloudless sky. If the bright weather was acting as a kindly portent to the day's proceedings, Chichester was concerned with more predictable activity long before the Rolling Stones carnival rolled into town. As usual for a late June morning, Chichester business started well before sunrise. The town's market-sellers were stocking up with freshly caught fish from the nearby harbour ports, and the summer abundance of fruit and vegetables was also on show. With schools and colleges deep in exam time, the town was fairly quiet for the best part of the day. With the annual Wimbledon Tennis Championships in its second day, British hopes rested on Ann Haydon-Jones and those locals not disposed to the trials of pop celebrities were ensconced before their television sets, unconcerned about the fate of two of The Rolling Stones.

Nonetheless, Chichester police were taking no chances, and on the basis of the scenes at the preliminary court appearance that May, they deployed extra personnel to deal with the anticipated invasion of crazed teenagers. Similarly, expected legions of news crews and rabid journalists from around the world had to be accommodated. Fleet Street had already been given a taster of what occurred that night at Redlands during the magistrates' hearing but the "not guilty" pleas meant further details would be forthcoming, a mouth-watering gift in the run up to the notoriously quiet "silly season".

To capture every moment of what was clearly regarded as the most sensational trial since the 1963 Profumo affair, sections of the media had camped out early at Redlands to capture Mick and Keith's journey towards the court. With typical zeal, a small clutch of photographers, including predictably those from the *News Of The World*, breached Redlands' modest defences to photograph Jagger and Richards as they were leaving.

These images show a somewhat sombre parade towards Keith's blue Bentley. With the likelihood of a hostile bench awaiting them, the deportment of Jagger and Richards offered a deferential nod to convention, while still maintaining a degree of fashionable chic. Mick wore a lilac and green, double-breasted jacket with white buttons, olive green trousers, a floral shirt and a green and black striped tie. Keith, in a similar quandary over what was considered appropriate and yet not too conventional, compromised slightly, decking himself out in a three-quarter navy frock-coat, a high, lace collar shirt, grey military-style trousers and black patterned shoes with a white scarf thrown over his shoulder. Behind them was Fraser, dressed conservatively with only his ubiquitous dark sunglasses suggesting nonconformity. With Tom Keylock waiting in the driver's seat, the Bentley made its way towards Chichester.

A modest group of fans had assembled before the court opened for business. This surprised the police, who had employed a large number of personnel to deal with the expected hordes. Inside it was more predictable, the 40 seats of the public gallery snatched up within five minutes of the building being opened, many having queued since the early hours to secure the best vantage points. Sharing space with fans were press representatives and members of Jagger and Richards' retinue. Several precautions were employed to ensure that a sense of order was maintained, and fans had been expressively warned by the court usher that any outward display of excitement would lead to expulsion. To reinforce this, two unformed police officers stood watch from the top of the gallery to ensure nothing untoward occurred.

Aware that they could be ensconced in Chichester for a few days, Mick and Keith's legal team established a base at the Ship Hotel, a few minutes' walk from the court. Situated at 57 North Street, it was an appropriate venue to establish a command HQ, having hosted General Eisenhower following talks concerning the D-Day landings in 1944.

Some 15 minutes after leaving Redlands, the Bentley made its approach to the court located on the road called Southgate. The imposing redbrick building cut an incongruous presence against the gentler architecture that defines the majority of Chichester. Built in 1949, its initial modernity had, even by 1967 standards, become swiftly dated. Still operating as a working courthouse, its cold, functional presence and the aroma of varnished oak panelling and freshly bleached floors – the smell of institutional England in all its sanctimonious glory – added many a heartbeat to those awaiting their fate.

To the disappointment of fans waiting outside, the trio entered the courtroom's rear entrance. Nonetheless, a bank of clicking shutters met Jagger, Richards and Fraser's arrival as did an ITN news crew. The news agency's cameras captured an extraordinary scene: Jagger taking some snaps with his own camera to preserve the surreal moment. Once inside the building they were greeted by Les Perrin, who was there to handle the media, while Keylock and Ian Stewart looked after any personal needs. (Allen Klein was temporarily detained in New York on business).

Also making their way into the building was the police presence from the Redlands' saga, their faces strangely familiar to Jagger, Richards and Fraser. Inside the courtroom itself, the lawyers concerned with the trial were attending to their various duties. To the left of the bench stood Michael Havers QC, to his right, prosecution lawyer Malcolm Morris QC. The 54-year-old was a seasoned barrister who, like Judge Block, had straddled a military and legal career. Eton and Oxford educated, Morris ominously pursued his social life at the same London clubs as Block, and had already earned a considerable entry in *Who's Who* for his deeds in legal circles, as evidenced by a résumé that emphasised his successes when it came to fighting courtroom battles. As later observed by Havers, just before proceedings begun the voluminous Morris was seen exchanging friendly asides with courtroom staff and, later, with the magistrates.

Behind the bench sat the three Justices of the Peace, with Judge Block to their left. The JP's daytime occupations were far removed from the accused: Mr Robert Elwes was a Chichester farmer, Mr J Gentle, a newsagent from Worthing and Sir Arthur Howard, a former Tory MP. Much like Block, Howard had left London to concentrate on agriculture, at Steyning in West Sussex.

With the court officials in place, the jury were led in. Composed of 12 men drawn from the Chichester locale, as the rigid protocol dictated, they had no inkling of the case on which they were about to hear. As they took their places to the left of the dock, their ruddy complexions and nervous expectations added to the drama of the occasion. Next, having been briefed on procedure by court officials, Jagger, Richards and Fraser made their way from a small waiting room into the court, and then over to the raised oak dock directly facing the bench. As they entered, a high-pitched squeal of excitement rose from the girls in the gallery. To most fans, The Rolling Stones were usually monochrome pixels on a TV screen, or fuzzy snapshots stolen by the tabloids to be gawped at over breakfast, and yet here they were, sitting incongruously in front of them, in the local courtroom.

After a few moments of nervous assimilation, the three took their seats in the dock, their fashionable attire clearly marking them out from everyone else in the room. Looking nervously around, they took in the unfamiliar scene, the functional surroundings of the wood-panelled interior where only the red and gold of the Crown decal hanging over the bench offered any semblance of colour. Above them, daylight cascaded through a predominately glass roof, while an archaic air-conditioning system whirred continuously in the background.

As a formality, police hemmed in the accused at either end of where they sat. Visibly nervous, Mick leaned over and chatted with the policeman alongside him. According to the vigilant press corps, these asides appeared fairly harmonious, if somewhat nervous. Breaking the strange reverie, the sound of a baby crying in another area of the courthouse echoed up the staircase and into the courtroom. Elsewhere, stifled giggles and screams would occasionally escape from the public gallery despite the efforts of police and court staff.

With everything in place, the business of the day could begin. As predicted, certain preliminary statements and objections were raised with the bench. Havers began with a request that the trio's charges be read separately; a device that while extending court time considerably, would serve to separate Jagger and Richards from Fraser's more serious charge. Equally, it would allow Fraser to distance himself from Jagger and Richards' overwhelming celebrity. This request, perfectly normal in the scheme of events, was granted by Judge Block.

The case against Michael Phillip Jagger was the first to be heard.

Morris rose and began the prosecution's case with a small joke, admitting that he was pleased he wasn't a journalist having to record the names of the pharmaceuticals that were to be read out that morning. He wasn't exaggerating, with Jagger's charge on possession of amphetamine sulphate and methyl amphetamine hydrochloride reading like a page from a pharmacopoeia.

This slight jocularity out of the way, Morris called the first witness, Chief Inspector Gordon Dineley, to take the stand. His delivery faultless and evidently well-rehearsed, Dineley reiterated the events that took his team of detectives to Redlands on the evening of Sunday, February 12. Presenting the warrant he had so proudly displayed to Richards as the first item of evidence, Dineley led the court through his version of events that night, restricting himself mainly to the number of people in the house and how many police personnel were involved.

Next to take the stand was Sergeant John Challen of Chichester Police who'd discovered the small phial of pills in Jagger's coat. Frequently referring to his leather bound police book, Challen recalled the moment when he discovered the amphetamines, and reiterated the singer's claim that the substances were prescribed by his doctor and had been used "to stay awake and work".

To substantiate the composition of the drugs, forensic scientist Michael Ansell was then called to the witness box. While amphetamine sulphate and methyl amphetamine hydrochloride meant little to anyone outside a pharmacy, their street vernacular – speed – was more familiar. Ansell said that the composition of the drugs came under the umbrella name of Benzedrine and were not legal in Britain. The appearance of the scientist among their witnesses reflected the prosecution's need to ensure that no chink appeared in the evidence against Jagger.

When Ansell stood down, a recess was taken to allow the defence team to prepare their retaliation. Central to the case was convincing the jury that Jagger's doctor would have prescribed the pills, even though there was no actual prescription. Additionally, with European amphetamine use a grey area, the defence would be at pains to point out that Jagger was a globally roving musician who could have purchased pills similar to these quite legally in many European countries. Since Jagger travelled in and out of Britain on a frequent basis, the possibility of his forgetting about them was a credible scenario. Furthermore, given the heavy workload he was undertaking, the defence needed to prove that Jagger's doctor would have happily prescribed him a similar preparation in this country if required.

Commencing his cross-examination, Havers called Detective Sergeant Stanley Cudmore to the stand. Havers wanted to make the court aware that his client had behaved in a courteous and obliging manner on the night of the raid, and his skilful questioning prompted Cudmore to state that Jagger, in particular, had indeed co-operated in a thoroughly adult manner. This device was designed to dispel any preconceived prejudices the jury and bench might have had with regard to Jagger (and Richards), which led to further discussion concerning Mick's conventional background and not inconsiderable educational achievements. "It may be a surprise to some people," said Havers, "that Mr. Jagger got seven 'O' levels and two 'A' levels."

The defence then called Raymond Dixon-Firth, of Wilton Crescent, Knightsbridge. A general practitioner since 1940, among other duties he had been a consultant to the Iraqi royal family. Dixon-Firth confirmed that he had been Jagger's doctor since July 1965, when the singer arrived for a check-up at his clinic.

Under Havers' guidance, Dixon-Firth attempted to rationalise the circumstances of the drugs that Jagger had been caught with. Knowing that amphetamine use had been demonised by some of the more hysterical elements of the media, the doctor pointed out that similar substances were still widely prescribed as appetite suppressants and for other issues such as hay fever and air sickness.

Havers: "Is there any type of person taking them?"

Dr Dixon-Firth: "People with a busy day ahead of them, long distance drivers, that sort of person."

Havers: "What would the average dose per patient be?"

Dr Dixon-Firth: "Five milligrams: one tablet three times a day would be perhaps the average dose."

Under questioning, the doctor recalled a telephone conversation he'd had with the singer earlier in the year concerning the pills in his possession. Dr Dixon-Firth stated that Jagger had told him he had acquired them to cope with a particularly difficult period in the Stones' busy itinerary. Furthermore, Mick had quizzed him about their safety, and was told that they were safe to use periodically, but to avoid any long-term use.

Havers: "Having been told this and being told he could have them, was he properly in possession of them?"

Dr Dixon-Firth: "Certainly."

At this juncture, Judge Block intervened to clarify matters.

Judge Block: "Had he had none, would you have prescribed something similar?"

Dr Dixon-Firth: "Yes."

With that authoritative conformation, ironically prompted by Block, Havers concluded by saying that as Jagger had conferred with his doctor, it amounted to a prescription and therefore he was in proper possession of the pills.

While the defence was compelling, the fact remained that the drug in that form was illegal in Britain except with an authorised prescription from a doctor in writing. With the prosecution holding what amounted to a whip hand, their council – led by the voluminous Morris – began a vigorous questioning of Jagger's practitioner. Not content with what Dr Dixon-Firth had told Havers, Morris queried the doctor's understanding of amphetamine composition. In clear, informed tones, the doctor reiterated that while the drug in Jagger's possession was not available in the UK in single tablet form, variants were legally available in numerous preparations, some of them over the counter.

Morris: "Did you ask him any more about these drugs?"

Dr Dixon-Firth: "He said they had been given to him by a friend and that he needed something to get him through the following day."

Morris: "Did you gather he was in possession of these pills?"

Dr Dixon-Firth: "Yes sir."

At that point, Judge Block interjected again.

Judge Block: "Did you ask to look at them?"

Dr Dixon-Firth: "No."

Seizing the advantage secured by the judge, Morris continued: "A doctor must know what he is prescribing. He must know the effects of what he is prescribing. You didn't know at all what you were prescribing?"

Dr Dixon-Firth: "I knew they were pep pills. I did not know the precise formula."

Smelling blood, Morris dug in deeper. "Are you really saying that if a patient came to you, as Mr. Jagger did, and said: 'I have some pep pills', you would say: 'All right, you can take them if you need them, but not too many'?"

Dr Dixon-Firth: "Yes, provided I was satisfied after discussion that they were appropriate for him."

Morris: "How can you know? You were not there."

Dr Dixon-Firth: "Because I know what pep pills contain normally."

Following the prosecution's cross-examination of Jagger's doctor, a lunchtime recess was called. With Jagger, Richards and Fraser still very much at liberty, they walked the short distance to the Ship Hotel in Chichester's North Street to lunch with their lawyers. As he entered, Jagger was besieged by several hardcore fans who demanded autographs, while a few photographers attempted to get pictures.

At just after 2 p.m. court resumed to begin summing up. Havers argued emotionally on his client's behalf, reiterating to the jury that Jagger had been in regular conference with his doctor, and that the drug in question was legally available in Europe and in various preparations in the UK. Aware that the prosecution were focusing on the definition of the word 'prescription', Havers argued that the verbal authorisation from his doctor was sufficient to exonerate Jagger of the charge against him.

Predictably, the prosecution pulled the case back to the absence of a written prescription and the illegality of the drug, which to them was unequivocal. Once these submissions were finished, Judge Block held a brief conference with colleagues on the bench before giving his own summation to the jury.

If the prosecution had any qualms about the validity of their case, they lifted as Block offered his own interpretation of what he'd heard. Ostensibly speaking as an impartial observer, in reality the judge spoke for four minutes and barely mentioned Jagger's defence. "You may think I am wasting your time in summing up," he began ominously. "I have no hesitation whatsoever in saying that the evidence given by Dr Dixon-Firth would not, in law, amount to the issue of a prescription by a duly authorised medical practitioner. So, really as a matter of the law, it therefore follows that the defence open to Mr. Jagger is not available to him. I therefore direct you that there is no defence to this charge. I now ask you to consider your verdict."

With this unequivocal assessment ringing in their ears, the jury made their way from the courtroom to a small anteroom to deliberate their verdict.

Judge Block's damning summation as to Jagger's innocence had shocked the defence team. Recounting events to AE Hotchner, Havers spoke of his utter disbelief on hearing Block's conclusive summary. "That was a vicious summation, tantamount to telling the jury to convict, despite the evidence and despite the principle that a man is innocent until proven guilty."

The defence team had barely time to assess the gravity of Block's words before the usher informed the court that the jury had reached a decision. They had been out for a little over five minutes.

With the atmosphere in the court charged, the foreman stood up to read the verdict. Given that they'd only spent a few minutes considering Jagger's fate, it was clear that there had been a unanimous vote.

Block then asked the juror to read out the jury's verdict.

"Guilty."

A wave of shock ran through the court. Jagger put his head down and stared into his lap. In among the hubbub of disbelief, Havers leapt to his feet and demanded right to leave of appeal.

Aware that the appeal procedure wouldn't stymie sentencing, Block happily granted the request, adding optimistically: "I wish you the best of luck."

Since the charges resulting from the Redlands saga would extend to a second day, Havers argued for Jagger's case to be wound up immediately, or for his client to be given bail, a tactic that might elicit an error from the judge. If Block were to sentence Mick there and then, any hastily contrived decision could have serious implications on the verdicts handed down to Fraser and Richards. Similarly, Jagger's sentence could easily provoke a huge public and possibly political backlash that could easily scupper the rest of the trial.

Fully aware what was being asked of him, Block refused, coolly recommending that bail should be refused and that Jagger be held in custody to await sentencing following the conclusion of the cases against his co-defendants. Albeit on remand, this meant a night in prison and, given the way events were panning out, it could be more than an overnight stay. Havers then argued that the present jury would then have to pass judgement on Fraser and Richards' cases which, given what had already transpired, might be prejudicial to their verdicts. Block retaliated by stating that he'd request a new jury to be empanelled for Richards and Fraser's trial the following day.

With the courtroom still in a state of shock, Jagger was taken down to the cells beneath, a warder gripping his arm in case he made an unlikely bid for freedom. It was a pitiful descent down three flights of cold stone steps to where Jagger was locked away to await transfer to a nearby jail. He now faced the stark reality of what could happen if Judge Block decided to roll out the full weight of the law in light of the verdict, the worst-case scenario being two years imprisonment.

Havers tried to counsel his distraught client, but it was clear that nothing could be done until the other trials were concluded. Aware that Richards' less straightforward charge could take up considerable court time, that could mean an elongated stay behind bars. Seemingly operating on the tightest of timetables, Jagger was allotted just 13 minutes to confer with his legal team before they were ushered out of his cell. Mick then had to wait until Fraser's trial concluded before knowing where he'd be taken on remand.

Meanwhile, Fraser was called to the stand. Like Jagger and Richards, he had originally registered a "not guilty" plea when charged. However, after seeing the conclusive manner in which Jagger had been treated, a decision was made to change his plea to guilty, hoping that the bench might show some sympathy for his contrition. Despite this turnaround, the prosecution wasted little time in going for the jugular. Without respect for legal protocol, they mentioned a wholly unrelated case against the gallery owner in which he had been prosecuted for exhibiting an erotic sculpture by American pop artist Jim Dine. Fraser had been fined £20 for this offence, and the reason it was cited in Chichester was evidently to throw suspicion over Fraser's defence and further sully his character.

With emotional candour, Fraser's counsel, the eminent QC William Denny, ex-RAF man and occasional lecturer at Jagger's alma mater, the London School of Economics, noted his client's impeccable credentials, both family and professional. From Eton College to army officer in the King's Rifles, a strong picture was painted of a character who'd come through a system similar to those attempting to rein him in. Spelling out his admirable military record, Denny stated that Fraser was in no way "a spineless individual", having served time in North Africa during the Mau Mau emergency in the fifties. Denny described a creative young man returning to build a thriving art gallery in Mayfair. Addressing his drug habit, Denny skilfully pitched Fraser as an innocent user of heroin, claiming that he had been introduced to the narcotic by a former employee. According to his council, Fraser took the drug, believing it would act as a temporary stimulant. However, despite his best intentions, after a few weeks of innocent imbibing, Fraser found himself hooked.

Speaking of Fraser's "private shame", Denny assured the court that his client had battled against his demons, and how prior to the Redlands incident, he had called his doctor for renewed help. Fraser's practitioner, London-based Dr John Quentin Craigmore, was brought to the stand to state that he believed his patient was now "clear of his addiction". In concluding his submission, Denny pronounced that there was "no reason why [Fraser] should ever go back onto heroin again".

Accepting Fraser's turnabout on his "not guilty" plea, Judge Block decided that he would defer sentencing until Richards' case was heard in full. That said, Fraser was remanded in custody with Jagger.

As Fraser ascended the steps to join Jagger, Richards was brought to the stand. Given that his offence of allowing his home to be used for the smoking of marijuana was the most complex of the three charges to prove, it was clear that the hearing could not be heard in the time remaining before court adjourned for the day. In the event Richards was given enough time to register his "not guilty" plea before the court closed. His plea having deferred the need for custody, Keith was bailed on £250 and was free to leave until the following day. Not surprisingly, he left Chichester in a hurry, Keylock driving him back to Redlands. There, he was able to take stock of what had occurred, and prepare for what might be a grim tomorrow.

A request from Jagger had filtered through to Richards, namely the provision of a suitcase containing fresh clothes, a razor and shaving soap. While he was gathering these items, Richards grabbed a book on Tibetan Buddhism, two on modern art and a 184-piece jigsaw. Keylock swiftly delivered them back to Jagger's legal team in Chichester. For obvious reasons the razor was later confiscated by prison authorities.

Because the court cells were purely a holding bay, Jagger and Fraser would be taken to the nearest prison with remand facilities, in this case Lewes Prison on the outskirts of Brighton. By dint of being found guilty and with bail refused, the pair suffered the humiliation of being handcuffed to a guard en route to the prison. Since there was no suggestion that they were violent prisoners or that the charges against them involved violent behaviour, the imposition of handcuffs appeared wholly ridiculous. Predictably, an hour after court closed, the press were there to capture the pathetic scene as Jagger, Fraser and four other prisoners also sentenced that day were driven from the rear of Chichester's courtroom in a grey prison van. With word of his imprisonment winging its way back to Fleet Street, some of the more tenacious photographers managed to grab a few images of Jagger in handcuffs as he left. Around a dozen girl fans began to bang on the steel gates that protected the rear of the building, shouting "We want Mick!"

The 37-mile trip along the rolling coastline from Chichester to Lewes is normally a pleasant enough experience but for Jagger and Fraser the journey in the back of the vehicle must have been miserable. Kept at separate ends of the van, each with their own police guard, Fraser would later recall his guard saying to him: "It wasn't you we wanted, it was that fucker Mick Jagger."

Some 90 minutes after leaving Chichester, the van arrived at Lewes Prison's imposing frontage. Taken through the huge oak doors, the convicted were processed in accordance with formal protocol. They undressed, were examined by the prison doctor, and then given a set of fatigues to wear. From the reception area, Jagger and Fraser were taken to a secure room in the hospital wing, their remand status not necessitating absorption into the general prison population. The hospital windows were fronted by metal bars and, looking through, the pair would have seen impossibly high stone walls tapered off by razor wire. The reality of his confinement was altogether too harrowing for Jagger, and he would frequently break down in tears.

Back at Redlands, a stunned Richards was pondering on what the following day had in store for him. A late arrival at West Wittering that evening was Marianne Faithfull. According to her recollections, Keith was phlegmatic about what had happened to Jagger and Fraser, and about his own fate, saying little beyond "whatever happens, happens". For those who knew Richards' moods, this was undoubtedly his way of dealing with the enormity of the situation.

Marianne, too, was desperately trying to come to terms with what was happening to her closest friends. While the details of her role in the Redlands saga had yet to surface in court, she knew that Keith's hearing the following day would almost certainly draw attention to her involvement. In a whirl of confusion, Marianne had escaped the first day of the trial by going over to the Chiswick residence of Steve Marriott, the puckish vocalist with The Small Faces. Friendly with the singer's girlfriend Saida, Faithfull, along with fellow Small Faces' Ronnie Lane and Ian McLagan, decided much in the spirit of the times that the best way to escape the underlying nightmare was to drop acid and dance away their woes. From Marianne's own accounts, it was a crazy, hugely psychedelic day, although the subconscious ticking away in her mind would manifest visions of Mick in court, twisting away in the wind with vultures ready to pick at his fragile body.

Somehow these vibrations had been picked up by Jagger. A phone call from Lewes Prison ordered Keylock to whisk Marianne over to give him some much needed support. Using his well-honed intrepidness, Keylock tracked Faithfull down to Marriott's but assuming that he was a presumptuous hack after a story, Saida kept the Stones' minder waiting at the door. Eventually, after raising his voice, the intimidating Keylock was allowed in to communicate Mick's need to see Marianne immediately. Still under the influence of LSD, she was driven down to Redlands to confer with Richards and then on to Lewes prison to visit Jagger and Fraser.

Also at Redlands when Marianne arrived was Michael Cooper who'd instinctively grasped the historical importance of Mick and Keith's dilemma. Accordingly, he'd been photographing every moment during the trial as it unfolded and he tagged along with Marianne to see Jagger and Fraser on their first night in Lewes prison.

Led into the hospital wing, they found Jagger inconsolable on the small cot that dominated his cell. Seeing his two close friends, he rushed over, his eyes damp since the Chichester jury had delivered their verdict a few hours previous. "You've got to get me out of here," he bleated. "I don't think I can make it behind bars."

Marianne, still in a blur from the acid residue, found some emotional strength from her reserves and delivered a blistering salvo at Jagger. "Pull yourself together," she recalled telling him that night. "Just try and relax. You'll probably be here only this one night, and after Keith's trial tomorrow you'll be free." Reportedly, Jagger continued to weep, saying through the tears, "I didn't do anything."

Pragmatic as well as sympathetic, Cooper began sizing up the room for photo opportunities. He was acutely aware that Jagger's incarceration was the most famous detention of a prominent artist since Oscar Wilde's imprisonment some 50 years previous, and he wanted to capture this iconic moment. Knowing that it would have been impossible to make his way into the jail with a conventional SLR camera, Cooper had smuggled in a microscopic device to capture an image of Jagger behind bars, a photograph that would prove a massive embarrassment to every tier of the stuffy establishment. He asked Mick to lie back on his cot so he could shoot him through the bars fronting his cell. As he snapped away, he said, "(I'll) give these to the newspapers and there'll be a tremendous fuss about it." Jagger liked the idea, even suggesting that it might make an excellent cover picture for the Stones' next LP.

Unluckily for all concerned, a guard heard the sound of the camera clicking and confiscated the film as Cooper made his way out. Nonetheless, other distressing images of Jagger handcuffed to a warder were given heavy prominence on the front pages of most national newspapers. While for the most part Jagger's face offered a brave smile, it wasn't that difficult to note that behind his professional veneer he was quaking.

Leaving Lewes Prison, Faithfull, Cooper and Keylock made their way back along the coast to West Wittering. With another emotionally draining day ahead of them, the inhabitants of Redlands eventually retired to bed.

In all probability, Judge Leslie Block would have turned in somewhat earlier than those at Redlands. If he was concerned that his actions that day would soon come under intense scrutiny, he was reassured by the knowledge that, in his world, putting a member of The Rolling Stones behind bars constituted a damn good day's work.

CHAPTER 8

Chichester (Day 2)

"Oh who is that young sinner with the handcuffs on his wrists?
And what has he been after that they groan and shake their fists?
And wherefore is he wearing such a conscience-stricken air?
Oh they're taking him to prison for the colour of his hair."

From 'Oh Who Is That Young Sinner'
by Alfred Edward Housman, 1896

The soaring temperatures outside Lewes Prison mattered little to Jagger and Fraser as they tried to get some sleep on the rock-hard beds. Their newfound surroundings did not offer the luxury of newspapers over breakfast but the rest of Britain were invited to relive the pair's traumatic day in court, illustrated with dramatic pictures of Jagger being driven to jail. The notoriously right-wing *Daily Express* ran with one such image under the headline, 'Jagger Spends The Night In Cell'. The *Daily Mirror* would devote three-quarters of its front page to a picture of Mick vainly trying to raise a smile while handcuffed. Even *The Times*, its coverage of pop music normally minimal, devoted column space to Jagger's imprisonment.

The day began in the same way as any other prisoner on remand. There was a wake-up call well before 7 a.m. and a meagre breakfast before the drive back to Chichester to await sentencing. While on their transfer to Lewes the night before they had been handcuffed to separate guards, on the return trip to Chichester they were manacled to each other, presumably to avoid prison guards being photographed by the press.

The copious news coverage generated had evidently electrified the entirety of Chichester's youth. Whereas on the first day of the hearing there was only a modest crowd, the street outside the courtroom for the second day was heaving with people long before Jagger and Richards made their separate arrivals. Given the captive audience, vendors were quick to cash in on the impromptu circus that had hit town. Ice cream, hot dog and tea vans arrived to feed Stones supporters and one opportunist hawker set up a mobile silk-screen printing machine to roll out T-shirts adorned with legends such as 'Mick Is Innocent' and 'Free The Stones'.

Just before 10 a.m., the grey prison van containing Jagger and Fraser arrived at the rear of the building. The vehicle's clear windows were ill-equipped to deal with the penetrative lenses lying in wait. Predictably, a battery of flashlights caught the two raising their wrists to block the flash-guns' glare, in the process, displaying their handcuffs.

Safely behind the steel gates of the courthouse, Jagger and Fraser were led out of the van with the media on hand again to film and photograph them on their way to the court steps – images that found their way to Fleet Street and photo agencies worldwide. Presumably confident at just how much embarrassment the imposition of handcuffs would cause to the establishment, Jagger and Fraser put on a comical dance as they were led from the van. With the chains impeding their movements, even the prison warders found the episode a trifle amusing. The pair were led down to the cells to await the call for sentencing.

Somewhat less conspicuously, Richards had arrived at court before Jagger and Fraser. Recording events was Michael Cooper, whose pictures from that morning include Richards en route from West Wittering with Havers by his side in the back of the Bentley. Aware of being fully under the spotlight, Keith arrived at the rear of the court building wearing a black, four-button Regency-style suit trimmed with black braid and a white, high-necked shirt with black stitching around its edges.

In a repeat of the previous day, the public gallery was full of Stones fans, media representatives and members of the trio's entourage. Marianne somehow managed to escape the paparazzi on her arrival, and took her place in the gallery, chaperoned by Keylock, Cooper and Les Perrin.

As agreed, a new jury had been called, drawn again from Chichester locals, a lone female joining the 11 men. To open proceedings, Richards was called to the dock to affirm his "not guilty" plea. With that formality out of the way, a certain amount of deliberation ensued as to the naming of individuals present during the raid on Redlands, but who had not been charged with any offence. While only minimal details had emerged thus far, the circumstances surrounding Richards' charge necessitated a more thorough description of what occurred that fateful night.

Worryingly for Faithfull, with little other collaborative evidence to hand, it was obvious the prosecution would undoubtedly focus on her allegedly louche behaviour to successfully prove the charge, suggesting the reason for this was her being under the influence of cannabis. With her involvement paramount to the prosecution's case, both sides were in agreement that Faithfull's identity should not be revealed and, accordingly, she would be referred to as 'Miss X'. Nonetheless, Judge Block ruled that regardless of the anonymity, every detail of what occurred that night was admissible as evidence. To the media possessed with numerous titbits of information, there was absolutely no doubt as to the identity of 'Miss X'.

Prosecuting council Malcolm Morris started by reading out the fairly tedious details of the law concerning householders permitting cannabis to be smoked on their premises. With a slight digression to determine the variants of cannabis strains, Morris then led the jury back to events occurring on February 12, detailing the scene inside Redlands. He then listed the various receptacles containing traces of cannabis and the overwhelming smell of incense mixed with stronger aromas.

Morris: "One of the things which is an effect of smoking cannabis resin is that it produces a strong, sweet and unusual smell. It may be that you will come to the conclusion, or you may not, that incense was being burned in these premises; and as you will hear – and as you will no doubt guess – if Indian hemp is being smoked, incense might be burned in the hope of masking a distinct smell. That there was a strong sweet smell in these premises will be clear from the evidence, and you may well come to the conclusion that that smell could not fail to have been noticed by Keith Richards."

To give credibility to these assertions, Morris stated that according to experts, the effects of smoking cannabis could induce tranquillity and could dispel inhibitions. This lively description would feed directly into their belief that the deportment of the mysterious 'Miss X' was as a result of the drugs Richards was allegedly allowing to be smoked.

"It had exactly that effect on the young lady on the settee," stated Morris. "All she was wearing was a light-coloured fur skin rug, which from time to time, allowed the rug to fall, disclosing her nude body."

Aware that he could be accused of voyeuristically describing the sort of behaviour that might occur behind closed doors, the QC swiftly put what he'd said into context. "How people behave in their own home is usually no concern to anyone else," continued Morris. "The only significance of that young woman's behaviour is when the police arrived, she remained unperturbed and apparently enjoying the situation. Although she was taken upstairs where her clothes were to be searched, she returned downstairs afterwards still wearing only that fur rug, and in the words of the woman Detective Constable looking after her, 'in a merry mood and one apparently of vague unconcern'. We are not in any way concerned with who that young lady was or may have been, but was she someone who had lost her inhibitions? And had she lost them because she had been smoking Indian hemp? You may conclude that the reason why he [Richards] was not surprised at her behaviour was that cannabis resin was being smoked then and there on his premises."

Again Morris attempted to rationalise his argument by asking the jury to separate what he called "unusual behaviour" from any prejudice (or indeed sympathies) that they might have concerning Richards' celebrity standing. Nonetheless, Morris had successfully painted a vivid picture that would (certainly by 1967 standards) help to create an impression of squalid decadence in the jury's minds. In fact, given the media's perception of The Rolling Stones, the prosecution could actually afford to be measured in their delivery.

Finally, Morris referred to the presence of David Schneiderman.

Stopping short of naming the Canadian, all Morris would say was that there was an individual present at the party "who is not before the Court, and indeed was not now in the country". To embellish pictures of a drug-ridden orgy, Morris gave details of the gargantuan quantity of substances found on Schneiderman's person that night.

To help qualify the prosecution's case, various police officers were called to the witness stand. The first was Detective Inspector John Lynch of Scotland Yard's drug squad. While not mentioned in court, Lynch was the first recipient of the *News Of The World*'s tip-off regarding the Redlands party, and who had baulked on pursuing the information. Regardless of his reservations concerning the whole affair, his seniority and experience in the London drug squad carried considerable weight for the prosecution's arguments.

With Morris steering his every word, Lynch talked through the effects he believed that cannabis had on the user, and of its unique smell. When it came to distinguishing cannabis from incense, the Inspector would say the more noxious substance had a "strong pieric (acrid) aroma" to it. This revelation was different to the "sweet and unusual" smell officers had detected that evening. While it might have appeared a small technicality, it would later weigh heavily against the prosecution.

Havers then cross-examined the inspector. Having taken copious notes, he picked away at the prosecution's belief that the smell of incense was being used to mask cannabis aroma. Havers drew attention to inconsistencies in Lynch's assertions, specifically the contradiction concerning the aromas in the house on the night of the raid.

Havers: "When there is a strong, sweet smell, is it because of the incense?"

Lynch: "I would not agree wholeheartedly."

Havers: "But say when one walked into a room there was a strong, sweet smell, is that the opposite of cannabis?"

Lynch: "Yes, sir."

To counter the prosecution's suggestion that 'Miss X' was behaving salaciously, Havers quizzed Lynch about cannabis use provoking carnal instincts in its users.

Havers: "Would you agree that one of the effects of cannabis is that it is not an aphrodisiac?"

Lynch: "I believe so, sir."

Havers: "In fact it diminishes sexual appetite."

Lynch: "Yes, sir."

The prosecution then called Detective Sergeant Cudmore. As one of the principal policemen involved in the raid, he too was asked about invasive smells at Redlands. Aware that the behaviour of the house guests was paramount to the conviction of Richards, Cudmore homed in on the activities of 'Miss X' and her languid state. Not surprisingly, the issue of the girl and the fur rug became the centrepiece of his evidence.

Cudmore: "On the sofa in the room were two males and one female wearing a light coloured, fawn skin rug around her shoulders. From time to time one could see she was wearing nothing underneath. The lady went upstairs and returned. There were 10 police officers in the room and she still had only the skin rug on and nothing else."

The police and prosecution's implications about 'Miss X' left little doubt about what the following day's headlines would contain. Up in the gallery, every journalist knew by a process of elimination that the lady in question was Marianne Faithfull. In an attempt to mitigate the impression that 'Miss X' was a shameless exhibitionist Havers questioned Cudmore further on the issue.

Havers: "Was it a large rug?"

Cudmore: "Quite large."

Havers: "Was it bigger than a fur coat?"

Cudmore: "Yes."

Havers: "Yes, but it's a bed cover isn't it? Here, take a look."

With the help of one of his junior council, Geoffrey Leach, Havers produced the first piece of solid evidence for the defence's case, namely the large bed cover that had covered Faithfull that February night. With its patchwork of fur pelts on one side and fawn material on the reverse, even Havers' not inconsiderable frame was dwarfed by its size. "It's enormous," he continued, puncturing the sergeant's suggestion that it was barely large enough to cover a person. "You can see. It's about eight-and-a-half foot by five foot."

With further assistance from Leach, the rug was held up for the jury to inspect, its size speaking for itself. With that point won, Havers asked

Cudmore about Richards' behaviour that night. Cudmore admitted, as he had with Jagger, that Richards and everyone else at the gathering had co-operated fully and behaved in a thoroughly mature fashion. In danger of undermining his assertions, Cudmore added that he couldn't vouch for what may have been going on prior to the police's visit.

The questioning then turned to how the raid was initiated. With Cudmore having admitted at the magistrate stage that he'd received a tip-off from a "well-known national newspaper", Havers asked Cudmore about the mysterious David Schneiderman. As the main conduit between the *News Of The World* and the authorities, Cudmore revealed what no one else at that point had; that Schneiderman – despite a warrant for his arrest – had skipped the country on February 14, just two days after the raid. Cudmore stated that as far as he was aware, the Canadian was not connected to any Sunday newspaper.

As agreed, Schneiderman was not named in person, and Havers passed Cudmore a piece of paper (on which Schneiderman's name was written) asking for confirmation. When Cudmore responded in the affirmative, Havers then asked the bench why the Canadian – so pivotal in the chain of events – should retain his anonymity. Judge Block replied that for confusion's sake, he should be referred to as 'Mr X' especially as, according to Block, he'd "done a bunk". The judge tagged the crude aside with a slight chuckle, which prompted many to believe that perhaps Block knew more about Schneiderman than he cared to let on. Dismissing the compromise, Havers pressed that he be named publicly. After some debate Block gave way, allowing 'Mr X' to become 'David Henry Schneiderman' while acknowledging that he was also known as 'David Britton'. Having the Canadian named scored a minor advantage for the defence, although in reality that and the size of the rug would be the only victories that day.

Next to the stand was Detective Constable Rosemary Slade. Guided by the prosecution, she again made reference to Faithfull's behaviour, stating that she saw her deliberately let the rug fall in front of the police.

Police Sergeant John Challen followed. Aside from noting the butt ends he'd found in Richards' room, he too was prompted to recall the behaviour of 'Miss X'.

Challen: "She had her back to me. She was naked. I heard a man in the bedroom using the telephone laugh."

The prosecution was unrelenting, calling up DC Evelyn Fuller to recall her experiences. Charged with searching Faithfull that evening, she made further reference to her bearing, remarking: "Her behaviour generally was that she seemed unconcerned about what was going on around her."

With much of the morning having been spent debating the demeanour, both mentally and otherwise, of 'Miss X', the lunchtime adjournment was called. Jagger and Fraser were led down to the cells but Richards, his trial still in progress, was free to lunch with his legal team. This impromptu act caught fans by surprise, the majority unaware that Keith had left the courthouse by the rear.

To enliven their deflated spirits, Jagger and Fraser were permitted a hearty lunch while languishing in the cells. As arranged by their lawyers, the Globe Hotel, situated across the road from the court, prepared prawn cocktail, roast lamb with mint sauce and a dessert of fresh strawberries and cream, at 21 shillings and six pence for Jagger. Fraser had iced melon, salmon salad followed by fresh fruit and cream at 22 shillings and six pence. The pair washed their meal down with a half bottle of Beaujolais. Delivered by the landlord, a service charge was levied on the transfer from the hotel to the cells.

An hour later, and with everyone suitably replenished, the court resumed its deliberations. Having heard from such a comprehensive array of prosecution witnesses, Havers decided to lay the defence cards on the table, appealing to the jury on an emotional level. Aware that the media were hanging on every nuance of the trial, his words were intended to travel further than the four walls of the court.

Michael Havers: "It is one of the sad things about any case which attracts public attention – whether it is a murder, fraud action, civil or criminal, or as now, a case involving a well-known pop group… one of the unhappy accidents with the nature of the crime is that interest mounts and mounts, and in the end rumour overtakes reality and there is a risk that prejudice creeps in."

Cutting to the chase, he centred upon the role of the *News Of*

The World. Ignoring the cloak of anonymity afforded to parties involved but not charged, Havers publicly named the paper, sarcastically labelling it a "well-known guardian of public morals". Its name now out in the open, Havers elaborated on its complicit role in events.

"How did they know that a raid ought to take place?" asked Havers. "Because the evidence you will hear is that the house party did not start until about midnight on the Saturday... The house belongs to Keith Richards, who bought it a comparatively short time before. In passing, he had told some friends, 'Come down and see my new house.' He had forgotten all about this invitation until he was rung up on the Saturday by another of the party who said the party was on, and that X, Y and Z were coming... They gathered at Redlands at about midnight on the Saturday. Included in the party was a man called Schneiderman, a man virtually unknown to Keith Richards. They had met in New York the previous year. How he got there and who brought him down was something no one may know [sic]. But Schneiderman was there, with all the trappings and kit of someone interested in drugs."

The court was engrossed with this astonishing news. While the prosecution had done its best to defer attention from Schneiderman, Havers placed him at the centre of the action.

"Let me tell you the background," he continued. "On February 5, a week before [the raid] the newspaper published, not in relation to Mr. Richards, but to Mick Jagger, an article which was untrue, was a grave and disgusting libel. The consequence was that immediately, on behalf of Mr. Jagger, a writ was issued by his solicitor and served upon the *News Of The World*... In the remaining five days, this man [Jagger] was subjected to being followed and observed wherever he went and whatever he did. A van or car was constantly outside his flat. And within a week, this well-known national newspaper tips off the police to go to West Wittering, not just for anything, but for drugs. We know it was for drugs because the warrant was issued for drugs."

Havers squarely addressed the jury. "If a newspaper publishes a story and it is found to be untrue, how many thousands of pounds would a jury like you award? It may be coincidence because a national newspaper publishes this libel on Mick Jagger and a well-known newspaper tips off the police the following week. In that party was a man not known to The Rolling Stones as a group. He was a stranger at the party, a stranger conveniently from across the seas and loaded to the gunwales with cannabis. Schneiderman was the only man who was found with cannabis. He has gone out of England with a return ticket in his pocket?"

Havers then paused for a few seconds to allow his allegation of collusion between gutter press and police to be digested. He was aware that up in the gallery reporters from the *News Of The World* were listening intently to every word being said – and no doubt under instructions to report back to head office any reference to their involvement in the saga.

Havers next turned his attention to the charge itself; namely that Richards had willingly allowed cannabis to be smoked on his premises. With the evidence regarding the actual smell of cannabis in doubt, Havers turned his attention to 'Miss X', thoroughly deconstructing the prosecution's allegations about her.

Havers: "They (the police) know now that a strong, sweet smell was the opposite of the smell of cannabis. If the place was drowned in this smell and this girl was in a euphoric state, they would expect the people to be rushing around getting rid of the traces. But a policewoman looked through the window and she would have seen them because she had a grandstand view. But nothing of this sort happened. Was the girl's behaviour such that they could draw from the evidence that she had been smoking cannabis? Had any of them stopped to think whether this was fair to the girl? She was not on trial or able to make a defence. She was a girl who remained technically anonymous, but the consequence of this was that she is described as a drug taking nymphomaniac, with no chance of saying a word in her own defence or cross-examining anybody. Did they expect him to force the girl into the witness box? How would they feel if in another place they were accused and witnesses were going into the box and discussing their behaviour and they could do nothing about it? I am not going to allow this girl into the witness box. I am not going to tear that blanket of anonymity aside and let the world laugh or scorn as they will."

Havers' emotional tour de force brought the day's business to a close. While he had successfully managed to clarify events in a relevant fashion, his speech went on too long for the trial to be concluded that a This allowed Richards to maintain his liberty since sentencing would now be deferred to a third day, but Jagger and Fraser faced another night at Lewes Prison. Despite Havers' best attempts at protecting the integrity of his clients, the press knew they had a genuine scandal on their hands. Their ears ringing with tales of wayward pop stars, drugs and a young woman clad solely in a fur rug, reporters rushed to the nearest phones to file their copy.

When the court adjourned, Richards and Faithfull visited Jagger and Fraser in the cells where they'd spent the entire day. To help cushion a second night at Lewes Prison, Marianne brought along a bag of fresh fruit, 60 cigarettes and a draughts board. Fifteen minutes later Jagger and Fraser were led out and placed in a cream prison van. Exiting from the rear of the courthouse, the vehicle was met with an all too familiar phalanx of paparazzi cameramen and enraged fans.

Back at Redlands, with Faithfull and Cooper for company, Richards again took stock of his fate. While neither side had thought it necessary to bring Jagger or Fraser to the witness box, it had been agreed that Keith should give evidence, not solely for his own sake but as a spokesman for the defendants in an effort to retaliate against the various accusations they faced.

On BBC2 TV that evening was a programme called *The Ravers*, part of their respected *Man Alive* season of documentaries. Much like the gulf of attitudes on display in Chichester's courthouse, it attempted to penetrate the mindset of young people in Britain engaged in activities far removed from their elders' rigid expectations. Somewhat ironically, the show's pre-publicity reported that it was "an attempt to show people, and particularly parents, the dangers which their daughters can face when they pursue pop stars".

Back in London, the press were having a field day. While according to the protocol of the court Faithfull's name could not be revealed, the media were quick to identify her by association. The *Daily Mirror* placed a full-length picture of Faithfull on its front-page while referring to a "nude girl in a merry mood" elsewhere. The *Daily Express* employed the same tactic, their headline 'Nude Girl At Party' accompanied by a prominent picture of Marianne. Other sections of the popular press followed this example. While *The Times* eschewed any salacious inferences, its eminently respected law report was illustrated with a demure image of Faithfull outside the court.

The Times and other papers were delivered to Redlands the following morning. With the scandal gathering pace, members of the press, eager for marketable shots of Richards or Faithfull, were camped outside. Staking out the grounds, they struck gold when Marianne appeared carrying the previous night's edition of the *Evening News*. With its 'Naked Girl At Stones Party' banner headline on its front page, it was a plum shot that swiftly made its way into the papers.

Unaware of the presence of unwanted photographers, Keith and Marianne posed on the front lawn of Redlands for a series of photos taken by Cooper in which they held two national newspapers across their chests, the headlines screaming the 'Nude Girl' saga. With Richards cheekily pointing at Faithfull while holding a paper, he was alluding to a fact that no one had yet dared print.

In tandem with the revelations concerning 'Miss X', further shots of a handcuffed Jagger were published in the morning papers. It was all too evident that his slightly ironic grin captured the day before had metamorphosed into a look of depression. If to the more sympathetic of observers, handcuffing the delicate figure of Mick Jagger appeared overzealous, more outraged protestations from the highest seat of British authority were starting to surface.

The most vocal of these came from MP Tom Driberg. Appalled by the gross indignity inflicted on someone he liked to call a friend, Driberg directed a parliamentary question to Home Office minister Alice Bacon regarding the handcuffing issue. While not referencing either Jagger or Fraser, Driberg was clearly out to call into question one element of what was already a deeply controversial trial.

From the floor of the House of Commons Driberg said: "I ask my right honourable friend whether she agrees that if the police themselves say that there has been every co-operation from an accused person he should not be handcuffed, as has been known to happen in certain cases?"

Bacon was quick to read between the lines, and deferred making any comment other than to say that the responsibility of the action lay with the governor of the prison the guilty were being driven to.

The answer wasn't enough to satisfy either Driberg or wily veteran MP Quintin Hogg. A distinctly maverick member of the Conservative party, Hogg had already written to the Home Secretary regarding the handcuffing saga, and now challenged Bacon to offer a more comprehensive response.

"Is it not clear that the instructions need some kind of revision?" Hogg asked of Bacon. "Do not they include a provision to the effect that if one prisoner is handcuffed all the others in the same batch must be handcuffed too? Is not this much too severe and liable to lead to unnecessary humiliation?"

Bacon referred Hogg's question to the previous answer she gave Driberg, but a statement was subsequently issued to the press from the Home Office. While unable to reference the Jagger incident directly, it attempted to clarify matters. "When, as on Wednesday," read the statement, "a number of prisoners are travelling together in the same vehicle, and some of them – for security reasons – have to be handcuffed together, it is the practice for a number of reasons that they should be handcuffed."

This did little to stop the furore, and in many quarters there was disquiet at the primitive form of restraint used for individuals connected with non-violent charges. With Jagger and Fraser not yet sentenced for their offences, the more erudite of observers had focussed on a controversy fast becoming a talking point around the legal community. One London lawyer articulated the disquiet by saying: "It does seem excessively dramatic. This isn't the kind of case where one would normally have expected handcuffs to be necessary." A letter to *The Times* articulated it further, reading, "a picture of Mick Jagger handcuffed to a police warder as if he were a dangerous criminal makes him a heroic figure and arouses sympathy, particularly as he had 'conducted himself in an exemplary way throughout'. Those who have a rebellious spirit will be incensed and aroused. Those who seek publicity will see a quick way to obtain it."

The (then) editor of *The Times*, William Rees-Mogg, was also concerned by the distressing photographs of Jagger in handcuffs.

While not disposed to follow the fortunes in the ephemeral pop scene, Rees-Mogg had taken a keen interest in the way that Jagger and Richards were being treated. "I thought that was particularly inappropriate," he reflects. "Putting people in handcuffs and showing them to the public does two things: it humiliates them, which is offensive in itself, and it creates an impression of guilt. It's an abusive use of authority. But to use handcuffs in order to prejudice the case, which was what this amounted to, was to my mind quite wrong."

While the restraining issue was turning the protagonists of Redlands into heroic martyrs in some quarters, it inspired a few cheeky shop owners in London's Soho to advertise handcuffs for sale. Prominently displayed in one window was a sign reading: 'Be Faithfull With A Pair Of Jagger Links'.

These distractions aside and barring any extraordinary events, Friday, June 29 was clearly going to be the day when judgement was passed, and an enormous sense of anticipation focused on Chichester's red brick courthouse. Jagger and Fraser were already en route from Lewes when Richards set off for Chichester a little after 9 a.m. As later noted by the *Daily Mail*, he had swapped the ragged jeans and polo neck shirt he'd worn around Redlands earlier that morning for a fashionable black suit with lace braiding around the edges. To protect his drawn appearance from prying lenses, he wore dark sunglasses. In the car with him for the six-mile ride were Michael Cooper and Marianne Faithfull.

Marianne was dressed demurely in a black, double-breasted jacket, frilly shirt and slacks. To prevent intrusive lenses capturing her fragility, she wore an oversize pair of rectangular tinted sunglasses. Again the scenes outside the courthouse were frenzied. With the word fully out about this free show, hundreds of teenagers and curious onlookers were in place to greet the separate arrivals of the two Rolling Stones. Michael Cooper's lens captured a millisecond of this craziness as they approached. With police attempting to usher the car safely through the throng of rabid fans and media, Stones roadie Ian Stewart was pictured vainly attempting to ensure a safe passage for Keith's Bentley.

It was no less charged for Jagger and Fraser's arrival. With fans having by now realised that the rear of the building was where Mick was being deposited, a sea of teenagers met the Commer van on its approach. Once inside, he and Fraser were taken down to the cells to await sentencing. With Richards' case expected to run for most of the day, there was a fair amount of anxious waiting below.

Inside the courtroom, it was a re-enactment of the usual procedure, with fans taking over most of the gallery. As had become customary, press with appropriate accreditation had specially reserved seats.

Whereas the previous two days had opened with lengthy legal preliminaries, the action cut to the quick when Havers called Richards to take the stand, his otherworldly presence and gaunt profile causing a ripple of excitement to pass through the court. One observer in the gallery noted that "an almost inaudible shudder greeted the least prepossessing defendant, with his fancy Beau Brummell clothes and his pale, sickly, wolfish face".

Painting a portrait of a man constantly at the behest of the world, Havers led Richards back through his short but hugely eventful life. Starting with his art school years, the potted biography moved through Richards' eventful convergence with Jagger to The Rolling Stones' early career; a period that Richards described as "very haphazard". Quizzed by Havers on how success affected the group, Richards replied, "There was a complete lack of privacy from 1963 onwards and continual work for four years."

Keith told of the mania that followed the group's movements, and the gargantuan amount of travelling the Stones undertook to secure their global success. He recalled running the gauntlet of marauding fans at every appearance, many of them ripping the clothing from his person. The recollection that he'd "nearly been strangled twice" by overzealous supporters provoked a wave of laughter around the public gallery from those who'd clearly engaged in such mad adulation.

Havers: "Do you need any sort of protection against fans?"

Richards: "Oh yes. We need an army."

The discussion moved to the rare moments of relaxation the group experienced, and the need to escape from the unrelenting demands of the music industry. With this in mind, Havers took Richards through events immediately prior to the raid, recalling in vivid detail the warm friendship that abounded in and around Redlands. Despite the shadowy figure of Schneiderman hovering in the background, Keith described a pastoral Sunday in the West Sussex countryside shared among a small coterie of close friends. When asked for his impression of the large troupe of police that appeared on his doorstep, Richards responded that his first impression was that they were fans.

Havers then asked Richards if the incense at Redlands that night was burned to mask the smell of drugs being smoked, to which he replied emphatically, "No sir." To qualify this, Keith explained that fans sent him joss sticks and other powders, and he liked to burn raw incense around the house. Visitors, too, liked to sprinkle the fragrant powder over the grate of his fireplace. He claimed that the Chinese joss sticks seized that night were brought to the house by Schneiderman. Despite all that had been said, Keith stated there was no intention of using them to cover up the smell of cannabis.

Turning to the physical evidence found in the house, Havers selected a briar pipe and bowl, one of the items proven to contain traces of cannabis. Displaying it to the court, Havers asked his client where it came from.

Richards: "That came from Los Angeles. It was given to me."

Havers: "By whom?"

Richards: "An American, a group's road manager."

Havers: "On trips such as those, I imagine you'd acquire a mountain of such items."

Richards: "Yes – always. When I get back to England, my suitcases are full up with rubbish."

Havers next steered Richards to the main gist of the prosecution's assertion: that the languid demeanour of 'Miss X' was as a result of the drugs she'd allegedly imbibed that night. Paying particular reference to the fur rug incident, Keith explained that she'd become dirty following a day's romping in the countryside and had run a bath. Without a fresh change of clothes, she'd utilised what was in effect a fur bedspread as a makeshift gown.

Havers: "Did she let fall the rug?"

Richards: "Absolutely not."

At this point Havers stood down to allow prosecution council to cross-examine. Having deconstructed Jagger's defence the previous day, Malcolm Morris was unlikely to be unsettled by Richards' impassive demeanour on the witness stand.

Predictably, Morris started by raking over the defence's sensational claims concerning the *News Of The World*. With one eye cocked towards Richards, he haughtily reviewed Havers' assertions, stating that he'd been "muddying the clear waters of the argument."

Morris: "He [Havers] spoke about various things, and in the course of that opening speech made it quite clear that your defence was that Schneiderman had been planted in your weekend party as part of a wicked conspiracy by the *News Of The World*. Is that part of the defence or not?"

Richards: "Yes it is, sir."

Morris: "Is your defence that Schneiderman was planted by the *News Of The World* in an attempt to get Mick Jagger convicted of smoking hashish? Is that the suggestion?"

Richards: "That is the suggestion."

Morris: "What you are saying is that because the *News Of The World* did not want to pay libel damages to Mick Jagger, which they might have to do if what they had printed about him was untrue, they had planted or arranged to have planted Indian hemp in your house?"

Richards: "Yes, sir."

Morris: "This misfired and the only result of that criminal conspiracy is that you are in the dock."

Richards: "Yes, sir."

Morris: "Are you quite clear of what you are saying?"

Richards: "Yes."

Morris then asked Richards about his relationship with his fellow house guests on the night of the raid. While Jagger, Faithfull, Gibbs, Cooper and Fraser were all close friends, Richards stated that the others were more of a party crowd, taking advantage of the relaxed door policy he maintained. One of these was 'flower child' Nicky Kramer. The other was Schneiderman.

Richards: "I can only say that in my profession there are people who are hangers on who you have to tolerate. On this occasion, there were two or three people I did not know particularly well, but did know well enough to allow them to come down."

Morris: "Can you say anything about these hangers on?"

Richards: "Two were hangers on, one of them Schneiderman."

Morris: "How did Schneiderman come to the party?"

Richards: "He knew one of the other friends. As far as I can gather, he knew a party was going on and he asked if it would be all right to go along. I had seen Schneiderman over a year ago in New York, and once since in a club in London the previous week."

Morris: "From what was found on him, it was clear he smoked Indian hemp."

Richards: "Most definitely."

Spying a weakness that could easily lead Richards into a further admission, Morris pressed on.

Morris: "Did you know that then?"

Richards: "Not at that time, sir."

To clarify his position, Richards told the court that to his knowledge, he wasn't aware that any of his friends smoked cannabis. Schneiderman, however, was an altogether unknown quantity. When Richards mentioned Schneiderman's early retreat from the beach on the Sunday morning, Morris decided to run with the assumption that the Canadian might have had other reasons for getting back to Redlands earlier.

Morris: "It would have been possible for Schneiderman to plant Indian hemp if he so wanted."

Richards: "Yes."

Morris: "In particular, if he had been injected into your weekend party for the purpose of incriminating Mr. Jagger, he could have put anything in Mr. Jagger's clothing or anything else?"

Richards: "Yes."

Morris: "Nothing was found in Mr. Jagger's clothing." (By this Morris was evidently referring to cannabis and not the amphetamines found in Jagger's coat.)

Richards: "No, sir."

Sensing a contradiction, Morris dug in quickly to puncture Richards' assertions.

Morris: "So if you are seriously suggesting that this was part of a plot, it is a curious plot in that nothing in fact was done to associate Mr. Jagger with Indian hemp."

Richards: "He was associated with the whole raid, which is enough I'm sure."

Morris then briefly diverted away from this line of questioning, and decided to concentrate his efforts on 'Miss X'.

Morris: "There was, as we know, a young woman sitting on a settee wearing only a rug. Would you agree, in the ordinary course of events, you would expect a young woman to be embarrassed if she had nothing on but a rug in the presence of eight men, two of whom were hangers-on, and the third a Moroccan servant?"

Richards: "Not at all. She doesn't embarrass easily, nor do I."

Morris: "You regard that do you, as quite normal?"

Richards: "We are not old men. We are not worried about petty morals."

With Keith's barb hitting its target, Morris took a step back to signify a sense of indignation. To those of Morris' ilk, that response was indicative of The Rolling Stones' anarchic, insolent image. Allowing a few seconds of silence to ramp up the drama, Morris then refocused on 'Miss X''s behaviour.

Morris: "After she'd gone upstairs with a woman police officer, did it not come as a great surprise to you that she was prepared to go back downstairs into the drawing room still wearing only a rug in front of a dozen [sic] police officers?"

Richards: "I thought the rug was big enough to cover three women. There was nothing improper in the way that she was wearing it."

Morris: "I wasn't talking about impropriety but embarrassment. You do not think it was because she had been smoking Indian hemp and had got rid of her inhibitions and embarrassment?"

Richards: "No, sir."

Morris: "You were all just sitting around the drawing room doing nothing in particular."

Richards: "Yes, sir."

Morris: "Was anyone smoking hashish or hemp?"

Richards: "Not to my knowledge."

Morris: "Would you have objected to anyone smoking Indian hemp?"

Richards: "Yes, because I knew that if the police came I would be standing here – and I am."

With that resounding reply, Morris drew the current phase of questioning to a close. While the prosecutor had attempted to paint a sordid picture of life inside Redlands as permitted by the householder, Richards had presented himself in an assured manner, offering a believable account of what transpired and deferring suspicion that he knew drugs were being consumed at Redlands that night.

Havers now had an opportunity to re-examine Richards. With the *News Of The World* revealed as the chief villain of the piece, Havers asked Richards to substantiate the allegations of covert surveillance. With startling candour, Keith told the court that the day following the libellous *NOTW* feature he'd seen a van outside his London flat. Later, he noticed the same vehicle outside Mick and Marianne's apartment in central London. He added that he'd seen another van following him around town later that week.

With the interrogation of Richards from both sides exhausted and with no other witnesses left to call, all that remained was for the opposing barristers to make their final addresses to the jury. Morris was quick to attack the defence's assertion that the *News Of The World* had been instrumental in events surrounding the raid and turned to Schneiderman's alleged involvement. If, as had been suggested, the Canadian was planted by the newspaper, why was it, Morris asked the jury, that "all the incriminating evidence was on him and not on Jagger?"

Morris concluded by referring again to 'Miss X'. Having employed her ambivalent state that night as a key element in Richards's prosecution, he reiterated her alleged behaviour on the night in a final attempt to sway the jury. "The jury may also find it strange that this woman at the party returned to the room filled with police wearing only a rug when her clothes were available to her... It has been said that she could not defend herself, but it would be wrong that the jury should be deprived of hearing relevant evidence against Richards."

Morris concluded with a defence of the *News Of The World* which had been freely referenced in court as an *agent provocateur* of events, a scenario he felt was iniquitous. Sensing the conspiracy angle had been drawn to distract attention from Richards' charge, Morris declared that all the evidence pointed towards the fact that drugs were being used that night.

It was left to Havers to begin his final submission to the jury. An acutely intelligent man, he realised that his address on Richards' behalf would carry with it the fortunes of Jagger, and to a lesser extent Fraser. Despite Judge Block's evident sympathies with the prosecution, there was a chance that at least one of the magistrates sitting alongside him might find it in their heart to argue against a custodial sentence.

Havers poured scorn on the prosecution's attempts to blow out of proportion the charge against Richards. Similarly, while Schneiderman had been caught and charged with cannabis possession, Havers asserted that there was no other evidence to suggest that anyone else had smoked drugs that same evening. While he conceded that Schneiderman might have attempted to pass the drug around, that in itself did not suggest that anyone had followed his lead. Repeating the police's admission that those inside Redlands behaved in a "thoroughly adult manner", the prosecution's assertion of 'Miss X's' languid condition was in conflict with the evidence. In relation to the prosecution's attempt to defend the *News Of The World*, Havers mentioned that if the police were that confident there was no collusion, then it would have been in order to ask the officer who received the tip-off, Sergeant Cudmore, to return to the stand and publicly refute that it was the paper that supplied the authorities with the information.

With that, both sides rested their arguments, allowing for the perfunctory lunch break. Jagger and Fraser once again had their lunch brought to them in the cells, while Keylock drove Richards to a country hotel for some tranquil sustenance before the all important verdict and sentencing were read out.

While the court's ruling of anonymity had to be respected in print, elsewhere the racier details concerning the alleged antics of 'Miss X' were already fevered currency around Fleet Street pubs. Given journalists' imaginative minds, Marianne Faithfull's antics on the night of the raid began to assume a sleazy momentum all of its own. Specifically, the image of Faithfull relaxing on the sofa clad only in a rug had transmogrified into Jagger performing a sex act on her. Evidently, the squalid details of this totally fabricated story came from someone with a vested interest in the Stones' downfall.

Whether intended or not, the prosecution's thinly veiled references to Marianne's scantily clad state viciously fanned the flames of a fiction that police caught Jagger eating a Mars Bar out of Marianne Faithfull's vagina when they entered Redlands. Transported on a bush network with frightening rapidity, this totally unfounded allegation became salacious currency for the sexually dispossessed, energising the worst elements in the self-conscious emotions of sexually repressed Britain.

In breaking down this lie, it is necessary to look at the cold facts. Given that the police recorded the minutiae of Redlands down to book titles and clothing, they would obviously have recorded this if, indeed, the act had taken place. With Richards' prosecution heavily reliant on the behaviour of those present to support the charge, it would clearly have been utilised in court by the prosecution to bolster the evidence (which was tenuous at best). PC John Rodway was close to all the personnel on the raid. He makes it abundantly clear that if indeed the Mars Bar scenario had an element of truth to it, the details would have been added to the written evidence that night. Furthermore, without a shadow of doubt, it would have become widespread police banter throughout the county.

"It was news to all of the detectives," recalls Rodway. "These weren't young policemen, these were police officers with a considerable amount of service. If they'd seen Marianne Faithfull with a Mars Bar, they would have documented that, and if they'd taken cameras with them (which they didn't) they would have taken pictures of it."

Uniformly, the police witness statements all testify that no such act ever took place that night. While never substantiated where the rumour started, it can only be assumed that a section of the media invented this myth out of thin air as some form of retaliation aimed at restoring their sullied reputation or, at the very least, to somehow avenge themselves.

At 2 p.m., the court reconvened to tie up Richards' trial and to deliver sentencing on all three accused. After a short period of deliberation, Judge

Block offered up his summation. As he'd done with Jagger, Block advised the jury to ignore any prejudice that they might have concerning the musician's fashion sense, or indeed, the defendant's outspoken reference to "petty morals". Stating the obvious, Block concurred on Richards' celebrity and also the enormous amount of publicity that the trial had generated. In an effort to appear impartial, he urged the jury to put out of its mind everything that they had read or heard in press reports concerning the other two cases (in itself, largely impossible).

Referring to the words of Dick Taverne MP who'd queried the massive pre-trial publicity on the case, Block attempted to charm the jurors, many of them cut from the same stock as his rural connections. "That gentleman," said Block of Taverne, "did not know the quality of a Sussex jury such as you are here now." This patronising gesture delivered, Block then dealt with the nub of the prosecution's argument. "The issue you have to try is a comparatively simple one," he said. "You have to be satisfied that cannabis resin was being smoked in the house when the police went there. And you have to be satisfied that Richards knew of it."

At 2:25 p.m., the members of the jury made their way to the small anteroom on the left of the court to make their decision. Just over an hour later, they informed the bench that they'd come to a decision. They were then ushered back in to formally read out the verdict.

On the count of allowing his house to be used for the smoking of cannabis resin, Keith Richards was found guilty.

With cries of disbelief audible from the gallery, a short recess was taken while the three lay magistrates determined sentence commensurate with the crimes. Crucially, their decision would be steered by Judge Block.

Their fate about to be read out, Jagger and Fraser were brought up from the cells to join Richards in the dock. The sight of Mick, Keith and Robert Fraser provoked a variety of emotions for Faithfull. "I will never forget those court appearances," she recalled to the BBC in 2004. "Having to watch them in court and realising the danger they were in, it was terrible. I will never forget how beautifully they dressed. It was absolutely wonderful the way they used that court case for their clothes."

Permitted a final plea to the bench before sentencing, Havers reiterated that variants of the drugs found on Jagger were freely prescribed in the UK.

With over 150 million tablets prescribed, Havers said that they couldn't really be classified as dangerous in any way.This, he said, was backed up by Jagger's physician. Furthermore, Jagger had endured three days of misery and "shockingly adverse publicity". Referring to photographs showing him in handcuffs, Havers queried whether someone not possessed of Jagger's celebrity would be treated in this punitive fashion. With overseas work paramount for such an internationally famous musician, Havers called for a measure of compassion to be shown.

Turning his attention to Richards, Havers said that there was no evidence to suggest that "wholesale cannabis smoking" was occurring at Redlands. Additionally, Havers pointed out that the Act employed to convict Richards was intended for the prosecution of organised drug-taking establishments operating solely for profit, something that evidently wasn't occurring at Redlands. Finally, Havers offered his own character summation. "He is a likable young man, who goes his own way... This young man of 23 has got to the age where all the temptations and emergencies thrust upon him by all the extraordinary lifestyle he has led over the past four years are so much greater than those the ordinary boy faces."

With that Havers rested his mitigation arguments, leaving the final act of the drama to be enacted by those on the bench. Judge Block was no doubt wary of the ramifications that could result from what had occurred over the last few days and, with the global spotlight allowing legal observers to eavesdrop on events, he knew that any slip would be seized upon by critics. Nonetheless, the law permitted the bench, under his advisement, to legitimately impose lengthy prison sentences. If, indeed, Block chose to employ the full weight of the law, Fraser could be imprisoned for seven years, Jagger for two years and Richards for a substantial 10 years.

While the jury in Richards' case had taken their time in reaching a verdict, it took only a few minutes of deliberation for Block and his colleagues to arrive at the sentences for the three defendants. With the sorry triumvirate of Jagger, Richards and Fraser standing as one in the dock, their charges were read out again before sentencing could take place. As protocol dictated, it was be delivered by the man who'd assumed the mantle of the establishment. Standing before him were characters with whom he felt little kinship, and whose reputation he'd attempted to trample underfoot. At the age of 61, and representing a generation that felt betrayed by the brazen, lawless antics of figures like The Rolling Stones, Judge Block could now roll out a judgement that was commensurate with the resentment felt against them from his quarter.

The time now was just past 3:45 p.m. A hush descended on the courtroom, lawyers on both sides of the legal fence resting their enormous library of paperwork and looking up at the bench. Outside, over 600 fans and curious onlookers had gathered to await the verdict. There was an ominous quiet in the room as Judge Block read out the first of the sentences.

"Keith Richards, the offence for which you have very properly been convicted carries a maximum sentence, imposed by Parliament, of up to ten years... That is a view of the seriousness of the offence... You will go to jail for one year. You will also pay £500 towards the cost of the prosecution. Go down."

There were immediate cries of 'No! No!' and gasps of shock from fans in the public gallery. A flurry of murmuring broke out between reporters and other interested parties. Richards, it was observed, did nothing. He simply stared blankly at the bench. Judge Block called for silence.

"Robert Hugh Fraser, you have pleaded guilty to possessing a highly dangerous and harmful drug. You will go to prison for six months. You will also pay £200 towards the costs of the prosecution. Go down."

On hearing this, Fraser noisily expended a large amount of air from his cheeks, and then clicked the heels of his black patent shoes together. With his celebrity restricted to London's art world, there were no cries or screams from the gallery.

With two of the Redlands Three sentenced to jail terms, any immediate hopes for Jagger's freedom appeared slim. While Keith's sentencing appeared grossly severe, the most pertinent question on everyone's lips was whether his fellow Stone would meet a similar fate, his greater popularity causing a pregnant hush to fall as Judge Block prepared to read out the sentence.

"Michael Phillip Jagger," he began ominously. "You have been found guilty of possessing a potentially dangerous and harmful drug. You will go to prison for three months. You will pay £200 towards the costs of the prosecution. Go down."

As the words left Judge Block's mouth, Jagger put his hand to his face and began to sway. With warders signalling that the trio should walk down to the cells, Richards momentarily clasped the wooden rail in front of him and glared over at the bench. During their descent, the public gallery erupted in a cacophony of screams, shouts and expressions of outrage. Jagger was evidently the most broken of the three and as he was taken away by a warder, he glanced up towards the gallery at a grieving Marianne Faithfull. In the few seconds allotted, the pair exchanged a sullen glance, and even from her remote vantage point she could see that he was crying. He turned and looked down the 12 stone steps leading to the cells, put his hands up to his face and staggered forward.

"I just went dead," Jagger would later recall. "It was just like a James Cagney film, except everything went black."

The *Daily Telegraph*, not then known for expending emotional hyperbole on pop stars, was fairly poetic in its coverage of the moment Jagger was convicted.

"Jagger almost broke down and put his head in his hands as he was sentenced," wrote their correspondent. "He stumbled out of the dock almost in tears."

The public gallery was in chaos. Two young girls clung to each other, weeping. Looking down at the broken figure of Jagger being led to the cells, one of them cried out, "They're only jailing him because he has long hair."

CHAPTER 9

Jail

"Calm down police. Calm down Sunday Papers. Calm down outraged magistrates. The laws will change and we'll all die soon and we will win – why not get things in perspective? We are not a threat to government or the law and order-we just don't want our people hurt."

Leaflet distributed at demonstrations against the *News Of The World*, June and July 1967

After the sentences were passed, the uproar in the court continued unabated. Such was the anger on display Judge Block ordered the gallery to be cleared. Court ushers and police steered fans downstairs out of the building. Elsewhere, those journalists present in the public gallery rushed to use the courtroom's two phone boxes. With schools now closed for the day, the numbers outside swelled to over 600, almost all of them incredulous at what had taken place. As the news spread, press and onlookers congregated around the court's rear entrance. Others ran across the road to the nearest pubs and hotels to deliver the verdict to expectant newsrooms in London.

Steve Abrams was a leading figure in the fight to decriminalise cannabis and, at that time, a contributor to the underground journal *International Times*. With seemingly the entire counterculture energised by the ongoing saga, Abrams had travelled to Chichester to report on the verdicts. Unsurprisingly *IT* had been unable to secure the necessary press credentials for Abrams to gain access to the court, and he found himself standing outside with Michael Cooper.

"When the verdicts were delivered," Abrams recalls, "we were standing across the road from the courthouse where the police had told everyone to gather. I clearly remember this electrifying moment when the large wooden door to the courthouse flew open and a young girl ran out screaming and in tears. A few minutes later, everyone knew what had happened."

The stampede from the public gallery left Marianne Faithfull dazed and unable to focus on what the immediate future held for her boyfriend, as she began a slow walk down the stone steps towards the cells accompanied by Cooper. Like the defence team, she had truly believed that even though found guilty, both Mick and Keith would be spared a custodial sentence. She and Mick held each other, sobbing.

A few minutes were allotted to Michael Havers and his defence team to confer with their clients. The two Stones were informed that appeal requests were to be promptly filed in London's High Court the following morning. While of little consequence, defence lawyers were able to predict that with remission, both Jagger and Richards' sentences could be reduced; in Mick's case by a month and Keith's by four months. Nonetheless, the focus was on the appeal hearing with the hope that bail would be instated.

The respective prisons to which they would be sent would be determined on the basis of available spaces. While not procedural, there was a suspicion Jagger and Richards would be split up. It was of little surprise then when news came down to the cells that while Richards and Fraser would be sent to Wormwood Scrubs in London's Shepherd's Bush, Jagger would be sent to the other side of London, to Brixton Prison.

Half an hour after the sentences were announced, a call went out that transport was ready to ferry the three to prison. Since fans blocked the rear entrance, many shouting 'Shame' and 'Let them go!' while those more adventurous attempted to climb over the steel gate to reach their fallen idols, it was decided the trio would leave from the front door of the court. While a decoy Land Rover left from the rear, Jagger, handcuffed to a prison warder, and Richards and Fraser manacled together made their way down the court's front steps, across the pavement and into a waiting police car that took them a few miles outside Chichester where a more conventional prison van awaited them. Inside were an unusually large team of seven warders to accompany Jagger, Richards and Fraser to their respective prisons, 40 odd miles away in London.

As they were driven away, Marianne wandered slowly from the court towards the Ship Hotel, followed by jostling cameramen, Les Perrin vainly trying to shield her from the intrusion. Like a wounded sparrow, her fragile innocence robbed by the ungallant machinations of the establishment, she allowed Cooper to take a few photos of her in the hotel lobby.

Eventually Faithfull was driven back to an empty Redlands before heading for London, as the inordinate amount of interest that had been directed towards her as the mysterious 'Miss X' escalated. As more salacious details arrived at the country's news desks, many of them fabricated, this "worst kept secret in Britain" began to assume a life of its own. By now, others within the Stones' inner circle had heard about the court's decision. Allen Klein, still wrapped up in business in New York, caught the first plane over to London.

At around 8 p.m. Jagger was dropped off at Brixton Prison, whereupon Richards and Fraser were driven the nine miles to Wormwood Scrubs in west London. Both custodial institutions were, in 1967, hugely typical of the British prison system; purpose-built Dickensian jails that served their purpose in an era when prison welfare was largely unheard of. Wormwood Scrubs was as horrendous as its name suggested. Built in 1874, the Gothic inspired building housed some of Britain's most notorious criminals behind its oak doors. Later described by its then governor as nothing more than a "penal dustbin", for those trapped inside there was nothing other than the thought of release to think about. Richards and Fraser's sentencing allowed for no special consideration, meaning the pair were expected to slot into the general prison population of around 1,300 convicts.

Having enjoyed some of the world's most extravagant hospitality, Keith was appalled at what he found on arrival. He and Fraser were processed by an administrator; Fraser allotted the prison number 7854, Richards 7855. Their tailored suits were removed, parcelled up and stored away and in their place they were given a set of denim fatigues and a pair of regulation shoes. They were then photographed in a room that Richards later described as resembling "an execution chamber". This whole procedure was clearly intended to dehumanise, and as Keith would later attest, it made him feel like a "minute turd". Presumably aware of the sensitivity surrounding these important prisoners, authorities decided not to subject Richards, Fraser or Jagger to any delousing or body cavity searches.

Following the entrance formalities, Richards and Fraser were led to their cells. As is customary for new arrivals, they were given a pencil and paper, standard prison stationary ruled with an HMS crest on the top. Both composed heartfelt messages to their presumably worried families, informing them that everything was being done for them on the outside to secure their release. Anita Pallenberg, away filming in Italy, was sent a telegram containing similar words of reassurance from Keith.

With transistor radios one of the few luxuries allowed inside jail, news of Richards' imprisonment had spread like wildfire around Wormwood Scrubs. As expected, a loud roar of support rang out around its dank walls as Keith was led to his cell. Walking through the depressing corridors, many inmates shouted words of encouragement; others attempted to pass him rolled-up cigarettes. "Don't worry," Keith said to one jailbird who offered his commiserations. "I ain't going to be here long." With that and other quips exchanged, the Stone was placed in his cell. Richards' celebrity was such that prisoners en route to their various ports of call would drop bits of tobacco and rolling papers through the bars to his door.

A welcome visitor to Keith's cell that night was John Hopkins. Popularly known as 'Hoppy', he was a co-founder of the underground paper *International Times* and an influential figure in London's counterculture. Hopkins had been sentenced to nine months' imprisonment on June 1, 1967 in similar circumstances to Richards. While eulogising in court about cannabis use, Hopkins' judge, Mr Gordon Friend, imposed a wholly exemplary sentence, declaring, "I have just heard what your views are on the possession of cannabis and the smoking of it. This is not a matter I can overlook. You are a pest to society."

Whether the two incarcerated Stones knew it or not, the sense of outrage manifested at Chichester had by now swiftly transferred across Britain. With reporters and distressed fans jamming prison switchboards to extract details on the condition of the famous duo, operators at both Brixton and Wormwood Scrubs were forced by protocol to pass on all such requests to the Home Office. It was rumoured that Mick and Keith would have to have their hair shorn to a prison regulation length but a Home Office official denied this, saying: "The crew cut is not compulsory. This is not an inhumane machine, you know."

While Richards' steely resolve was in keeping with his resilient character, Jagger's sensitivity meant that life in Brixton was going to be an altogether horrendous experience. Like Richards and Fraser, he underwent the stiff processing formalities before being led to his cell and given pencil and paper. Among a few emotional letters, Jagger managed to write down some lyrics from his prison bed. These words would later inform some of the Stones' tracks, notably '2,000 Light Years From Home' and 'We Love You', a work in progress influenced by the mad pantomime of the ongoing saga.

By the close of the day the media was full of the day's events in Chichester. Both of London's evening newspapers, the *Evening News* and *Standard*, gave voluminous space to the sentencing on their front pages. To offer some immediacy to the story, the *Evening Standard* commissioned a swift vox pop to gauge public reaction. Asked the question, "Did the Rolling Stones get their just deserts?" a slim majority agreed with the sentences of incarceration, while others objected to their severity. One telling fact from the survey was how those who believed the sentence was appropriate were aged over thirty.

Other, less regulated media outlets offered up support in whichever way they could. Offshore 'Pirate' radio stations began giving Rolling Stones records heavy rotation. Similarly cast as social pariahs, these illicit broadcasters had much in common with Mick and Keith's victimisation and would soon be shut down under the Marine Offences Act. Beyond Britain, news of the arrests was prompting many ex-pat sympathisers to picket their nearest embassies to register their disgust.

In London, many who felt a kinship with the Stones began to consider a course of action. Propelled by what they saw as an attack on their culture, fans and activists were unified as never before and, although it was the middle of the so-called 'Summer of Love', there was a hard core of left-inclined militants based in London who weren't averse to utilising direct action.

Proactive attitudes overriding idealism, a snap decision was made to march on the *News of the World*'s offices at 30 Bouverie Street, just off Fleet Street in the heart of London's newspaper land. Mick Farren, a prime activist at the head of the task force and singer with the garage band The Deviants, was switched on well beyond the flaky dreams of the hallucination generation. Already a respected contributor to *International Times,* Farren and some of his cohorts collected as many protesters as possible on the night of the sentencing.

Mick Farren: "For the next three hours we called people solidly telling them to show up at midnight in Fleet Street, and call others to tell them about it. At about a quarter to twelve we arrived at the *News of the World* to find that about fifty freaks had shown up. It was disappointing, but it didn't last. From then on hippies began to show up in droves. By 12:30 a.m. the narrow streets around the newspaper building were thronged with a weird assortment of people. Hippies came with drums and flutes, political heavies in leather jackets. Superstars drove around the building in limousines. A rock band's equipment manager blocked the street with his truck."

The advancing crowd, now numbering several thousand, was met by an unprepared squad of just seven policemen. The narrow streets that ran around the *News of the World*'s headquarters were soon blocked by a sit-in and the large amount of protesters ensured that little police action could be taken. While this largely peaceful demonstration was taking place, the nearby dailies were putting to bed the following morning's first editions. Predictably, with the summer bereft of any hard news, Jagger and Richards' jail sentences handed them a golden egg. The *Daily Mirror* devoted four pages of its June 30 edition to the jailing with the headline 'Can The Stones Survive A Spell In The Wilderness?' The *Express* also devoted its front page to the case, spelling out in banner type, 'Stones Go To Jail' with a feature that ran over two pages inside. In addition to the Stones' drama in London, papers had another – more distressing – entertainment story to fill their pages: the death of actress/singer Jayne Mansfield in a motor accident in Mississippi.

In 1967, as now, the *Daily Mail* articulated the voice of Middle England and, in addition to a predictable news story on Jagger and Richards' imprisonment, ran a hugely idiosyncratic feature written by Monica Furlong. With most papers deferring judgement, Furlong's piece: 'The Shallow Idols of Society and the Smell of Decadence,' took pot-shots at numerous targets, drawing a wider metaphor than the characters involved in the saga played out in a Chichester courtroom.

"What is the whole Mick Jagger case about?" asked Furlong. "It is not easy to thread one's way past the drug-taking, the naked girl, the home life of pop stars and models and the long hair, to something more solid underneath... Inevitably reactions to this case reveal horror that people in the public eye can set such an example to their admiring young fans... Some forms of protest, no doubt, are healthy. [They] help to produce a useful tension against the rigid traditions of society. But in others, as I believe in this case, there is the smell of decadence, which is to say the absence of real ideas and real joy."

In the more heavyweight journals, events were more soberly reported, the *Daily Telegraph* and *Guardian* offering little other than facts. *The Times* also gave front-page column space over to the trial, reporting 'Gaol Sentences on 2 Rolling Stones.'

With more demonstrations against the *News Of The World* planned, other events were mooted to highlight the injustice of the sentences. One was a gigantic concert in support of the pair at London's Hyde Park. Another idea, much in the spirit of the times, was a plan to buy Judge Block a large bouquet of flowers with some of the proceeds from the benefit concert. The more irreverent activists even suggested enclosing a note reading: "With forgiveness".

Sympathy was extended from the group's peers. The Who, a band that had articulated the thoughts of disenchanted youth in 'My Generation', were the first to act. As well as The Rolling Stones being his favourite group, Pete Townshend had good reason to empathise with Mick and Keith's situation as he'd been named in the same *NOTW* drugs exposé. The night Jagger was found guilty and remanded in custody (28 June), The Who had gone into De Lane Lea studios in Holborn, *sans* John Entwistle (who was on his honeymoon) and in a quick session, recorded two Jagger-Richards compositions, 'Under My Thumb' and 'The Last Time'. With speed of the essence and, it has to be said a keen eye on the resultant publicity, their co-manager Kit Lambert took out an advert in the London *Evening Standard*. Too late to meet the final evening edition of June 30, it nonetheless appeared in the paper the following afternoon.

The text read: "Special Announcement: The Who consider Mick Jagger and Keith Richards have been treated as scapegoats for the drug problem and as a protest against the savage sentence imposed on them at Chichester yesterday, The Who are issuing today the first in a series of Jagger-Richards' songs to keep their work before the public until they are again free to record themselves."

Similar support was shown by teen prefabricated group, The Monkees – in town for three largely hysterical concerts at London's Wembley Empire Pool, Peter Tork and Michael Nesmith wore black armbands to tacitly display their support. Nesmith, the most thoughtful of the group, was asked for his views on the pair's sentencing, and was typically erudite in his response: "The encounter with the law of Mick Jagger and Keith Richards will do for the psychedelic scene what Joan of Arc did for Christianity."

Ironically, the night of Jagger and Richards' transference to jail The Monkees were lodging at the Royal Garden Hotel in Kensington, where a fellow guest was Brian Jones. Paranoid by what had occurred to Mick and Keith, he'd opted to flit between various London hotels lest the drug squad hound him in the hope of repetition of what had happened at Chichester.

With the likelihood of Stones supporters up and down the country engaging in their own acts of solidarity, the 10,000 paid-up members of the Rolling Stones Fan Club were contacted and urged not to take part in any of the demonstrations. While many were eager to mobilise themselves into action, a full-scale campaign could easily have had a reverse effect on both public and legal opinion. It was clear to Jagger and Richards' defence that those who sat on the appeal bench were cut from the same cloth as those who'd judged them in Chichester, and overt public remonstrations might be counter-productive to the case.

This uncertainty lay heavily with Michael Havers who returned home from Chichester late that night dejected and depressed. "He was devastated," confirms Nigel Havers. "I'd never seen him so low. Dad was shocked and upset by the ruling and he vowed to get them off on appeal."

While their defence team worked frantically through the night to prepare the necessary paperwork, Judge Block having reluctantly given his blessing to formally license an appeal request, Jagger and Richards faced up to the harsh reality of prison life. Keith, more used to looking at the Sussex countryside at an hour that normally suited him, was woken at 6 a.m. with the other prisoners in Wormwood Scrubs. For a change of scenery from the grey, pitted walls that dominated his cell, he pulled up a rickety stool and climbed towards the small window that offered a glimpse of sky. A bark from the warder brought him back to reality and he joined the other prisoners queuing for breakfast. Richards, along with several other new arrivals, was then herded around other areas of the prison, the chapel and the library included. Keith was allotted his morning duties in the prison workroom where he joined an assembly line of fellow convicts sewing mailbags or, in Richards' case, piecing together small plastic Christmas trees destined to sit on the top of festive cakes.

After he'd completed his session of mind-numbing work, Richards made his way out into the yard for an hour's 'association'. Kept walking around the prison quadrangle by guards, he nonetheless made contact with other inmates, many of whom, in low voices, offered him a wide assortment of the substances that had led to him being there. Following the enforced exercise, Keith retired to the relative safety of his cell. Early that afternoon a moment of sheer amazement occurred when the radios of the prison, all presumably tuned into the same station, played the Stones song 'It's All Over Now'. With seemingly the entire inhabitants of Wormwood Scrubs singing along, Richards became aware that whatever his fate, he would never be short of supporters on the inside.

While Keith had served just one night in jail, this was Mick's fourth day behind bars and to visitors, his appearance made for a deeply depressing sight. In addition to the drab prison garb cutting him down to size, Mick's profile was drawn and pitted with stress. Sharing a cramped cell and without the usual protection of his security, Mick was concerned about his personal safety, if not from opportunist convicts then from someone harbouring a grudge. Marianne, one of the first permitted to visit, attempted to console him but it was all too evident he was a broken man.

Early the morning of June 30 Havers and his team were present at London's High Court in the Strand before Judge William Kenneth Diplock and his two colleagues, Mr Justice Brabin and Mr Justice Waller. While the bulk of the paperwork could take months to prepare, achieving bail was the primary objective at this stage. Diplock, aged 60, was a doyen in the field of the appeal process, and while not disposed to the culture that Mick and Keith represented, he was sufficiently in touch with the gravity of the decision made in Chichester. Those present in the small courtroom heard Havers plead with the bench that Jagger and Richards were the subject of exemplary charges, delivered with little regard for the actual evidence laid before the bench.

Reiterating the evidence heard, Havers affirmed that Jagger had the support of his practitioner, and although he conceded that his client was found in possession of drugs, he had a "moral authorisation" to have them. In impassioned tones, Havers indicated how Jagger's reputation had been heavily sullied by media coverage of the case, a slur that Havers was eager to defend. "There is no question of peddling," he pointed out. "'No question of vast quantities [of drugs] and there is all the difference in the world between this case and the case of the person who has large quantities for gain as a peddler or pusher." Equally, Havers argued that the photographs of his client in handcuffs had built up an inordinately distorted picture from the media. This compelling reiteration of Jagger's defence prompted the bench to issue the certificate to appeal. More pertinently, Judge Diplock agreed that bail should be granted, allowing Jagger immediate release.

With that success won, the question of Richards' sentence came before the bench. Havers argued that the conviction of allowing his house to be used for the smoking of cannabis was heavily flawed because of the discrepancies between police officers in determining the aroma of cannabis from incense. Furthermore, the allegedly ribald behaviour of the enigmatic 'Miss X' – deemed to be under the influence of cannabis – had been contradicted by Scotland Yard's Inspector Lynch.

The bench agreed with Havers that the points concerning Richards needed re-examining, and conceded to the request for his immediate release on bail. Freedom for Mick and Keith secured, there were still a few bows to the demands of legal officialdom. Imposing an enormous, although presumably commensurate, bail of £5,000 on both Jagger and Richards, the bench demanded further sureties of £1,000 from two named individuals; in this case the group's press agent, Les Perrin, and their accountant, Stanley Blackmore. Despite a plea from Havers that the pair had musical and contractual commitments abroad, the bench demanded that Jagger and Richards' passports be surrendered until the formal appeal hearings took place. The summer recess was fast approaching which meant the appeal could take over three months to come to court. With this in mind, Havers argued for the appeal to be brought forward at the earliest opportunity, but with stenographers' paperwork from Chichester as yet not transcribed, the chances were that it might run over the summer break and into early October. Nonetheless, despite these obstacles, the fact remained that Mick and Keith's immediate freedom had been secured. If time was a measure of how conclusive the appeal request was, it took just 26 minutes to grant the pair their release.

Both Stones heard the news in different ways. Richards recalls being in his cell when he heard a loud roar emanate from outside, those prisoners with transistor radios having heard the news that bail had been granted. When a fellow jailbird shouted through his door that he'd won his release, Keith leapt off his bed and began kicking the door to his cell shouting, "Let me out, you bastards! I've got bail!" He was then officially informed of his imminent release and told to prepare for it. While collecting his things, he claimed he heard one warder say, "You'll be back." Jagger reportedly read of his release when a copy of an evening newspaper was pushed through the bars of his cell.

Despite the clemency displayed towards Jagger and Richards, Fraser's request for bail was refused. His counsel William Denny QC argued that his client was caught with just one day's supply of heroin, and that the sentence he received – especially now that he was cured of his addiction – was altogether excessive. Denny also pointed out that the publicity the trial had generated had denied his client a fair hearing. None of this failed to impress the bench, and they ruled that Fraser should remain behind bars. "Where heroin is concerned," said Lord Parker, "this court is satisfied that in the ordinary way, if there are no special circumstances, the public interest demands that some form of detention should be imposed."

Nonetheless, Fraser's request for an appeal hearing was granted. Incarcerated, he would have to wait for the wheels of law to turn before he could taste freedom again. While there was a smidgen of hope that his appeal might be heard before the legal session went into recess that July, it was by no means a certainty.

Driven by the redoubtable Tom Keylock, Keith's blue Bentley firstly made its way to Brixton prison to collect Mick. At exactly 4:20 p.m., and with a small posse of fans (most of them in school uniform) waiting outside, Jagger was driven out of the prison gates. Dressed in a beige jacket and yellow shirt, he smiled to fans and photographers. Fifty minutes later, the Bentley approached Wormwood Scrub's imposing entrance. Dressed in the same clothes in which he had stood trial in Chichester, relief was written over Keith's pale face as he walked from the prison building. At the gate, photographers swarmed in on the vehicle, causing it to stop momentarily. Both Mick and Keith were predictably engulfed with flashlights, the images capturing their weary but relaxed profiles in the backseat. Within five minutes of its arrival, the car had turned around and was on its way to central London for Mick and Keith to rendezvous with their defence team in the Temple area of London. Once there, the two Stones were able to put calls through to those that had supported them over the last few days, including Paul McCartney who apparently sent messages of support to Jagger, Richards and Fraser.

While it appears Mick was just happy to be free, Keith was reportedly incandescent with rage over his enforced incarceration. At the nub of his anger was an anomaly that had manifested itself while he was inside Wormwood Scrubs. Nigel Havers recalls being told of what lay behind Richards' disquiet. "Keith said: 'I want to prosecute the Queen.' My dad was rather taken aback by this and replied, 'What do you mean?' And Keith said: 'I'm being done for drugs being smoked on my premises. I was offered dope in jail – joints, everything. Who owns the prisons? The Queen.' At that my Dad said: 'Ah, I see where you're going, but I think we'll move away from that.'"

The debriefing concluded, Mick, Keith and Les Perrin trooped over for a drink at a nearby pub, The Feathers, at 36 Tudor Street, a popular hostelry for the legal community (now renamed The Witness Box). Clearly enjoying their freedom, the pair chatted happily with members of the press who had followed their progress throughout the day. They also consented to have their photos taken as they propped up the bar. The conversation, mainly at the prompting from reporters, was fairly stilted, although in hindsight, their answers were well-guarded, presumably on the advice of lawyers and management.

Keith: "The publicity will not break up the group. There are definitely no plans to split up. We hope our fans will remain loyal."

Mick: "We were treated very kindly and everyone was very helpful. We do not bear a grudge against anyone for what has happened... After all, a cell is not much different to a hotel room in Minnesota."

Keith: "All I'm doing at the moment is just digging my freedom."

With flashbulbs continuing to flicker, Mick quietly sipped his vodka and lime while Keith drank whiskey and coke from a half-pint glass. Perrin attempted to keep some semblance of order until a time-out was called with reporters, Jagger bidding them farewell with the words, "It will take a few days to readjust. But we must get back to completing a record we were making."

Press questioning brought to a close, the pair left the pub, and such will on display its landlord cheerily waived the bill for p up this ersatz press conference, a few final photos were outside in the street. With their arms around each other, the pair looked drawn and tired. Mick, reunited with Marianne, and Keith were driven to Allen Klein's suite at the Dorchester Hotel. While relieved that his artists had received their freedom, Klein reportedly became incensed at what occurred in his hotel room.

"When Mick, Keith and Marianne got back to my hotel room she pulled out a hash pipe and lit up," Klein recalled. "I mean how goddamn stupid can you get? I grabbed the thing away from her and fucking threw it out the window. She stood there saying the law was unrealistic: well, I don't give a shit if it is. I didn't want them to go to jail. And it's not the money. I don't care only about that. It's just if I'm involved then I'm responsible. It becomes my cross to see that they stay out of prison."

London's two evening papers were the first to get the story of Jagger and Richards' release onto the streets. Most imaginatively, the *Evening News* split its editorial into two, with opposing opinions debating the wisdom of the decision. Elsewhere, the presses for the next day's papers were already turning. With word of the release coming late in the afternoon, papers with less demanding deadlines were debating the Stones' continued incarceration.

In the most respected seat of British journalism in 1967 was William Rees-Mogg, editor of *The Times*. Later to become Baron Rees-Mogg, he was one of the most erudite commentators of his generation, equipped with a vast understanding of politics, judiciary and the machinations of the media. In 1956, he'd stood as a candidate for the Conservative party in a by-election in Chester-le-Street, Durham. Although he failed to win the seat, it didn't hamper his journalistic career one jot. He transferred from the *Financial Times* to become editor of the *Sunday Times,* before taking on the reins of the daily *Times* just before the Jagger-Richards saga erupted.

Monitoring Britain's diverse landscape, Rees-Mogg had noted escalating drug use among the young. Like many, he was unimpressed by the ambiguity of a law that failed to differentiate between soft drugs like cannabis, and harder narcotics such as heroin. The Jagger-Richards

Mick and Robert Fraser arrive at Lewes Prison to begin their first night in jail on June 27. Jagger would eventually be transferred to Brixton Prison to begin a three-month sentence for drugs possession. (DAILY SKETCH/REX FEATURES)

Arriving at Chichester Court to await sentencing, Robert Fraser and Mick Jagger show off their steel linkage to waiting photographers: June 28, 1967. (TED WEST/CENTRAL PRESS/GETTY IMAGES)

Just hours after the details of the raid have been read out in court, Marianne Faithfull is photographed at Redlands carrying an early edition of the London *Evening News* – its headline forever connecting her with the scandal. (DAVID MCENERY/REX FEATURES)

Photographer friend Michael Cooper vainly attempts to shield a distraught Marianne Faithfull from the press following the guilty verdicts handed down on Mick and Keith at Chichester Court. (MIRRORPIX)

Moments later in Chichester's Ship Hotel, Marianne attempts to process the enormity of the prison sentences for Mick and Keith. (MIRRORPIX)

Special Announcement

The WHO consider Mick Jagger & Keith Richard have been treated as scapegoats for the drug problem and as a protest against the savage sentences imposed on them at Chichester yesterday. The WHO are issuing today the first of a series of Jagger/Richard songs to keep their work before the public until they are again free to record themselves.

"THE LAST TIME" and "UNDER MY THUMB"

written by Mick Jagger & Keith Richard

TRACK 604006

Track Records

Above: The jailing of Mick and Keith brought an extraordinary amount of support from their peers. In an act of solidarity, The Who rush-released a single containing two Jagger/Richards songs: 'The Last Time' and 'Under My Thumb'.

Right: Following their release from jail on Friday, June 30 1967, Mick and Keith went straight to their lawyers' offices to confer with their legal team (MIRRORPIX)

After a debriefing with their legal team, Mick and Keith enjoy a well-deserved drink at The Feathers, a pub situated close to their lawyers' offices. (MIRRORPIX)

Despite Jagger and Richards' release from jail on bail, demonstrations against the *News Of The World* continued. Here, Who drummer Keith Moon and his wife Kim show their support for the cause on June 30. (C MAHER/GETTY IMAGES)

Mick and Keith at Redlands on July 4, 1967, the day news surfaced that their appeal hearing had been brought forward. "It's a great relief," said Mi
(DAVID COLE/REX FEATURES)

Michael Havers Q.C. Mick and Keith's defence barrister during the Redlands' trials. (MIRRORPIX)

William Rees-Mogg, in 1967 editor of the *Times* newspaper and author of the historic editorial 'Who Breaks A Butterfly On A Wheel'.

Judge Leslie Kenneth Allen Block, Chairman of the bench at Chichester Court. Stern, intransigent and unforgiving, Block clearly revelled in the opportunity to put Mick and Keith behind bars. (HENFIELD VILLAGE MUSEUM)

Detective Sergeant Norman Clement Pilcher. Having busted Donovan, Brian Jones, John Lennon, Yoko Ono and George Harrison during the late 1960s, Pilcher earned a reputation as rock's Oliver Cromwell.

A few hours after Mick's prison sentence was reduced to a conditional discharge, he was flown from Battersea Airport to Spain's Hall in Essex to appear on a *World In Action* TV special. With him are Marianne Faithfull and Granada researcher John (now Lord) Birt.

Mick and Keith's successful appeal hearings on July 31 was met with relief from all who'd championed their case. Beatle Paul McCartney – returning from holiday in Greece with girlfriend Jane Asher and friend 'Magic' Alex Mardas – was eager to show his delight at the news. (GEORGE STROUD/EXPRESS/GETTY IMAGES)

Robert Fraser, art dealer and Mayfair gallery owner. He wasn't as lucky as Mick and Keith, serving out the majority of his sentence at Wormwoo[d] Scrubs jail in west London. (FRED MOTT/EVENING STANDARD/GETTY IMAGES)

Richard Hamilton's extraordinary take on the Redlands' saga was entitled Swingeing London. The artist's embellishing of Mick and Robert Fraser's transference to jail while handcuffed has become one of the most striking images of the sixties. (MOMA, HOMER SYKES)

It wasn't just Mick and Keith who found themselves up against the law. Brian Jones had numerous infractions with the police during 1967/8. Despite his smile, Brian – seen here at West London Magistrates Court on May 11, 1967 – would find himself jailed on the drug's charge. (ANN WARD/DAILY MAIL/REX FEATURES)

May 21 1968. Just hours after a raid on his Chelsea flat, a distraught Brian is driven from Chelsea Police Station on May 21, 1968. (RON CASE/KEYSTONE/HULTON ARCHIVE/GETTY IMAGES)

A degree of mercy. Brian, with girlfriend Suki Poitier beside him, is driven away from court after escaping a jail term for possession of drugs on September 26, 1968. (MIRRORPIX)

trial not only spotlighted this but also called into question the nature of exemplary sentencing. When images of Jagger in handcuffs circulated around the nation, Rees-Mogg felt obliged to articulate the growing sense of unease of what had occurred via the *Times*' editorial column.

Since Mick and Keith's cases were still to be reviewed by the appeal's bench, it was by no means a foregone conclusion that their sentences would be quashed or reduced. Equally, any published opinion while a case was still active as such might be interpreted as *sub judice*. If indeed the authorities had seen fit, they could have held the editorial in contempt and pursued Rees-Mogg and *The Times* through the courts.

As such, it was a brave move for Rees Mogg to stick his neck out. While in reality, *Times* editorials were often written by a cast of anonymous journalists, Rees-Mogg took it upon himself to compose this in its entirety, and in doing so created one of the most historic editorials of the 20th century. Such is its importance that the full text is reprinted here verbatim by kind permission of Lord Rees-Mogg.

Who Breaks a Butterfly on a Wheel?

Mr. Jagger has been sentenced to imprisonment for three months. He is appealing against conviction and sentence, and has been granted bail until the hearing of the appeal later in the year. In the meantime the sentence of imprisonment is bound to be widely discussed by the public. And the circumstances are sufficiently unusual to warrant such discussion in the public interest.

Mr. Jagger was charged with being in possession of four tablets containing amphetamine sulphate and methyl amphetamine hydrochloride; these tablets had been bought perfectly legally in Italy, and brought back to this country. They are not a highly dangerous drug, or in proper dosage, a dangerous drug at all. They are a Benzedrine type and the Italian manufacturers recommend them both as a stimulant and as a remedy for travel sickness.

In Britain, it is an offence to possess these drugs without a doctor's prescription. Mr. Jagger's doctor says that he knew and had authorized their use, but he did not give a prescription for them as indeed they had already been purchased. His evidence was not challenged. This was, therefore, an offence of technical character which before this case drew the point to public attention any honest man might have been liable to commit. If after his visit to the pope, the Archbishop of Canterbury had bought propriety air sickness pills at Rome Airport and imported the unused tablets into Britain on his return, he would have risked committing precisely the same offence. No one who has ever travelled and bought proprietary drugs abroad can be sure that he has not broken the law.

Judge Block directed the jury that the approval of a doctor is not a defence in law to the charge of possessing drugs without a prescription, and the jury convicted. Mr. Jagger was not charged with complicity in any other drug offence that occurred in the same house. They were separate cases, and no evidence was produced to suggest that he knew Mr. Fraser had heroin tablets or that the vanishing Mr. Schneiderman had cannabis resin. It is indeed no offence to be in the same building or the same company as people possessing or even using drugs, nor could it reasonably be made an offence. The drugs that Mr. Jagger had in his possession must therefore be treated on their own as a separate issue from the other drugs that the other people may have had in their possession at the same time. It may be difficult for lay opinion to make this distinction clearly, but obviously justice cannot be done if one man is to be punished for a purely contingent association with someone else's offence.

We have therefore, a conviction against Mr. Jagger purely on the grounds that he possessed four Italian pep pills, quite legally bought, but not legally imported without a prescription. Four is not a large number. This is not a quantity which a pusher of drugs would have on him, nor even the quantity one would expect in an addict. In any case Mr. Jagger's career is obviously one that does involve great personal strain and exhaustion; his doctor says that he approves the occasional use of these drugs, and it seems likely that similar drugs would have been prescribed if there was a need for them. Millions of similar drugs are prescribed in Britain every year, and for a variety of conditions. One has to ask, therefore, how it is that this technical offence, divorced as it must be from other people's offences, was thought to deserve the penalty of imprisonment. In the courts at large it is most uncommon for imprisonment to be imposed on first offenders where the drugs are not major drugs of addiction and there is no question of drug traffic. The normal penalty is probation, and the purpose of probation is to encourage the offender to develop his career and to avoid the drug risks in the future. It is surprising therefore that Judge Block should have decided to sentence Mr. Jagger to imprisonment, and particularly surprising as Mr. Jagger's is about as mild a drug case as can ever have been brought before the courts.

It would be wrong to speculate on the judge's reasons, which we do not know. It is, however, possible to consider the public reaction. There are many people who take a primitive view of the matter, what one might call a pre-legal view of the matter. They consider that Mr. Jagger has 'got what was coming to him.' They resent the anarchic quality of the Rolling Stones performances, dislike their songs, dislike their influence on teenagers and broadly suspect them of decadence, a word used by Miss Monica Furlong in the Daily Mail.

As a sociological concern, this may be reasonable enough, and at an emotional level, it is very understandable, but it has nothing at all to do with the case. One has to ask a different question: Has Mr. Jagger received the same treatment as he would have received if he had not been a famous figure, with all the criticism his celebrity has aroused? If a promising undergraduate had come back from a summer visit to Italy with four pep pills in his pocket would it have been thought necessary to display him, handcuffed, to the public? There are cases in which a single figure becomes the focus for public concern about some aspects of public morality. The Steven Ward case, with its dubious evidence and questionable verdict, was one of them, and that verdict killed Steven Ward. There are elements of the same emotions in the reactions to this case. If we are going to make any case a symbol of the conflict between the sound traditional values of Britain and the new hedonism, then we must be sure that the sound traditional values include those of tolerance and equity. It should be the particular quality of British justice to ensure that Mr. Jagger is treated exactly the same as anyone else, no better and no worse. There must remain a suspicion in this case that Mr. Jagger received a more severe sentence than would have been thought proper for any purely anonymous young man.

Rees-Mogg employed his editorial title from a line in Alexander Pope's 1735 poem *Epistle To Dr Arbuthnot*. Broadly speaking, the analogy of breaking a butterfly on a wheel was employed to symbolise an exemplary act on something relatively innocuous – or using a sledgehammer to crack a nut, as more modern vernacular would have it.

William Rees-Mogg: "The quotation from [Alexander] Pope reflected this extraordinary contrast one had between the sort of slim figure of Mick Jagger being exposed to the full weight and force of the law. It was this sense that because he was famous, because he represented gressive approach towards our existing culture that he was not receiving justice which made me feel very strongly that our existing culture was letting itself down."

Aside from Rees-Mogg drawing attention to whether Jagger's fame influenced the savageness of the sentence, he expressed the clear division concerning the substances Jagger was caught with.

Rees-Mogg: "Four Benzedrine-type tablets were certainly not regarded as a serious offence. Benzedrine had been taken since the war when aircrews were fed on it to keep them awake while they were out over Germany. It was used by students to keep awake in exams; not as a mind altering drug, so much as a drug that would allow you to be mentally active when you were very tired."

Rees-Mogg's views carried considerable weight and influence. Other editors inspired by the editorial ran with their own opinions over the coming days. The weighty Sunday *Observer* would also contend that the judgement achieved "no firm conclusion" other than provoking "martyrdom symbolised by the handcuffs which seemed to have no other purpose than except to add one further humiliation".

Rees-Moggs' sister paper, the *Sunday Times,* also offered a stinging barb directed at the rough justice meted out at Chichester. "The generation gap widened considerably in West Sussex this week, leaving in its wake a detritus of shock, anger, smugness and brooding over it all, to paraphrase the council for the prosecution, the strong smell of ignorance."

Predictably, the right-wing *Sunday Telegraph* attempted to justify the verdicts. In doing so, it articulated what many had believed were the private thoughts of Judge Block. "The object of those sentences," wrote traditionalist TE Utley, "was not to censure pop culture, but to give firm and clear proof of society's determination to put down drug taking by the young.... There are many of them (and I am among them) who would regard punishment of twice the severity of those which have been decreed perfectly defensible if they could be shown to be likely to produce this result." Utley concluded his argument with: "If the hand of authority could administer a similar check to the drug craze, there is no responsible parent in this country who would not welcome its application."

Surprisingly, Britain's music press was split down the middle over the issue. *New Musical Express,* a journal that would later build a reputation for displaying its political colours, barely referenced the Stones scandal engulfing the music community. *Melody Maker,* in those days much more supportive of its core industry members, printed its own response on its front cover (dated July 8): "The *Melody Maker* has read them all," ran its vibrant editorial, "and we found ourselves a little surprisingly offering not one flower, but a bouquet to the *Times*. For last Saturday, the *Times* ran a leader on the Jagger case. It was objective, informed and fair. Thankfully, it lacked hysteria."

Mick and Keith's regained liberty did little to quell demonstrations against the *News Of The World* and, appropriately enough, UFO, the capital's most prominent psychedelic club, on Tottenham Court Road was utilised as the command centre. A preferred hang-out for musicians, freaks and left-field dilettantes, the UFO enjoyed a street level vibe that made it both slightly dangerous and very attractive. Details of a second demonstration against the *News Of The World* were broadcast on the club's PA system on Friday, June 30, and as a result another sizable crowd made its way from the club towards Piccadilly Circus. There, they met up with other protesters, many of whom had been on the previous night's march. With Eros' enduring symbol of love a gathering point, the party then moved off down the Strand towards Fleet Street and the *NOTW*'s headquarters.

This time, however, the police were waiting for them, equipped with batons, shields and dogs, and during the sit-down protest scuffles broke out and many, including Mick Farren, were injured. 'Hoppy' Hopkins' girlfriend, the larger than life Suzy Creamcheese (aka Susan Ziegler), was in the thick of the action, and was later arrested. Present also to make his feelings known was The Who's Keith Moon who, along with his wife Kim, carried two placards, his reading 'Stop Pop Persecution!', hers, evidently unaware of the irony, reading 'Free Keith'.

"I went out and bought a hundred broom handles and a bunch of cardboard and made signs that said 'Free Mick And Keith'," Moon recalled in 1978. "I gave them out to the crowd in front of the building from my Bentley."

Unperturbed by the behaviour of the police, some of the more militant elements in the movement planned a further protest the following night, with demonstrators planning to block the exit route for vans carrying Sunday's edition of the paper. While the numbers were slightly less, the efforts by those present served to keep the issue of Mick and Keith's sentencing in the public eye.

OZ magazine, fast gaining an ascendancy among the counterculture for its outspoken, uncensored opinions, rush released a newsletter to coincide with the protests. Handed out among demonstrators as they walked towards Fleet Street, the flyer exemplified the sense of outrage at the wider implications of the sentencing; a large measure of their anger directed at the editor of the *News Of The World*, Stafford Somerfield.

"Just as the Stones symbolise the new permissiveness – hence the vicious exemplary punishments – this man's [Somerfield's] rag epitomises the money-grabbing, witch-hunting, God-playing fascism of a decaying hypocrisy. Yet this paper's amorality has proved typical of all press ethics. Though the court guaranteed the anonymity of the female guest, almost every paper juxtaposed 'Nude Girl' headlines with irrelevant pictures of Marianne Faithfull. This cruel innuendo was basic press strategy – too ungenerous to protect her completely, they were too gutless to name her outright.... The national press has been quick to cash in on the colourful antics of the Stones in the past... Now Richards and Jagger are in the dock, the boot is on the other foot, the Youth Kick [sic] is aimed to the groin."

With such a torrent of bile hurled at the paper, it was a formality that the *News Of The World* would retaliate in its own idiosyncratic way. Many were the voices that poured scorn on the paper's evident collusion with police, but it was the demonstrations that took place outside their front door that had clearly rattled the paper's executives. There were other, more unconventional, attacks on the rag and its staff that week. An advert in *International Times* encouraged its readers to call the tabloid and register disgust at the covert operations. Of little surprise, the paper's switchboard was jammed for most of the week. Other, more intrepid callers, managed to bypass the switchboard and be put through to the editorial department, causing serious inconvenience to reporters piecing together the next edition of the paper.

Somerfield found himself a target too, with protests directed to his home. Evidently, someone in possession of the embattled editor's address had called the drug squad, claiming that drugs were to be found on Somerfield's property. With police none the wiser as to Somerfield's occupation, they arrived to search his house. With her husband behind his desk in London, Mrs Somerfield was confronted with a team of detectives. Inviting them in, she told one of the detectives that she was going to call her husband at the *News Of The World*.

"Why?" asked the confused detective.

"Because he's the editor of the *News Of The World*," she replied.

With that revelation, the penny dropped.

"Jesus Christ!" said the police officer, clearly embarrassed.

"Not quite," remarked his wife. "Though sometimes he acts like it."

Threats against Somerfield and editorial staff continued throughout the week, so much so that police took up residence in his home. Officers reportedly enjoyed the editor's hospitality, allegedly sharing out whatever they found in his drinks cabinet and larder. Eventually, Somerfield dispensed with their services. "I got their chief to call them off," recalled the editor, "on the grounds that I couldn't afford them any longer."

With the gloves off, the *News Of The World* hit back, their July 2 edition screaming innocence on its front cover. Under the headline 'A Monstrous Charge', the paper defended the allegation that had gathered momentum since the trial concluded. "A monstrous charge against the *News Of The World* was made during the trial of Rolling Stones' Keith Richards at West Sussex Quarter Sessions," ran the bold type. "It was a charge made within the privilege of a court of law. It was a charge made in circumstances which denied us the opportunity of answering back at the time."

Over the course of two pages, the paper attempted to absolve themselves from the host of allegations directed their way. Not surprisingly, they were keen to dismiss any claims that they had planted an *agent provocateur* within the Redlands gathering. "We have had no connection whatsoever with Mr. Schneiderman," ran the editorial, "directly or indirectly, before, during or after the case."

Despite the denials, Somerfield confirmed what had been suggested in court, namely that the paper had tipped off police regarding the Redlands party. Since police and defence lawyers were in possession of this fact, the paper had little option but to come clean. "Let us make it quite clear, that it was the *News Of The World* that passed information to the police. It was our plain duty to do so."

Dramatically illustrating this brazen claim were two photos of Mick and Keith, evidently taken in a surreptitious fashion in what appeared to be a fairly ramshackle flat. Obviously acquired from an insider, it was clearly an attempt to portray the pair in as sleazy an environment as possible, the caption beneath the picture of Jagger reading, "At ease in the clutter".

The paper's admission that it tipped-off police about the party did little to quell the anger directed towards it, and many were quick to condemn its role. Lord Lambton, Conservative Member of Parliament for Berwick-upon-Tweed, publicly damned the tabloid saying, "Their action seems by any standard indefensible. It is the business of a newspaper to present the news and try to form or guide events according to the opinion of its proprietors. It is surely not the function of a newspaper to become an agent of the police."

Members of the artistic community also voiced their condemnation. John Osborne, *enfant terrible* of Britain's playwrights, fired off a letter to *The Times*, pouring scorn on the *News Of The World*'s behaviour. "Are we expected to accept the principle that newspapers' editors consider it their 'plain duty' to pass random tip-offs from informers about what may or may not be going on in someone's private house?"

Responding to Osborne's claim, Somerfield wrote to *The Times* in an attempt to clarify matters. "We did not plant a man at the party," he claimed. "We did not plant drugs at the party; we did not 'follow and observe' Mr. Jagger; we did not take action to influence libel proceedings."

While Somerfield's retaliation cut no ice with his critics, in 2007, *NOTW* reporter Robert Warren gave a retrospective view of events to the BBC. "Obviously if we'd had a plant there we would have left him there and got the full story, the raid cut the whole thing short. Jagger's defence brought it all up at the trial and everybody clutched at it... It wasn't our intention to have Jagger jailed; our intention was just to prove that what we were telling people was true. But the police took it to court; we didn't urge them to do that. But it was an offence and we're not sorry for it, and we're very glad it did end up in a prosecution... It was one of those banal things that snowballed really."

Elsewhere, comments were still pouring into newspapers, magazines and journals from members of the public touched by the case. Mrs F Smith of Birmingham wrote to the *Daily Mail* with her thoughts. "I wouldn't cross the road to see or hear The Rolling Stones, but I am perturbed at the savagery of the sentences passed on them." Miss R Deere of Kingston, Surrey was more eager to uphold the letter of the law: "The Stones should be jailed straight away and any protest march on their behalf banned by the police." Sylvia Disley's letter to the *Daily Mail* was perhaps the most pertinent letter received by the media concerning Jagger's dilemma. She highlighted a quandary that faced many British housewives concerning innocent possession of drugs – ironically a subject the singer had written and sung about in 'Mother's Little Helper' (off *Aftermath*). "I am a housewife in my thirties," wrote Disley. "I have had a bottle of Benzedrine tablets in a cupboard for a long time, but for the life of me I cannot remember where I got them. It is only now, after Mick Jagger's sentence that I realise that I, and possibly thousands of others, could also be liable to up to two years' jail and a £1,000 fine."

Given the depth of feeling, a nationwide poll was commissioned to assess the public's views. With Jagger and Richards' cases dividing opinion, the results were quite startling, the National Opinion Poll reporting that 56% of those between the ages of 21 and 34 actually believed that Jagger in particular, should have been jailed for longer.

News of the results predictably enlivened sections of the right-wing press, a *Sunday Express* editorial remarking: "What a lesson for those who mistake the chatter at a few avant-garde parties for the voice of youth. The vast majority of young people want nothing to do with drugs. They look upon them, rightly, as only for the sick in mind."

Others eschewed the media and made their feelings known to

those directly concerned. A mother from Tooting, south London, was compelled to put pen to paper to offer her support for the police's action. Her letter to the Commissioner of Police at New Scotland Yard on July 3, 1967, was one that police felt was worthy of preserving in their dossier on the case. It remains there to this day.

Dear Sir,

In this world of ours today where youngsters do not give traditional respect to Queen, country and our people at the top, but has to be wrung from them, I thought this information might cheer you up.

My young son (17 turned) has read the Rolling Stones case, and all the sordid details I am afraid, but has come through unscathed. In spite of adult opinion sometimes on the Rolling Stones (he reads the Times, Sunday Times, *and* Sunday Express*) he summed up with "I am on the side of the police, 15 of them wouldn't lie." This from today's youngster is praise and respect too.*

I felt I had to write you this letter as I felt so pleased myself, but if I have wasted your time I apologise.

Yours faithfully,
Myrtle K Smith

CHAPTER 10

The Court of Appeal

Ransom Stoddard: "You're not going to use the story, Mr. Scott?"
Maxwell Scott: "No, sir. This is the West, sir. When the legend becomes fact, print the legend."

From *The Man Who Shot Liberty Valance*, screenplay by
James Warner Bellah and Willis Goldbeck, 1962

With the Redlands saga engaging the country, the more pertinent issues the drama raised were overshadowed by rumours in circulation regarding Marianne Faithfull. Although sections of the press became inflamed with the tittle-tattle in their hands, no one dared print it. Nonetheless, it became strong currency around Fleet Street before seeping out to roll unchallenged around the nation's pubs, clubs and bars.

Not surprisingly, it was the irreverent *Private Eye* that first hinted at the grubby rumour – albeit obliquely. With typical coded zeal, the magazine dropped in a reference to the scandal printed around the groin shaped 'Y' of its *EYE* logo. Reading, 'A Mars Bar Fills The Gap', the comment was designed to rattle the sensitivities of everyone privy to this information. Making more capital out of the Redlands' issue, *Private Eye's* July 7 cover featured suitably doctored images of Prime Minster Harold Wilson and his deputy leader George Brown. Pictured stumbling out of 10 Downing Street with superimposed beatnik hair cuts, it was accompanied by the headline, 'Drugged With Power – Two Held'. *Private Eye*'s interest in the case extended over several issues, lampooning anyone and everything connected to the saga.

Others were attempting to present the issue more intelligently. Artist Richard Hamilton was a friend of Robert Fraser, and like many London-based artists, had been represented by him professionally. Given this close proximity, Hamilton was moved by the case; in particular the sight of Jagger and Fraser in handcuffs. Keen to dramatise the demeaning situation artistically, Hamilton used a photo by *Daily Sketch* cameraman John Twine showing the pair attempting to shield their faces with their manacled hands. Utilising his trademark Pop Art style, Hamilton set to work on colourfully embellishing Twine's monochrome image, transforming it into a remarkable series of garish lithographs. Entitled *Swingeing London*, Hamilton's reinterpretation of the historic moment created a landmark image that best exemplified Jagger and Fraser's most indignant treatment.

However, Hamilton wasn't finished there. With Mick and Keith now out on bail, he decided to further highlight Fraser's continued incarceration with another dramatic piece of art in the form of a collage. In pursuit of something that captured the media frenzy, Hamilton was handed a miscellany of newspaper clippings concerning the Redlands trial by Fraser's secretary. Collating them into an uneven collage of newsprint, Hamilton also included a few appropriate items in the work. These included a swatch of wrapping paper from an incense packet, a section of a painting by artist Bridget Riley (a client of Fraser's) and, most controversially, a slither from a Mars Bar wrapper.

Meanwhile, Mick and Keith attempted to reassume their lives. Within a week of their release, they were taking care of business well away from the glare of the spotlight. Given that recording had been impossible during the trial, Jagger and Richards slipped back to Redlands to begin running through numbers for the Stones' sixth album.

Noting their absence from London, reporters from the *Daily Mirror* tracked the pair down to West Wittering on July 4. The timing of the visit was fortuitous in that an exemplary decision had been taken by the Lord Chief Justice, Lord Parker, to bring forward Mick and Keith's appeal hearings to July 31. Evidently anxious to get this headline-grabbing issue out of the way as soon as possible, this was the final day of the legal calendar before the summer recess, and it ensured that their cases wouldn't be carried over to the new session beginning in October. "It's a great relief," Jagger told the reporters. "It was a drag having to wait all that time not knowing what was going to happen to us in the end." Fraser was also a beneficiary of the Lord Chief Justice's determination to wrap the cases up early. His appeal date was set for July 28, three days before Mick and Keith's hearing.

Elsewhere in the Stones' camp, Brian Jones wasn't enjoying the same measure of public support as his colleagues. His trial for drug possession was not due to be heard until October, which left him in a state of intense anxiety. Convinced that he was to be the target of further raids by Sergeant Pilcher, Jones, feeding off the reports from Jagger and Richards' case regarding covert surveillance, believed his phones were being tapped. With (reportedly) numerous calls received by local emergency services containing reports of break-ins, fires and, not least, the state of Brian's health, a steady stream of vehicles turned up at his flat to investigate these matters.

Fearful that someone was attempting to inflict a nervous breakdown on him, Jones called a press conference at Courtfield Road, addressing the media from the balcony of his first floor flat. Wrapped in a silk kimono and standing perilously close to the flat's modest parapet, Jones informed curious reporters that a war was being waged against him by anonymous forces. The voices in his head were amplified by the massive coverage afforded to Jagger and Richards' trial. Visiting his physician at the time of his colleagues' sentencing, Brian's condition was deemed so grave that a recuperative stay in a Hampshire clinic was arranged to sort out his numerous traumas. He checked out after only two days.

Fate would take a hand in sidelining Jones more permanently. Still wounded by Anita Pallenberg transferring her affections to Keith, Brian continued seeing Suki Poitier, whose profile and features were an almost carbon copy of Pallenberg's. Back in London and reassuming his roistering around town, he collapsed after a party at the Hilton and, with Poitier distraught at his condition, the pair were rushed off to The Priory in Roehampton. Jones' physician Dr Anthony Flood was on hand to oversee treatment and the state of Brian's mental health was evaluated as "anxious, considerably depressed and potentially suicidal". Feeling desperately isolated Jones requested a double-room for him and Poitier, plus accommodation for several of his retinue – all of which were politely refused. Following nearly three weeks convalescing at The Priory, Brian took off with Suki for a holiday in Malaga on Spain's Costa del Sol.

His absence did little to derail sessions for the Stones' next album which formally resumed at Olympic Studios on July 7. There was considerable pressure to have new material out as soon as possible and with the 'Summer of Love' close to peaking, suspicions abounded that the Stones take on psychedelia might well arrive after the party had ended. To temporarily fill the void left by the dearth of Stones releases in the States, a tepid collection of B-sides, out-takes and leftover album tracks entitled, somewhat wearily, *Flowers*, was compiled by London Records in America. The group's individual faces on the cover (taken from the UK *Aftermath* record sleeve) were underpinned by flower stalks. The absence of any leaves below Jones' image would later lead some observers to over-speculate that this was a reference to his miniscule contribution.

Procol Harum's 'A Whiter Shade Of Pale' and Scott McKenzie's 'San Francisco (Be Sure To Wear Some Flowers In Your Hair)' topped charts around the world in July but, predictably, it was The Beatles who carried off the honours with their anthem to the era, 'All You Need Is Love'. With the song at number one and absolutely no chance of The Beatles appearing live on *Top Of The Pops*, the BBC's only option was to repeat the Our World film of the recording session.

The Redlands issue still *au courrant*, someone from the BBC hierarchy decided that the image of a singing, smiling Jagger in his psychedelic finery was far too provocative for viewers' sensitivities. With *Top Of The Pops* producer Johnnie Stewart preparing to insert an audience shot in place of Jagger's cameo appearance "as a precaution", Beatles manager Brian Epstein heard about the deception and stepped in. At Epstein's insistence, the film was broadcast uncut. The press got wind of the brouhaha and The Beatles' management issued a terse statement reading: "If the BBC had insisted on the cut, we planned to tell them that they could not show it. We certainly would not allow any censorship of that kind. We have control over the film – absolute control." In its defence, all a BBC spokesperson could offer was that the suggestion to edit Jagger out "came from very high up".

This sensitivity was more than likely being fuelled by column inches devoted to the trials. The drugs debate was gaining ascendancy, and some were attempting to capitalise on the hysteria by influencing public opinion. Many of those on the front line were busy formulating this dissent into a more proactive desire for change.

Like many at the sharp end of the debate, Steve Abrams had been actively monitoring events escalating across the UK. Energised by the Labour government's clear lack of understanding on the issue, in January 1967 Abrams inaugurated SOMA, a pressure group cum think-tank charged with tackling the inequality concerning cannabis use. The acronym, coined from the omnipresent drug in Aldous Huxley's novel *Brave New World*, stood for Society Of Mental Awareness.

Cannabis laws failed to distinguish in matters of composition, use and supply, and many – including Abrams – were aware that the Redlands trial highlighted such iniquities. Those less celebrated offenders who had been jailed for longer periods needed representation. Furthermore, the rough justice handed out after some raids was raising deep concern on how much freedom police had in pursuing users for what was a non-violent, victimless crime.

John 'Hoppy' Hopkins' imprisonment on the same law that had convicted Keith Richards drove a stake into the heart of London's counterculture. The Rolling Stones had access to legal brains that other less celebrated or financially endowed persons were denied, and debate quickly transformed into activity. The then Labour government had commissioned its own inquiry into narcotics under the umbrella of the Wootton Committee, headed by Baroness Barbara Wootton, which asked Home Secretary Roy Jenkins to explore drug use in the UK and make recommendations. Despite her lofty prefix, Barbara Wootton was receptive to arguments on both sides of the debate, having previously forged a distinguished career as a sociologist and criminologist.

With the report due for delivery the following year, Abrams and his growing band of sympathisers were eager to seize the high profile afforded to the drug issue by the Redlands case. While LSD use was a major consideration for the report, SOMA's brief was to steer the committee's finding towards the more pressing issue of recreational cannabis use. SOMA had compelling information to support their argument, and with reports commissioned overseas in broad agreement with their aims, there was a possibility that they may be able to influence the committee's decision.

While SOMA meant little to the wider British public, Abrams was savvy enough to realise that celebrity involvement could add considerable weight to the campaign. The concept of freedom of the press was very much alive in Britain, and it was proposed that an advert should be produced stating what many, both erudite and creative, believed was the appropriate approach to cannabis use. Abram's drew reference from a *Times* newspaper advertisement of March 30, 1967 opposing the Vietnam War. Headed 'Disassociate Britain', its stark edict was accompanied by signatories from leading personalities allied to the arts, politics and learned professions. Utilising the Vietnam advert as a template, supporters of the cannabis issue would similarly be invited to sign up in support of the campaign.

Abram's project duly green-lighted, it appeared obvious to offer it to *The Times* which, because of William Rees-Mogg's editorial, was deemed to be most receptive. Despite this impression, in actuality Rees-Mogg did not concur with the aims of the advert. Nonetheless, he agreed for it to be published even though he knew it would attract considerable criticism.

William Rees-Mogg: "I decided on freedom of arguments grounds that although I didn't agree with it, it never became the official position of *The Times*. But on the other hand, the case for thinking that cannabis was a drug that ought to be legalised on various grounds was one that was certainly strong enough to be argued. And therefore if there was an advertisement of that kind and we were asked to take it, we were open to other views."

The terms having been approved, Abrams and his team turned their attention to the practicalities of bringing it to the page. In 1967 the cost of a full-page *Times* advertisement was in the region of £1,800 so it was vital to secure support from those who could accompany their sympathies with hard cash. Aware that the fame of The Beatles could elevate the campaign globally, Abrams visited Paul McCartney at his St John's Wood home on June 2 to see if the Beatle would assist. With the group's *Sgt. Pepper* album officially one day old, McCartney was in an ebullient mood.

Steve Abrams: "Unless my memory is playing tricks on me, McCartney thrust a copy of *Sgt Pepper* into my hands and said, 'Listen to it through headphones on acid.' The conversation that followed was, however, sedate. McCartney was well aware of the power of public statements coming from The Beatles. He realised that if they spoke out on too many issues, their influence would be diluted. But pot was going to be an exception."

In contrast to the 'cute' status inflicted on him during the early days of the Beatles, McCartney had more recently gained considerable respect within London's alternative community as the most approachable Beatle. He'd helped out on numerous occasions to assist the embattled *International Times* and was an active supporter of the trendy Indica Gallery in London's Piccadilly. Whereas the other Beatles had kept quiet regarding their chemical intake, McCartney confirmed using LSD via an ITV news interview on June 19 following a similar admission in *Life* magazine. "God is everything," he excitedly told the *Life* reporter. "God is in the space between us. God is in the table in front of you. God is everything and everywhere and everyone. It just happens that I've realised all this through acid."

In a somewhat circuitous fashion, McCartney's comments had come to the attention of 58-year-old Home Office minister Alice Bacon. With special responsibilities for drug abuse, she had been shocked to read an article about drug use by celebrities, including McCartney and Brian Epstein, in *Queen* while at her hairdressers. Scuttling furiously back to parliament, Bacon, in a meandering monologue littered with contradictions, promptly addressed the House of Commons on the issue of pop stars and their responsibilities.

Alice Bacon: "I believe that at present we are in danger in this country... I am not speaking only of cannabis but also of some other drugs which have been mentioned, particularly LSD of some people misleading young people by not only taking drugs themselves, but trying to influence the minds of young people and trying to encourage them to take drugs. Today there are those who see in society's attitude to drug taking the opportunity for questioning traditional values and social judgements of all kinds and for advocating aims and conduct going far beyond the 'kicks' and pleasures of a few pills. For them drug taking is a way – the way – of life to which they beckon the impressionable, the curious, the frustrated, and the demoralised. Insidiously or openly, wittingly or unwittingly, the young are being taught the paraphernalia of psychedelic experience, and the catch phrases of drug cults."

Despite such moral admonishments, McCartney was happy to stump up the necessary cost for SOMA's advertisement and also to guarantee the signatures of his fellow Beatles. "McCartney had gone over the top with LSD," recalls Steve Abrams today. "I was suggesting a way to change the subject from LSD to cannabis, and to associate The Beatles with a lot of prominent people in a protest within the system."

While agreeing to the advertisement, *The Times* demanded the written consent of each and every name supporting the case be made available to their lawyers. This lengthy formality held up the planned advertisement date by one week but the strength of feeling ensured that the list contained some prominent names.

Steve Abrams: "We found people of the highest repute prepared to put their names to this petition; in particular, Francis Crick, the greatest scientific mind of the twentieth century, and the leading figure in English letters, Graham Greene. Graham Greene wrote back [saying] that when he got the letter he was high on opium, and he walked two miles into town to send the cable to Rees-Mogg confirming his signature to the advertisement."

On Monday, July 24, *The Times* ran the advertisement on page five of all of its editions. With its unequivocal headline reading, 'The Law Against Marijuana Is Unworkable In Principle And Unworkable In Practice', the advert was underpinned by a litany of collaborative evidence that verified

SOMA's claims that cannabis was neither habit forming nor overtly dangerous to health. Furthermore, the advertisement documented the worrying rise in police harassment towards cannabis users, and while not specifically stated in the advert, it resonated deeply with the treatment that the likes of Donovan and Brian Jones had suffered at the hands of Norman Pilcher's team.

"The prohibition of cannabis has brought the law into disrepute and has demoralised police officers faced with the necessity of enforcing an unjust law. Uncounted thousands of frightened persons have been arbitrarily classified as criminals and threatened with arrest, victimisation and loss of livelihood. Many of them have been exposed to public contempt in the courts, insulted by uninformed magistrates and sent to suffer in prison. They have been hunted down with Alsatian dogs or stopped on the street at random and improperly searched. The National Council for Civil Liberties has called attention to instances where drugs have apparently been 'planted' on suspected cannabis smokers. Chief Constables have appealed to the public to inform on their neighbours and children."

Summarising the debate, the piece made five recommendations to the Home Secretary towards a saner drug law:

1. *The government should permit and encourage research into all aspects of cannabis use, including its medical applications.*
2. *Allowing the smoking of cannabis on private premises should no longer constitute an offence.*
3. *Cannabis should be taken off the dangerous drugs list and controlled, rather than prohibited, by a new ad hoc instrument.*
4. *Possession of cannabis should either be legally permitted or at most be considered a misdemeanour, punishable by a fine of not more than £10 for a first offence and not more than £25 for any subsequent offence.*
5. *All persons now imprisoned for possession of cannabis or for allowing cannabis to be smoked on private premises should have their sentences commuted.*

With Richards' recent charge referred to in Sections 2 and 5 of SOMA's recommendations, it couldn't have failed to hit its target.

Despite the compelling evidence present in the advert, it was the 65 signatories that carried the most gravitas. There were 15 doctors of medicine including Jonathan Miller and RD Laing in agreement with the broad aims of the campaign, as well as MPs Tom Driberg and Brian Walden, but it was the names of all four Beatles and manager Epstein that courted most attention.

As anticipated, the advert provoked a massive wake-up call for a nation already in a quandary over the spiralling drugs issue. In Parliament, Conservative MP Paul Channon called for an adjournment debate to examine soft drug use in Britain, citing the massive coverage of narcotics use raised in the press. Taking care not to address the Stones' case directly, Channon made several references to the *Times* advertisement.

Jagger's parliamentary acolyte MP Tom Driberg tabled a question to Alice Bacon regarding clarification on amphetamine use. Although not mentioning Jagger by name, the question re-ignited the issue over banned drugs acquired legally elsewhere that were brought back onto British soil. This was a key element of Jagger's appeal, although the Home Office minister was savvy enough to short circuit the reply lest it turn out to be prejudicial.

Alice Bacon: "I would not like to comment on that because it might lead me into talking about a specific case which is before the courts. But obviously 'dangerous drugs' means what it says. According to our law the tablets which my honourable friend has described are dangerous drugs."

Predictably, Rees-Mogg's decision to run the advert met a mixed reaction from his peers. Conservative MP Quintin Hogg, while previously championing Jagger's corner over the handcuffing issue, found the advert "an absolute disgrace". "There were people who were much more worried about cannabis than obviously the people who signed the advertisement were," Rees-Mogg says. "Quintin Hogg was one of them. I found myself on balance not supporting the advertisement, but nevertheless thinking it was right to run it."

With their appeal hearings just days away, Jagger and Richards wisely kept their support to themselves although it was obvious that, by association, the advertisement would raise the profile of their plight. However a potential setback occurred during Fraser's appeal on July 28.

While his counsel attempted to separate Fraser's links with his associates' more celebrated case, the larger crime of heroin possession would ultimately put Fraser at a huge disadvantage. Incarcerated at Wormwood Scrubs, Fraser was unable to attend and was represented by his barrister, William Denny QC who, once again, spoke of a man overworked and under continual pressure of the rigours of running a successful London gallery. His client having already served five weeks of a six-month sentence, Denny asked for lenience but all hopes were slapped down by the bench. Indeed, his impeccable background was interpreted more as a hindrance to any potential clemency.

"Those privileges if anything," said Lord Justice Parker, "raise greater responsibilities and would tempt the court to give more rather than less by way of sentence than to a person whom I will deem as the man in the street."

In his summing up, Parker focused on Fraser's heroin use, invoking the popular demonisation of the drug. "Heroin has been termed in argument a killer, and it must be remembered that anyone who takes heroin puts themselves body and soul into the hands of the supplier. They have no moral resistance to any pressure being brought to bear on them."

After such damning words, it was of little surprise that Fraser's appeal was rejected and albeit with remission, he was ordered to serve out the rest of his sentence – a miserable four months, where as prisoner 7854, he spent his days either in his cell or working in the prison kitchen. The news sent a dark omen to Jagger and Richards. Adding to the sense of unease, their counsel Michael Havers received an ominous, unsolicited call – ostensibly from a member of the prosecution team – informing him that it would be a waste of time to pursue the matter.

With time of the essence, the Stones completed a stopgap single. Entitled 'We Love You', the song had been in an embryonic form for well over a month. Musically, it was a collage of sounds popular at the time, with a strong Middle Eastern ambiance serving as backdrop. Underpinning the piece was a driving piano lead dreamed up and played by session musician Nicky Hopkins. Brian – despite his haphazard contributions to the Stones' current oeuvre – contributed a memorable psychedelic background to the song courtesy of the swirling Mellotron.

Lyrically 'We Love You' oozed a bittersweet irony; its loving sentiments not only directed squarely to Stones fans standing by them but also at the forces of authority that attempted to curtail their activities. Jagger, keen to inject a degree of verisimilitude, used the sound of cell doors slamming, chains rattling and footsteps echoing on stone floors on the track. With various Beatles and Stones exchanging visits across London's studio network, Paul McCartney and John Lennon had stopped by Olympic Studios on July 19, 1967 to lend some vocal harmonies to the chorus and another track, 'Dandelion'. With them they brought visiting American Beat poet Allen Ginsberg to join in the jamboree.

Sounds duly recorded, a promotional film was required. For 'We Love You,' it was evident that the song required a suitably dramatic scenario to illuminate the subject matter. In 1967, film inserts – a forerunner of today's pop video – were fast becoming fashionable for groups tiring of the rigmarole of making mimed television appearances on the likes of *Top Of The Pops*. Originally simple performance shots, these short vignettes had recently undergone a minor revolution, and were veering into much more experimental fields. The Stones commissioned Peter Whitehead who had directed their unreleased 1965 tour documentary *Charlie Is My Darling* as well as original clips for their last two singles, 'Have You Seen Your Mother, Baby, Standing In the Shadow?' and 'Let's Spend The Night Together'. Whitehead was one of the most fashionable film-makers of the mid-sixties, having been commissioned by *Top Of The Pops* to shoot pieces to accompany songs from the likes of Jimi Hendrix and Pink Floyd.

Peter Whitehead: "As far as we knew, on the Monday they were going to go into that court and could well be sent to prison. Andrew Oldham sent me their new record and said, 'It's great, it's called 'We Love You'.' I listened to it, and I thought it was unbelievably bad. I thought, 'They're going to prison and there's going to be revolution on the streets and there's this ghastly piece of music.' So Andrew said, 'Well, do you have any ideas of how we should film it?' I had the idea that as far as I was concerned, Mick and Keith's trial had been as symbolic as the trial of Oscar Wilde. The attitude to Wilde in his time about homosexuality was very little different to the attitude I felt in the sixties towards pills and cannabis, it was just exactly the same kind of hypocrisy that was going to send them to jail. Now looking back on the Oscar Wilde thing, we cringe at the very thought that we could do something like that to someone like that. How could we have done it? So I said, 'Right, dress Mick up as Oscar Wilde and we'll do a sort of send up of the Wilde trial.'"

Mick, Keith and Marianne met up with Whitehead at a Methodist church hall in London's King's Cross on the morning of Sunday, July 30. With assistant cameraman Anthony Stern, the church's sparse interior was turned into an ersatz courtroom.

"We were dashing around like wild things," recalls Stern. "It was a totally improvised experience. We made up the film as we went along. We got rolled up newspapers to make a wig for Keith. He also used my square spectacles to give himself a rather judicious look."

The costumes were to be as symbolic as the concept. Jagger, cast as Oscar Wilde, wore the same emerald green jacket in which the police had discovered the four amphetamine pills. In case anyone missed the inference of injustice, he wore a green carnation that Wilde's associates had adopted to symbolise their support.

Marianne, recognised now as a component part of the affair, wore a short bobbed wig in order to take on the appearance of Lord Alfred Douglas or 'Bosie', the Edwardian dandy who betrayed Wilde in court. Behind the bench sat Keith as the Judge. While his resemblance to Wilde's trial adversary, The Marquis of Queensbury, was minimal, with the addition of Stern's spectacles he transformed into something of an authority figure. Adding considerable irony, the rolled newspapers that formed his full-bottomed wig were pages from the *News Of The World*.

Whitehead had another visual idea up his sleeve. "I said, 'Listen can you bring the fur rug?' The one that Marianne was supposed to be naked under when they were busted. In one stroke, we said that this was going to be as scandalous as the Wilde trial – plus we would end up hopefully with a movie which could go on to promote the song."

Towards the end of the film, with Keith presiding over events in magisterial fashion, attention focuses on the rug placed on top of the bench. A nonchalant Marianne pulls the rug up on 'Judge' Richards' command to reveal a naked, smirking Jagger beneath it.

Peter Whitehead: "When it came to the rug, I thought it was too obvious to put Marianne under it, so let's fool everyone and put Mick under it. So the film developed a kind of androgynous element in the end, which was right in the sense of Oscar Wilde."

Filming inside concluded, Whitehead and Stern also shot close-ups of the two Stones faces and the pair (with Marianne still in her short wig) walking around the forestry outside the church (this was used for a film to accompany 'Dandelion'). Believing that the courtroom sequences were far too sensational to dominate the film, Whitehead inserted recent footage he'd shot of the Stones recording at Olympic Studios. This footage was in itself remarkable, thanks to candid images of a deeply stoned Brian Jones, who appeared barely able to operate through a chemical haze.

Despite the ad hoc ingenuity detailing their ongoing plight, a sense of gloom overwhelmed the filming. "It wasn't much fun because they were in a terrible mood," recalls Whitehead. "They thought they were going to jail. They were just low, they were just completely empty and void of feelings. I was trying not to be jolly. We were all just trying to be very cool and getting the job done. It was very mechanical actually."

The next morning saw London bathed in sunshine but Keith discovered he was covered in spots which his doctor diagnosed as chicken pox. The two had a scheduled meeting with their counsel Michael Havers.

Nigel Havers: "The morning of the hearing, the boys came to our flat first. Keith said, 'I've got chicken pox' and dad said, 'Well, we'd better ring the court because you might find one of the appeal judges might not have had it.' In fact, one of them hadn't. I just have this vision of Keith sitting on my mum and dad's bed, and my mum dabbing him with calamine lotion."

Beforehand both Stones had visited the eminent Savile Row tailors Gieves & Hawkes to purchase suits as Havers had advised them to deck themselves out as conventionally as possible. Looking every bit the respectable young businessman, Jagger sneakily wore a tie with a painted decal of a naked woman at its base though with his suit buttoned up, no one other than Mick was any the wiser.

Anticipation of the appeal proceedings had been considerable, and journalists, film crews and scores of fans were already outside the Royal Courts of Justice well before court commenced. Held in check by police, some on horseback, the crowd were joined by curious onlookers and office workers. One optimistic fan had brought along a portable record player and was playing 'It's All Over Now' continually. While some were confident that Jagger and Richards' cases would be quashed, others were not so sure. For those possessed with sufficient worldly rationale, what Judge Block had imposed in Chichester could easily be affirmed by those of his ilk sitting in the High Court.

As per the Chichester hearings, the public gallery was jam-packed with Stones fans, many of whom had queued overnight to gain entry. Just before the business of the day started, Jagger and Richards arrived in Keith's Bentley, Tom Keylock at the wheel. Not wishing to draw undue attention to herself, Marianne Faithfull arrived independently in a red Mini. As always, she looked the epitome of 'Swinging London', dressing in a figure-hugging skirt and psychedelic floral blouse.

His chicken pox highly contagious, Richards was excused from the courtroom and isolated in an anteroom adjacent to the Crown Office. This left Jagger, Havers and the defence team to hear the appeal judges read out their decision. Draped in attire that befitted his high office was Lord Chief Justice Hubert Parker of Waddington. At 67, Parker's steadiness and experience had carved out a formidable reputation among his peers. While this impartiality was to be welcomed, it also meant that there was no chance whatsoever of him being swayed by the groundswell of publicity that had risen in the Stones' favour.

Assisting Parker in his duties were Lord Justice Winn and Justice Cusack, two highly experienced judges similarly resilient to any hint of outside pressure. Before the judges took the bench, officials announced that any disruption from the public gallery could lead to the court being cleared, but this did little to quell the excitement from the gaggle of teenagers for whom a courtroom was no different from a concert hall.

"It was extraordinary," recalls Havers' eldest son Philip who watched events with his brother, Nigel. "First of all, the public gallery was chock-full of Rolling Stones fans and they were making quite a lot of racket. My father had to say to Mick, 'Can you get them to shut-up, because they will upset the judges.' So Mick turned around, put his finger to his lips and they instantly obeyed and quietened down."

The gallery duly muted by the only authority they recognised, the business of the day could begin. The charge against Richards of allowing his house to be used for the smoking of cannabis was decided in his absence; Havers respectfully presenting the key points of his client's appeal, Lord Parker and his two colleagues occasionally probing him on various points. Although all three judges were in possession of the Chichester court transcripts, there was a reiteration of the events at Redlands by prosecuting QC Malcolm Morris, and Faithfull, her anonymity now in shreds, had to endure the whole saga being made public again.

Richards' hearing took a little over two hours to complete. Following a five-minute recess, those on the bench returned to read their deliberation and judgement. Aware that this decision would be minutely scrutinised, Lord Parker read out a detailed summary, tackling each point of the appeal in turn. Principally, this referenced the police evidence and the copious transcripts from the trial itself.

After deliberating with his two colleagues, Parker informed the court that the evidence presented in Chichester by Inspector John Lynch was not – despite his experience in such matters – concurrent with events at Redlands. With officers evidently in conflict regarding what constituted cannabis odour, this further highlighted a major inconsistency in the prosecution argument. Since comments about states of cannabis intoxication were normally the domain of a physician and not a police inspector, the bench judged that Lynch's observations in particular were evidently based from what he'd read from a "textbook" rather than personal, informed experience. Moreover, Judge Block's inability to balance the prosecution evidence, especially regarding the state of 'Miss X', was additional proof that the correct legal protocol had not been observed.

"One was left," remarked Parker, "with the evidence which was extremely prejudicial; her undress. No jury could possibly be sure that she had smoked cannabis resin on merely that evidence."

Without wishing to pour scorn on Block's stewardship of the trial, Lord Parker nonetheless informed the court that it was the belief of all three judges that the evidence concerning 'Miss X' would have been declared inadmissible had they themselves sat in judgement at Chichester.

"The Chairman was in a difficulty," said Parker in polite referral to Judge Block. "It might be that with hindsight he should properly, in his discretion, have excluded the evidence."

Creating a sense that the bench was intending to go further than just a reduction in Richards' sentence, Parker pronounced: "What finally influenced the Court in deciding to quash the conviction was that, granted that the Chairman was right in admitting the evidence, yet at the end of the day he must have properly told the jury what the position was, and have warned them that there was really no proper evidence other than purely tenuous evidence which could persuade them so as to make them sure that she had smoked cannabis resin and that the appellant must have known it. It would be unsafe to allow the verdict to stand and accordingly it is quashed."

While Parker's words were delivered without any visible emotion, they translated in much clearer terms throughout the courtroom. A cheer rang out from the gallery. Totally absolved of the previous judgement, Keith, at that point elsewhere in the building, would have been unaware until someone went over to his temporary isolation to inform him.

After a 15-minute recess, the judges reconvened and turned their attention to the case of Michael Phillip Jagger. Havers reinforced his client's innocence, legitimised by the "verbal" doctor's prescription. Approximately 20 minutes of dogged reiteration followed from both sides before the bench gave its deliberation without calling for an adjournment.

At first, it appeared that the ruling was going to be layered on several tiers.

Despite the defence's argument, Parker ruled that it was impossible for Jagger's doctor to know the exact constituents present in the pills by dint of a conversation. Equally, Parker stated that there was no doubt that the properties within the drug were illegal in the UK, and were only permissible if legally prescribed.

"It was impossible to say," said Parker, "that even if a prescription could be oral – and the court was not deciding that point – that what happened amounted to a prescription."

Parker's words brought some feelings of anxiety into the court. With excitement from Richards' acquittal still evident, there was no guarantee a similarly sympathetic gesture might be extended towards Jagger.

The courtroom descended into a fearful hush as Lord Parker concluded, "Accordingly, the appeal against the conviction was dismissed."

Given that Jagger's appeal against conviction had been thrown out, there was still a chance that his sentence might be reduced or even dismissed. Equally, there was a possibility that it could be affirmed or, heaven forbid, increased.

Parker drew attention to the modest amount of substances found in the pocket and conceded that there was absolutely no evidence of over-indulgence or peddling – a point that Havers had been eager to affirm. Parker concluded that Jagger had taken the drug with the full knowledge of his practitioner, which in itself was the strongest mitigation there could be.

Asking Jagger to stand, Lord Parker read his decision out to the court.

"The proper course,' he said on behalf of the bench, "was to give a conditional discharge."

A large measure of relief descended as the judge detailed the conditions attached to the ruling, specifically that Jagger's conviction would be deferred for a year. If after that period, he had not been involved in any further trouble, it would not stand as a conviction and be wiped from the records. However, if the order was breached, Jagger would be sentenced not just on the original charge, but on the newer offence as well.

In summing up, Lord Parker diverted from his strictly indifferent attitude towards Jagger's status. "I think it is right to say that when one is dealing with somebody who has great responsibilities as you have, because you are, whether you like it or not, an idol of a large number of the young in this country. Being in that position you have very grave responsibilities, and if you do come to be punished it is only natural that those responsibilities should carry a high penalty."

Following that unusual deviation from protocol, Jagger's case was brought to a close. Swiftly reunited with a jubilant Richards, the pair, along with their legal retinue made their way out of the court, and were driven away from the courthouse with the predictable stampede of fans and media personnel in their slipstream. Back at Havers' flat a small celebration took place. Jagger changed from his court apparel into something more appropriate, in this case a white Nehru shirt with mauve embroidered collar, billowing satin trousers and white shoes.

Courtesy of his chicken pox, Richards was in need of immediate isolation. Jagger's day however, held much in store, and from Havers' flat he was driven over to the offices of Granada Television in Soho's Golden Square, where a press conference had been convened. Escaping the media rush, Marianne followed on behind in her Mini.

Mick sidled through the legion of newsmen and reporters crammed into a tiny office to take a spot close by the window. Conducted by Les Perrin and with Allen Klein furtively monitoring events, the questioning was as furious as the mass of pictures being taken. Jagger's relief at being spared jail time was sufficient enough to placate him in acquiescing to the reporters' questions, many of which echoed Lord Parker's words regarding the special responsibility he had to his legion of followers. While appearing slightly phased, Jagger was nonetheless loquacious when it came to the thorny issue of this accountability.

"One perhaps doesn't ask for responsibilities," he told a news crew, in his best bourgeois accent. "Perhaps one is given responsibilities when one is pushed into the limelight in this particular sphere, rather than asking to be… My responsibilities as far as that goes are only to myself. The responsibility, which as one of my friends has said before me, is also on that of the gentlemen of the press, who create those responsibilities, perhaps for themselves, and by trying to report every personal detail of one's life, which one doesn't wish to be made public, which one tries to keep private. In the public sector as such, as to do with my work and my records etc, I have a responsibility… The amount of baths I take or my personal habits are of no consequence to anyone else."

Someone then implied his fanbase looked up to him for leadership – and then asked him whether he should set an example?

"But I have never come out in any kind of argument for or against drugs or anything like that," replied Mick. "I don't propagate religious views, such as some pop stars do; I don't propagate drug use, such as some pop stars do. This whole sort of thing was pushed upon me, by the mere fact that I had been prosecuted and also with Keith being prosecuted, we didn't make a public statement on religion, on drugs or anything like that."

The subject of private drug use at the core of the debate, Jagger was asked whether he condoned the taking of narcotics behind closed doors.

"I don't know," replied Jagger to ITN reporter Michael Nicolson. "It's against the law. It was against the law at one point not so long ago in the judicial history of this country to attempt to commit suicide, and some of those people who attempted to commit suicide were put in prison. Looking back at it, it seems rather a barbaric law. And we might at one stage look back upon these sets of laws and think about them in the same way."

Another more opportunist reporter asked Mick if he'd ever consider taking pep pills again.

"Oh yes," replied Jagger to the delight of certain quarters of the press. He then clarified his position. "Provided they are on prescription."

Sensing the questioning might progress to more controversial areas, the conference was brought to a halt after 15 minutes. The choice of Granada's offices for the event was not without reason. Following secret negotiations, Granada Television's hard-hitting news programme *World In Action* had secured an agreement with Jagger for an exclusive interview when the hearings drew to a close. Confident that he'd escape further incarceration, the programme makers had already finalised details of the shoot before the appeal hearing took place. Shadowing Jagger's every move that day, Granada production staff were present in court when the verdicts were read out and later at the news conference.

First broadcast in 1963, *World In Action* had earned considerable respect for its challenging style of guerrilla journalism that exceeded the staid investigations of the BBC. A member of their production team was John Birt, later to become Director General of the BBC, but in 1967 a 22-year-old researcher. Moved by the extraordinary set of circumstances that had befallen Jagger and Richards, Birt suggested that their case would be appropriate for *World in Action*. As its centrepoint Birt envisaged Mick Jagger being quizzed by several pillars of the British establishment on the enormous gulf of understanding between generations that was, for many, at the core of the issue.

Following a preliminary meeting with Andrew Oldham to discuss the film, Birt held two meetings with Mick Jagger; one at his Harley House flat and the other at a Stones recording session. Together, they devised a scenario that would best present Jagger and the establishment figures discussing the generation gap. John (now Lord) Birt recalls the timeline of events: "I was very much a child of the sixties myself, so I was interested in the avant-garde and breaking the mould of television and other art forms. I imagined there would be a very sixties style party in a beautiful country garden with lots of people floating around and in the middle of it all we would encounter Jagger and talk to him. In discussions it turned to a harder edged idea in which 'Mick Jagger meets the establishment'. Jagger was a quite surprisingly hard-headed young man, and he wanted something less amorphous than I had originally discussed; something harder, but the English country garden element survived."

In search of a location fitting Birt's vision, Spain's Hall, close to Ongar in Essex, was chosen to host this extraordinary meeting of minds. The then home of the Lord Lieutenant of Essex, Sir John Ruggles-Brise, the 15th century property, as now, was available for hire. With the omens looking good, the plan was to broadcast the debate live, which in itself would add an element of excitement to proceedings.

Imaginative concept aside, there was the not insignificant issue of whether the Court of Appeal might decide to uphold Judge Block's decision. This would not only send Jagger back to prison, but also leave *World In Action* with 30 minutes of dead-air and a costly expenses bill. "I was not very experienced and in retrospect, at just 22-years-old, I was being a little reckless," says Birt. "I actually assumed that he would get off his appeal which I think was a bigger assumption than I should have made at the time."

In the event, Birt's faith in the outcome of the trial was rewarded, and the brief to elicit a "dialogue between generations" brought four different figures to debate with Jagger. William Rees-Mogg was an obvious choice, his evident understanding of the issues Jagger was confronting making him best placed to act as a *de facto* host. The other three were Jesuit Father Thomas Corbishley, Lord Stow Hill, a former Home Secretary and Attorney General, and Dr John Robinson, the Bishop of Woolwich and author of a controversial assessment of Christianity entitled *Honest To God*.

While these establishment pillars waited in Essex, Jagger, Faithfull and Birt were taken at high speed from Granada's garage to Battersea Heliport in a white Jaguar sports car driven by a stunt man in order to escape the attentions of the paparazzi. For reasons best known to themselves, the press decided not to follow, with just a solitary photographer waiting at Battersea. Transferred to a small helicopter, the cramped conditions did little to curtail Mick and Marianne's ardour, as Birt recalls:

"When we arrived at Battersea, the helicopter wasn't very big, and was quite rudimentary. It had one pilot in the front and quite a small old seat in the back in which there was me, a big lad at six foot two, with the slender Jagger and the pretty slender Marianne Faithfull. It was a very tight squeeze indeed and Marianne was in the middle, and she was all over Jagger throughout the majority of the flight. Seemingly oblivious to my being there, she was kissing and fondling him, not to any extreme, but both of them made out as though I was not there. It was quite an embarrassing thing."

Twenty minutes later the helicopter landed on a lawn at Spain's Hall. Presumably for the sake of TV cameras, Jagger alighted from the aircraft before the others to create a dramatic entrance and exemplify his otherworldly celebrity. Jagger had undergone a further change of apparel en route, and was now dressed in a mauve tunic, purple satin trousers and white shoes.

"Before the programme went out," Birt recalls. "I took Jagger and Marianne Faithfull to a room in this stately pad, and I had no illusions at all about what was going to happen once they got inside. I'd had a tough day, and I went back downstairs to have a cup of tea only to have my colleagues say to me, 'Where is he?' So I said that I'd told Mick he'd got time to relax, and they said, 'No, there's been a change of plan, we'll have to record straight away because we've tested the links and they don't work properly, and we're going to have to record it now and then

take it back to London in time for the broadcast.' So I '
upstairs to try and extract Mick. I knocked on the door anu
no reply. I knocked again and a rather exhausted voice said, 'Yeah? ı
in a nervous voice, 'Sorry, Mick, there's been a change of plan. You're required on set.'"

Out in the sunshine, the lush atmosphere appeared to loosen Jagger up, and with Rees-Mogg acting as genial host, he was gently eased into the conversation.

Rees-Mogg: "Mick. You've had a difficult day and you've had a difficult three months to put it mildly. And now you're sitting in this garden with a bench full of the establishment opposite you... What we'd like to do would be to discuss with you the things that you believe in, and think are important, and see what we feel about them... You're often taken as a sort of symbol of rebellion, and mothers deplore the influence of The Rolling Stones, because they think that The Rolling Stones are rebellious. Do you think that the society that you live in is one you ought to rebel against? Or do you think you are rebelling against it?"

Smiling, and sounding slightly slurred, Jagger adopted his best erudite stance to process the reply. "Yes, definitely rebelling against it. I mean, not in the obvious way that a newspaper or a pop sort of headline would do it, but obviously we feel there are things wrong with society. But I haven't until very recently, been into this kind of discussion at all because I haven't really felt it hasn't been my place, or through my knowledge, which I don't think is enough to start pontificating on these kinds of subjects."

Lord Stow Hill focussed on the extraordinary amount of interest Jagger – and by association – pop culture received, and in what way the singer would like to be received by his audience. Jagger's response was fairly evasive, and yet exemplified what lay at the hub of the new youth revolution.

Mick: "The very way I started myself when I was young, which was just to have as good a time as possible, which is what most young people try to do without regard to responsibilities of any sort."

Warm and polite, the freshly emancipated Jagger easily charmed his inquisitors with his inoffensive stance and unassuming persona. While the chances of the panel meeting Jagger socially were remote in the extreme, any initial scepticism was replaced with a respect normally reserved for figures drawn from more conventional arenas.

On a personal level, Jagger was deeply touched by Rees-Mogg's decision to fight his corner. "He was always grateful for the editorial," reveals Lord Rees-Mogg. "Much later, he ran into my daughter and he said that he was very grateful to me because I'd saved his career. This was on the point that he wouldn't have been able to go to America if the conviction had stood in its original form."

The interview concluded, Mick and Marianne were able to take the helicopter back to London. With the press still on their tail, they were later discovered in a Soho restaurant. Huddled together, the pair happily chatted to reporters, discussing their plans to set up home together in the near future.

Years later, Jagger would reflect on the rather crazy day that had seen him at the highest seat of judiciary and then helicoptered away to face the panel of highbrow inquisitors. "I was a bit sort of shell-shocked," he recalled. "Especially after being locked up in a little room for a while, which is never very nice. And then to be flown off to this thing. I didn't really make a lot of sense in that interview. It was so embarrassing."

While Jagger was rubbing shoulders with the establishment, Stones fans held a small 'Thanksgiving ceremony' at Westminster Abbey, where a modest crowd of 15 laid flowers in the grounds of the cathedral. A mile or so away, a much larger 'Love-In' was convened in Hyde Park to give thanks for the result. With just three policemen watching them, over 150 participants dressed in hippie garb and engaged in a celebratory circle, banging drums, chanting and shaking bells.

With the media close to exhausting all available strands of the case, from his manor in Henfield, West Sussex, Judge Block was asked if the appeals decision had come as a surprise. "I am not shocked by the matter," he replied confidently. "I have had many reversals. After all, we make our decisions, and always thank God for the Court of Appeal."

On the surface, Block's statement appeared nothing more than a polished media response. With his intransigent judgement in Chichester still provoking an avalanche of consternation, he would deliver his true feelings before the year was out.

CHAPTER 11

London I

"Wherefore rejoice? What conquest brings he home?
What tributaries follow him to Rome,
To grace in captive bonds his chariot-wheels?
You blocks, you stones, you worse than senseless things!
O you hard hearts, you cruel men of Rome."

William Shakespeare, *Julius Caesar*

The morning after the successful appeal hearings brought a predictable slew of newspaper comment on Lord Parker's ruling. In an era when the media was still wary of pop stars it could be regarded as historic that five national press editorials were concerned with the court's decision.

The *Daily Mirror,* which had tacitly championed Jagger and Richards' corner from the start, were fairly chuffed with the decision. "Many people felt that the sentences – twelve months and three months in jail – were out of proportion to the alleged drug offence," ran their leader. "Lord Parker, the Lord Chief Justice, put the whole miserable business in its proper respective. He has brought a disquieting case to as satisfactory a conclusion as anybody could have expected."

Other left of centre newspapers were pleased that a sense of proportion had finally been applied to the issue. The *Guardian* philosophised that the resolution of the issue should prompt the Home Office to conclude its long awaited report on drugs "at the earliest opportunity".* The *Daily Sketch* applauded Lord Parker's decision, but opined that, "British parents would have also welcomed from their Lord Chief Justice a clearer lead on the duty of the law to protect the young from the perils of drug taking."

The *Daily Telegraph,* the broadsheet least disposed to pop culture, took a predictably sober approach to the appeal court's decisions. "This cannot be regarded either as a victory for the permissive voices in society which seek to legalise the preferred use of 'soft' drugs or as a defeat for the advocates of control and discipline."

With the extraordinary amount of support from their peers and fans, the Stones took out full-page advertisements in Britain's leading music papers by way of a thank you. Both *New Musical Express* and *Melody Maker* carried warm, if somewhat cryptic, acknowledgements for backing they'd received. Much of the text was reworked from the Stones' soon-to-be released single 'We Love You', in itself an oblique résumé of events surrounding the trials. "To all dear *NME* readers everywhere," read one advert. "We want you to love them too." *MM* featured a full-page notice reading, "We love you for all the help from our friends to a happier end."

'We Love You' was released on August 18. In Britain, where the group was guaranteed a chart placing, it only peaked at number eight. Across the pond, American sales were disappointing, with the record just creeping into the Top 50. The record's chances weren't helped by the nervous response to Peter Whitehead's promotional film. The BBC, still sensitive to any reference to the Redlands trials, refused to broadcast the film on *Top Of The Pops* unless the courtroom scenes were excised. Notified that the BBC wanted to feature its dance troupe, The Go-Jos, in place of these sequences, Whitehead refused to countenance the plan. When the

* The *Guardian* was still doing so as this book was being prepared for publication. Its June 5, 2011 edition contained a letter urging a review of drugs laws signed by many from the ranks of the great and the good.

furore became public, the BBC issued a statement attempting to clarify matters: "The producer has seen the film, and he does not think it is suitable for the type of audience that watches the programme. There is in no sense a 'ban' by the BBC – it was entirely the producer's decision."

While the Stones themselves kept silent on the refusal, Whitehead was compelled to respond: 'I guessed it would be banned by *Top Of The Pops* because of their extraordinary naïve attitude to pop music. I was very annoyed at the decision. Pop is not all sweetness and light, as the programmers would like to see it, and my film is valid social comment... it's an insult to the pop industry. About 80% of the songs played on *Top Of The Pops* every week are making a social comment. Pop music today is a socially committed form and the BBC are being irresponsible to ignore what is happening in the pop business today."

Ultimately, 'We Love You' was played on the show without visuals, the show's producer circumventing the embargo by playing the song over a montage of still photographs with snatches of the programme's audience gyrating away. In parts of Europe broadcasters were kinder, allowing the unedited film a screening. Ultimately, Whitehead's film remains an extraordinary landmark in the genre of pop video.

Those involved in the Redlands saga found it hard to shake off the associated notoriety. When word of his involvement started circulating in the public domain, Christopher Gibbs found himself having to retaliate. Pursued by the media for any juicy titbits concerning the raid, Gibbs broke cover to claim that the Redlands party was nothing more than a "thoroughly decorous" gathering of close friends. "I had this shop in Elyston Street, Chelsea," he recalls today, "and I was there when the whole saga became public. I remember various journalists came and made a nuisance of themselves and I got labelled with the whole issue. I got a lot of flak from my family being involved with 'these raffish, disreputable people'."

Having little chance of retaliating from behind bars, Robert Fraser's perceived fall from grace was devoured by sections of the press. The *Daily Sketch* summed up the gallery owner's decline under the headline, 'Comfort, Money, Respect... Drugs', while London's *Evening Standard* chipped in with, 'The Shame And Courage Of

A Financier's Son'. The *Daily Mail*'s relentless prurient moralising continued with a feature entitled, 'The Private Shame Of Robert Fraser: The Gallant Old Etonian Who Won Too Late His Battle Against Drugs'.

Other contemporaries in Fraser's wide circle took over his Mayfair gallery for a month-long exhibition. Entitled, 'A Tribute To Robert Fraser', 19 artists, including the likes of Peter Blake, Richard Hamilton and Claes Oldenburg, donated exhibits – "Half in sympathy, half anger" – to highlight the severity of his sentence and, equally, to keep the premises running. Fraser's prison stay was enlivened by a plethora of letters from those closest to him. One letter, surviving to this day, was a joint missive created by Jagger, Faithfull, Richards, Brian Jones and Anita Pallenberg. The sentiments were clearly heartfelt, Mick's reading: "Everything will be so much more beautiful when you come back. There will be so many things to do. I'm sure you've thought of a million things so we'll put them all together." Richards would later add his own contribution, signing the note with his own Wormwood Scrubs prison number, 7855.

Meanwhile, Stones recording sessions continued at Olympic Studios. Accompanied by pianist Nicky Hopkins and with Glyn Johns in the control booth, they worked at a prodigious rate – often through the night – laying down tracks. Brian's appearances however were patchy, and when he did appear, his need to escape his ongoing paranoia was all too evident. His impending court trial acting as an unnerving spectre, he'd talk continually of escape, and at one point arrived brandishing travel brochures for locations predominately in the Middle East. "Look at these fantastic Roman remains," he enthused to reporter Keith Altham during one session. "I'm going to find somewhere in the middle of the Sahara where there are no photographers."

Another avenue of escape emerged in August in the form of the Maharishi Mahesh Yogi and his Transcendental Meditation techniques. Over the August Bank Holiday weekend, Mick and Marianne travelled by train with The Beatles to Bangor in north Wales to take part in the Maharishi's gentle form of mind expansion. The Beatles announced their abstinence from drug use while in Wales, but Mick and Marianne kept quiet on the issue, presumably unwilling to ally themselves with any inference concerning narcotics lest it be misconstrued.

The Maharishi interlude failed to excite Mick and Marianne, and they arrived back in London a few days later, fairly disillusioned by the exercise. Jagger's close interaction with The Beatles throughout the year led to discussions for a joint business venture that would lever them out from the constriction of traditional record company politics. Though these plans were momentarily suspended by the untimely death of Brian Epstein during the Maharishi sojourn, they'd continue to discuss them throughout the year. Jagger and McCartney seemed the most vocal about merging their business interests but like a lot of ideas that year it didn't get beyond the talking stage. Nonetheless McCartney – far more pragmatic when it came to business – built on the idea when establishing the Beatles' Apple Records and attendant companies.

Similarly, Keith and Anita were unconvinced by Transcendental Meditation's newly fashionable status. Still wounded by the court trials, Keith opted for anonymity away from home, spending most of the late summer travelling to and from Italy to be with Anita Pallenberg while she was filming Roger Vadim's *Barbarella*. Schmoozing with luminaries from the art and movie world in Rome, the couple fell easily into a bohemian lifestyle far removed from the rigid conformity of Britain.

Seemingly in the rearguard of his colleagues, Brian sought out the services of the Maharishi in early September, having eschewed the trip to Bangor with the Beatles in favour of flying to Amsterdam to confer with the giggling guru. His supplications at the feet of the Maharishi duly discharged, Jones then headed over to Libya in search of the anonymity he'd been long been seeking.

Other figures associated with The Rolling Stones were also buckling under pressure. Andrew Oldham had succumbed to the over-excesses of the period and his detachment from the group during the Redlands episode had not gone unnoticed. Oldham's attempts to reassume a production role had been met with a lukewarm reception during sessions at Olympic, the group evidently preferring to work with Glyn Johns. Since Allen Klein and Jagger were jointly tending to the Stones' business affairs, Oldham's presence on all tiers seemed surplus to requirements. "I had placed enough strain on my relationship with The Rolling Stones," recalled Oldham in 2007. "I decided it would be better if I said, 'We should part'."

Oldham's removal was formally approved after talks in America at the beginning of September when all five Stones travelled to New York to meet with Klein to discuss business. The drug trials having garnered worldwide coverage, it was therefore no surprise when both Jagger and Richards were collared by immigration officials on their independent arrivals into New York. Keith was first to be detained, taken into a private office and quizzed over what had transpired back in England. Denied entry to the States, Richards was handed a "deferred entry" certificate that allowed him to stay overnight before being hauled back for further questioning the following day. Jagger was treated in a similar fashion and, like Richards, was required to meet with customs officers at an office on Broadway the following morning. In the meantime US officials asked their counterparts in England to provide them with details of what had transpired in the courts.

The following morning Mick and Keith, with Brian and Michael Cooper in tow, attended an immigration hearing where, presumably due to their unique status and Klein's persuasive talking, they were granted short-stay US visas. Predictably, this was picked up by the press back home, the *Daily Mirror* headlining their story: 'Two Stones Barred In US: Jagger, Richards In Airport Drama'.

Once the red tape was out of the way, the Stones convened with Cooper for the photo shoot for the sleeve to *Their Satanic Majesties Request* – the title being a cheeky dig at the establishment appropriated and corrupted from the British passport text that read, 'Her Britannic Majesty Requests'. At a Manhattan studio, the group and Cooper set up a backdrop, then decked themselves out in a garish array of clothes more befitting wizards than pop stars. Sat incongruously in this ersatz Neverland, the pose referenced a period that was already seen as passé.

With hippies in San Francisco symbolically burning the ephemera associated with the 'Summer of Love', promoting an album with all the trappings of the era was going to be problematic. If anything, the cover was a throwback to a theme better realised with The Beatles'

Sgt. Pepper album. Incidentally, since Cooper was involved with both sleeves, as a thank you for the use of the doll with the 'Welcome Rolling Stones' top on the *Pepper* cover, The Beatles' heads were concealed amid the shrubbery surrounding the Stones on the album's 3-D design mount.

Returning to England, the group attended to business. On September 27 a brief press statement was issued to the effect that Oldham had "no connection whatsoever with The Rolling Stones". With Klein based mainly in New York, plans were formulated to run a dedicated office for the group in central London, with representatives of Klein's sent over to facilitate this. Jagger took on the running of day-to-day Stones management, with Les Perrin retained as PR and Marianne Faithfull's PA Jo Bergman taking on the bulk of the administration.

Thoughts then turned to Jones' dilemma. The press speculation about the group's future if he received a lengthy prison term was met with a denial from Jagger that the Stones would split up, nor would Jones be replaced. Brian, meanwhile, was keeping a low profile, having gone on another Spanish sojourn with Suki Poitier to marshal his energies in the run-up to his trial.

Still intensely paranoid that he would be busted again, he'd moved from his Courtfield Road flat to a mansion block at 17 Chesham Street in nearby Belgravia. While not noted in police documents or by the press, it has been alleged that Detective Sergeant Pilcher made an impromptu visit to the flat, ostensibly to quiz Jones in relation to a murder inquiry. While no reference of this or Pilcher's presence has been found in documents – murder not part of his remit – it could easily have been a ruse to spook Jones prior to his all-important hearing.

When October 30 arrived he was chauffeured to court by Tom Keylock, and as newsreel footage of the day testifies, Jones was clearly eager to adopt a conventional profile, his attire as conservative as the chauffeur-driven Rolls-Royce he arrived in. Beneath his dark blue and grey pinstripe suit, he wore a white lace shirt and blue polka dot tie. Making his way up the stairs into London's Inner Sessions Court, despite his sorry circumstances, he cut an impressive dash.

A few loyal Stones fans were waiting outside to offer their support.

Present, too, was a modest contingent from London's press pack, no doubt delighted that the 'pop stars and drugs' issue was dragging on. News of Jones' arrest back in May had been eclipsed by his fellow Stones' Chichester saga but now the press were able to feature the Stones' habits on their front pages again.

Arriving at court with Brian was his co-defendant, Stanislaus "Stash" de Rola whose chances of successfully defending the charges against him were quite high. "You have to understand that I truly loved Brian," de Rola told Peter Markham in 2010. "Shortly after the bust they stopped our car again on an alleged tip-off that it was headed for the West End and full of drugs which of course was nonsense but Brian and I were told by our respective attorneys not to hang out with one another and Brian was specifically told to avoid the company of his fellow band members… Sadly every time I saw Brian he insisted that 'they are too strong for us' and carried on in a defeatist manner."

Ominously, the set-up of the court was a virtual carbon copy of that which greeted Jagger and Richards in Chichester: a chairman and three lay magistrates, all of whom would have been well aware of Jagger and Richards' recent tangle with the judiciary. Clearly Jones needed as much support as he could muster. Under normal circumstances the other members of the Stones might have been in court to support their bandmate but with commitments elsewhere, it wasn't to be. Jagger and Richards were travelling to New York that same day to master the new album and, ironically, Keylock was obliged to leave the hearing early to chauffeur them to Heathrow. Nonetheless, Jagger's brother Chris, SOMA head Steve Abrams, UFO Club DJ/MC Jeff Dexter and others from London's counterculture turned up to offer support. Present, too, was Suzy Creamcheese, the cheeky, outspoken warrior on the front-line of London's underground. Another notable attendee in the gallery that day was artist and activist Caroline Coon. With these and other supporters forming a small but solid army of supporters, there was the possibility of trouble if events took a downward spiral.

Before the day's hearing began Jones had been advised to offer a guilty plea on both cannabis charges but maintain his innocence on the more serious cocaine and methadrine offences. In view of this, police dropped those charges. Given their fervour in pursuing Brian, this was a remarkable gesture although it didn't neuter the prosecution's attack in any way. One positive outcome of Jones admitting the cannabis offences was that there was now no reason to prosecute de Rola. The whole unnecessary process of the Swiss national's dismissal took just a few minutes. To supplement any legal cost he might have incurred, he was granted a meagre £78 and 15 shillings for his trouble. He'd incurred particular inconvenience regarding the affair, having had his passport confiscated by police following the raid (although thanks to his important connections, this had been returned) as well as a sizable raking through the media.

The prosecution's case began by describing in detail the narcotics found in Jones' flat on the afternoon of May 10. Jones' counsel, James Comyn QC, submitted in his client's defence that although Brian had taken drugs in the past, they had only brought him trouble and disrupted his career. In a plea of mitigation, Comyn stated that despite substances being found in Jones' home, he had "never peddled or pushed drugs, never bought drugs and never circulated them or carried them around".

Comyn then spoke of Brian's extraordinary creativity, marking him out as an exceptional individual. Describing his client as a "young man with a brilliant career", he mentioned Jones' virtuoso skills as a musician and his abilities on a variety of instruments. Comyn added that Jones truly hoped that the charges laid against him would act as a deterrent to his younger fans, then detailed Brian's descent into a mental breakdown due to his past excesses, and pleaded that the bench spare his client a custodial sentence. "He has never been in prison," said Comyn, "and it is my urgent plea that it is not now necessary for him to go to prison... People in the public eye who offend are sometimes inflicted with a higher penalty, which sometimes can be harsh and even cruel."

This final statement was clearly a thinly veiled reference to the Redlands saga. If it was intended to deter the bench from provoking the same sort of outrage that had occurred when Jagger and Richards were jailed, it was a desperate move.

Dr Leonard Henry, Jones' therapist, was called to validate Comyn's assertion that his client's mental condition was perilous. Taking the stand,

Dr Henry stated that sending Brian to prison would, "completely destroy his mental health. He might even go into a psychotic depression… He might even attempt to injure himself."

His admission of guilt precluding a major grilling from the prosecution, Brian went into the witness box to affirm his fragile state. It was a gamble, and whereas Richards had battled it out at Chichester with steely aplomb, there was always a chance that Jones might let slip some information that could undermine his defence.

With Comyn gently coaching his fragile client, Brian explained that by dint of having a constant stream of visitors to his flat, he couldn't keep tabs on everyone that passed though his door. While he agreed with the prosecution that he should have been more proactive in removing individuals who smoked cannabis in his flat, he had in no way encouraged drug taking on his premises. Comyn then asked Jones to publicly affirm his abstinence from all future drug use.

Barely audible, Brian's response mirrored his council's own words. "That is my precise intention," he said. "They have only brought me trouble and disrupted my career, and I hope this will be an example to anyone who is tempted to try them."

A 90-minute adjournment was called. If Jones' counsel felt they'd competently constructed a defence that urged for compassion, they hadn't counted on the reputation of the court's seasoned chairman, one Reginald Ethelbert Seaton. Like Judge Block, the 68-year-old magistrate was enlivening his retirement with part-time judiciary. In a scenario all too reminiscent of what had met Jagger and Richards, Seaton tore into Brian with a vengeance that reeked strongly of revenge from the establishment.

"I would be failing in my duty," began Seaton, "if I failed to pass a sentence of imprisonment. These offences to which you have pleaded guilty are very serious. It means that people can break the law in comparative privacy and so avoid detection in what is a growing canker. No blame is attached to you for the phial of cocaine that was found, but it shows what happens at that sort of party. People go there who are smokers of cannabis. Others take hard drugs and that is how the rot starts. You occupy a position by which you have a large following of youth and therefore it behoves you to set an example. You have broken down on that. I take into account the fact that you are a person of good character and have admitted your responsibility for these offences."

Despite acknowledging the mitigating evidence presented before him, Seaton handed down two prison sentences on Brian for the cannabis offences; one of nine months for allowing his flat to be used for the smoking of cannabis, and another of three months for the possession charge. Furthermore, Brian was ordered to pay £262. 10s in court costs. After the sentences were handed down, cries of "Oh no!" were heard from the public gallery. A furious chant of opposition arose from Chris Jagger and his fellow activists before they were removed by the police. The court in uproar, Brian's counsel asked for bail to be considered but this was met with a resounding "No" from Chairman Seaton. The court then witnessed Jones being led down to the cells to await transfer to prison. While this took place, Brian's defence team argued, and won, the right of leave to appeal.

Caroline Coon was privy to the pathetic spectacle, and draws a poignant picture of Brian's – and by association many of his peers' – plight. "I think it very shocking for men to be overwhelmed by the power of other men in uniforms. When you see a youth being caught, especially if they are somebody who thinks they are a little bit privileged and they've been overpowered by men in uniforms, they are utterly emasculated, and it's very shocking. Although all of those pop stars that were busted put on this incredible bravado, sort of 'we don't care' or 'fuck the establishment' attitude, that was just a bravado front, underneath what was going on was real psychological damage which had to be worked through, and some people survived and some didn't."

Thirty minutes later, with his Rolls-Royce waiting outside the court, a dark grey van containing Brian and other prisoners headed off for Wormwood Scrubs. Once there, Jones met the same dehumanising formalities that had met Richards and Fraser. While many stories emanating from Jones' tenure in prison might appear apocryphal, it was later claimed that Scrubs guards – reportedly upset at being unable to detain Richards – were planning a suitably rough welcome for Jones. The inmates, too, allegedly greeted Jones with jeers and catcalls; some of them calling for his hair to be cut down to regulation length.

With Jones imprisoned, those who'd borne witness to his sentencing were angry beyond comprehension. Following the hearing they travelled the relatively short distance from the court in Fulham to the Man In The Moon pub in King's Road, Chelsea. Following a hastily convened meeting, they decided to demonstrate in the middle of the road outside. Since her studio was relatively close, Caroline Coon had rushed there to collect some unusual props to highlight the severity of Brian's sentence.

"I had in my studio a thousand fake joints," she remembers. "We demonstrated smoking these fake joints up and down the King's Road protesting 'Free Brian Jones'." Because it was a wet and miserable day, the eight protestors continued with their antics fairly unhindered until police arrived to inspect what was going on. Citing that no formal licence to demonstrate had been obtained, they attempted to stop the group's activities.

"The police said, 'Well, you can only march on this side of the pavement'," recalls Coon today. "Steve Abrams and Jeff Dexter and Chris Jagger kind of fell across the invisible police line and they were all thrown into the back of a Black Maria. As the vehicle was driving away, I managed to bang on the back and say, 'Don't worry, I'll be there to bail you out' at which point the doors were flung open and I was flung in the back of the police van."

Taken into custody, each was asked to identify themselves. On hearing the name Jagger police were wondering if Chris was actually his more famous brother. In the event he was charged on suspicion of damaging a police van, while Suzy Creamcheese (calling herself a "professional demonstrator"), Coon, Dexter and Abrams were detained on charges ranging from obstruction to abusive behaviour. In the spirit of the times, Coon refused to accept bail, and was sent to Holloway women's prison. She stayed there until broadcaster Bernard Braden heard of her incarceration and paid for her release.

Coon's presence at Jones' hearing was more than just support for him. She'd become painfully aware of how the punitive attention directed towards users of drugs had escalated in tandem with casual narcotics use. A London-based art student, in 1966 Coon had seen her Jamaican boyfriend jailed on a marijuana charge. While visiting him in prison, she'd assisted with lawyers working for his release and had become aware that many arrested for minor drug offences were being denied their basic rights. The Redlands case having highlighted the issue of drug use among the young, Coon was propelled into action, and with a core of like-minded supporters established Release, a charitable organisation that provided essential, impartial information to anyone arrested on a drugs charge.

Caroline Coon: "While I was aware that Mick and Keith's sentences were horrific, they weren't as bad as those who hadn't got the great and the good to protect them. The reality was that you had people disappearing off the streets, so you wouldn't know where they were. That's why Release became important. The first thing that I demanded from the Home Office was that people were allowed to make a phone call. The police would arrest somebody, and if you didn't know your rights, you would just disappear for a few weeks. People were being arrested and you wouldn't hear about them. It was a very frightening time. It was a jungle out there."

With the likes of Sergeant Pilcher and his ilk seemingly running rampant around London, stories flooded into Release's offices about the brutal treatment inflicted during raids. While the Stones had been treated with a certain measure of civility during their contact with police, other less-celebrated targets were undergoing human rights abuses at the hands of overzealous officers.

Caroline Coon: "The police thought they really could do what they liked. They'd walk into a person's house, steal their money, plant them, punch them, be violent towards them. It was really horrific. It kind of shocked us all, it shocked Jagger, it shocked everybody who was educated to believe that the British justice was wonderful, that the British Empire was the most liberal in the world, and we were the moral leaders of the world. It all came crashing down against this police state that the authorities, if not condoned, turned a blind eye too."

News of Jones' sentence soon reached the rest of the Stones' circle, and an appeal was readied for delivery in the High Court the following day. The members of the group were tight-lipped about their feelings, and with speculation rife that Brian's incarceration could be the final nail in their coffin, the group's PR team reiterated their statement that the group would not be splitting up.

The following morning, Jones' representatives were at the Royal Courts of Justice petitioning for bail on both medical grounds and on the severity of the sentence. After consulting the medical evidence, the appeal judges acceded to the bail request on the understanding that psychiatrists, appointed by the court, independently evaluate Jones' state of mental health. With these conditions agreed upon and bail set at £250 and with further sureties of £250 from two independent guarantors, the request was granted. One hour after the necessary paperwork was signed off, Brian was formally discharged from Wormwood Scrubs at 7 p.m. With Tom Keylock behind the wheel and accompanied by lawyer Peter Howard, Jones headed out of London to a country location in Middlesex. Because the legal calendar was full towards the end of the year, the full appeal couldn't be heard until December 12.

Remarkably, after what had occurred, Brian killed his anxiety by embarking on another round of drinking and drugging in London. This might have been his way of coping with the pain but the flip side was that he could be back in prison in a trice if he was caught. Still convinced that his movements were being trailed by police, he quietly traded in his silver Rolls-Royce for a blue model. One night while being chauffeur driven around town, Jones and a companion were pulled over by police alongside the Embankment. Either recognising the car's famous occupant, or working on prior information, the vehicle was meticulously searched. Jones had a small quantity of cannabis on his person and while the police were searching elsewhere he popped the drugs (wrapped in silver foil) into the mouth of Brian Pastalanga, his chauffeur. The dupe worked but after the police left the scene, in a fit of repressed paranoia, Brian attempted to throw himself over the embankment wall into the Thames. Luckily Pastalanga was equipped to cope with Jones' behaviour and pulled him back. In the throes of a further collapse, Brian was driven straight back to The Priory in Roehampton.

While Jones was trying to pre-empt his appeal hearing in the worst possible way, others involved in this ongoing saga were actively reviving past setbacks. The most prominent of these was Jagger and Richards' old adversary, Judge Leslie Block. While his performance in Chichester had been interpreted by many as nothing more than a final burst of indignation from an aging pillar of society, he'd nonetheless become something of a champion among like-minded folk. While the magnitude of Block's decision had been nothing short of monumental – from major editorials in all of the British press, discussions in parliament and at the highest seat of the country's judiciary – he had been guarded in his response to the successful appeals. It was predictable then that the opportunity to make his true feelings known would arise at some point.

Between his part-time duties at Chichester court, Block enjoyed hobnobbing with West Sussex's agricultural community, among whom he was a much-revered figure. Each autumn, as the farming calendar drew to a close, members of the community gathered to give thanks at harvest festival services in the medieval parish churches that proliferated locally. The hardcore of the agricultural community would attend less Godly dinners and dances that similarly marked the time of year. Block occasionally enlivened these occasions as an after-dinner speaker who could be relied upon to both inform and entertain, and finally propose a toast to a popular cause. Thus he was a popular choice to deliver some words of wisdom at the Horsham Ploughing & Agricultural Society dinner on Saturday, November 11, when over 80 local farmers gathered to discuss events relating to their industry. Held in the small but hugely affluent village of Rudgwick, Block's presence and profile caused the local press to be present to record his words.

The speeches at gatherings like these normally concerned themselves with the obstacles that regularly befall the farming community, and Block employed scant irony in his oration. To the titter and guffaws of the ruddy-faced guests, the judge's words veered somewhat from tales of errant livestock, harvesting and farm machinery towards the case in which his name had lately been associated. Talking about unwanted detritus that frequently dogged farmers, Block mentioned that he'd come across other "sordid" debris in his legal work.

"I refer to certain objects of no use to farmers," said Block, his tongue firmly in cheek. "I may say they are of no use to man or beast unless they are otherwise dealt with by being ground very small to surface roads, or be cut down in size for other uses. I refer to stones."

Block's metaphor was quickly interpreted and the room descended into laughter. On a roll now, he mined further hilarity from his comrades. "Shakespeare said about things in *Julius Caesar*: 'You blocks, you stones, you worse than senseless things.' Be that as it may, we did our best your fellow countrymen – I and my fellow magistrates – to cut these stones down to size. But alas it was not to be because the Court of Criminal Appeal let them roll free. I can only suppose that the Court of Criminal Appeal were influenced also by the words of Shakespeare when he wrote his own epitaph in these words: 'Blest be the man who spares these stones'."

Since the subject of the speech was clearly of interest beyond the parochial limits of Horsham and district, the local journalists' copy was filed over to Fleet Street, creating a wholly new angle to the saga.

Once Block's comments were published in the national press, condemnation was swift. Understandably, the Stones' management charged straight into the fray, issuing a terse statement from Les Perrin: "We shall be consulting lawyers to see what action we can take over the judge's regrettable remarks. All the Stones are very upset about this. There is a lot they could say. But they will not say anything. They will observe the law of *sub judice* in the proper manner by maintaining a dignified silence."

Others outside of the Stones' coterie were outraged by Block's outspoken remarks. William Wilson, Labour MP for Coventry, called the comments "quite deplorable" before raising the matter with the Lord Chancellor. "Since a member of The Rolling Stones is at present on bail pending an appeal hearing," said Wilson, "the remarks of the judge may be taken as *sub judice*."

Block's farming community were swift to defend their controversial speaker. "Judge Block did not explicitly name the pop group, but his implication was quite clear," remarked John Holman, president of the agricultural society. "The MP who is complaining ought to realise that the judge was joking."

The president of the society may well have been protecting his esteemed guest, but Block's damaging words couldn't have come at a more inopportune time while Jones' appeal hearing was being prepared.

On November 27, *Their Satanic Majesties Request* was released, complete with its lavish 3-D effect sleeve, the cost of which topped £15,000. With many of their hardcore followers embarrassed by the Stones' immersion into psychedelia, the record divided those who'd religiously bought their records in the past. To most a patchy effort, the album bore all the hallmarks of a group torn in different directions. Given the events of 1967, this was probably hardly surprising.

The opener, the ragged 'Sing This All Together', was a dissonant aural reflection of a time that for many had well and truly passed; the jangling bells, exotic instruments and mystical ambiance making for an uneven and outdated experience. Other tracks tested the mettle of even the broadest minded aficionado of the group. Bill Wyman, never previously venturing beyond bass and occasional backing vocals, conjured up a composition for the album, the fairy-tale ambiance of 'In Another Land', which featured the backing vocals of Steve Marriott of The Small Faces, who happened to be in the studio next door at Olympic during recording. 'She's A Rainbow', a song with a catchy arrangement, ended up lost in a mire of distortion.

Though largely absent for the recordings, Jones augmented some of the tracks with some suitably esoteric sounds. This was best exemplified in arguably the album's finest moment, the eerie and autobiographical '2,000 Light Years From Home', the song Jagger cheekily referred to as being written "under the influence of jail". With the refrain "It's so very lonely" underpinned by thoughts of desert landscapes and startling nebulae, it was as powerful a statement of isolation as has ever been committed to tape. Jones ran a nightmarish, trippy Mellotron over the entirety of the song, elevating it considerably. While never considered for single release in the UK, the group shot a hazy promotional film to accompany the song, directed by Peter Clifton.

Advance orders sales of the album were healthy, and in the weeks leading up to Christmas the record occupied places in the Top 5 in both Britain and America. Critical reaction, however, was mixed with many media observers' nonplussed by the direction the group had chosen.

While the Stones were far from formulaic, full-blown psychedelia was perhaps a step too far. The influential *Rolling Stone* was forthright of its assessment of the work, as evidenced by Jon Landau's review: "*Their Satanic Majesties Request*, despite moments of unquestionable brilliance, puts the status of The Rolling Stones in jeopardy. With it, the Stones abandon their capacity to lead in order to impress the impressionable. They have been far too influenced by their musical inferiors and the result is an insecure album in which they try too hard to prove that they too are innovators, and that they too can say something new... It is an identity crisis of the first order and it is one that will have to be resolved more satisfactorily than it has been on *Their Satanic Majesties Request* if their music is to continue to grow."

In less erudite journals, the reaction was one of disbelief. *Daily Mirror* pop columnist Don Short was unimpressed by the album, commenting, "Count me out of this scene, I can't get to grips with it."

For a band famously associated for a complete absence of pretence, *Their Satanic Majesties Request* left many in a quandary, and more perceptive critics would point out that the album was nothing more than a reflection of a torrid year. Future Stones PR Keith Altham was equally thrown on hearing it. Speaking today, he recalls the sense of incredulity that met the album's release. "They'd seen what The Beatles had done with *Sgt. Pepper* and decided that they ought to try something similar, but it wasn't them at all. I reviewed it for the *New Musical Express* and gave it as good a review as I could. I just wrote this kind of drivelly hippy-trippy nonsense associated with what I thought was a hippy-trippy album."

The review was indeed as far-out as the material being reviewed. Under the headline, 'Stones Satanic Majesty's [sic] LP Is Trip To Infinity Between Stars And Beyond' Altham took his own trip to the cosmos in attempting to sum up the mass of contradiction embedded in its 10 tracks. "Gladly raise your hands in the air. Empty your mind onto the desk and your brains into the ashtray, now let us see what we have here. Item: a small bag of fears. Item: two dozen assorted ethics. Item: a large jar of obsolete standards. Item: two packets of preconceived moral judgements: Item: a large chunk of well-used conscience. Item: half a dozen black and white lies on one shiny white magic soul. Now you will put all these in a sack and shake them around a bit. Now what have you got? Answer: roughly the equivalent of some close attention to The Rolling Stones' latest album *Their Satanic Majesties Request.* I expect to see the critics call the album everything from 'brilliant' to 'nonsense'. You must make up your mind. I have.

A final word about the three-dimensional album sleeve: 'Eek!'"

Altham recalls a similarly strange reaction once the piece hit the newsstands in early December. "A few days later, I was walking down Wigmore Street very early in the morning after a concert I was reviewing, and a black Rolls-Royce came towards me from the other side of the road. It was fairly surreal as it was just me and this car. Anyway, the back doors of this Rolls suddenly sprung open and this figure came running across the road towards me in a fur coat, and it was Marianne Faithfull. She said, 'Darling, I just adored your review of the Stones' *Satanic Majesties* album, absolutely wonderful tripe!' and she rushed away! To this day I have never been sure if she was referring to the album or the review!"

Four days after the album's release Brian Jones' appeal hearing at the High Court was heard. With the result in no way predictable, the anticipation caused Jones to become acutely anxious. Conditional with his bail, he underwent four sessions with the psychiatrist appointed by the court, Dr Walter Neustatter, at his Harley Street clinic. A psychiatrist of great distinction, Neustatter held many eminent positions in the science of the mind and had penned a respected textbook on criminality entitled *The Mind Of The Murderer.*

Neustatter's evaluation was as thorough as could be expected. The first meeting was unusual in that Brian waxed lyrical about LSD, urging the doctor to "educate the establishment" regarding drug use. Nevertheless, the pair forged a reasonable relationship, not least because both shared a fanatical interest in cricket. Since Jones' mental health was the core of his acquittal chances, the psychiatrist tackled the numerous contradictions in his patient's psyche. He identified Jones' extraordinary intelligence, pitching his IQ at 133. While not finding any signs of formal thought disorder or psychotic influence, Neustatter did detect other disturbing elements of the musician's fragmented state. Much of the report – which appears below – details a man seemingly at war with himself and the world around him.

"Mr. Jones' thought processes do reveal some weakening of his reality ties as a result of intense free-floating anxiety. He currently tends to feel very threatened by the world about him as a result of his increasingly inadequate control of aggressive instinctual impulses. This repressive control seems to be breaking down, and he often resorts to conspicuous denial of the threat created by the breakthrough of these impulses into consciousness. At times he projects these aggressive feelings so that he feels a victim of his environment; at others, he interjects them, resulting in significant depressive tendencies and associated suicidal risk. Mr. Jones' sexual problems are closely interrelated to his difficulties of aggression – that is, he experiences very intense anxiety surrounding phallic and sadistic sexuality because of its implicit aggressive strivings [sic]*. However, these phallic strivings are also in conflict with his gross passive dependency needs. This conflict prevents any mature heterosexual adjustment; indeed, he withdraws from any genuine heterosexual involvement. These sexual difficulties reinforce Mr. Jones's considerable emotional immaturity and effect gross confusion and identification. He vacillates between a passive, dependent child with a confused imager* [sic]*; an adult on the one hand, and an idol of pop culture on the other… In conclusion, it is my considered opinion that Mr. Jones is, at present, in an extremely precarious state of emotional adjustment as a result of his unresolved problems with aggressive impulses and sexual identification. His grasp on reality is fragile because of the debilitating effect of intense anxiety and conflicts surrounding these problems. Much of his anxiety is currently localised onto his potential imprisonment, but its underlying sources are more deeply rooted. He thus urgently needs psychotherapy to assist in mustering his considerable personality resources and capacity for insight to contain his anxiety. Otherwise, his prognosis is very poor. Indeed, it is very likely that his imprisonment could precipitate a complete break with reality, a psychotic breakdown and significantly increase the suicidal risk for this man."*

To back up his written evaluation, Dr Neustatter took the stand. Painting a picture of a broken man beset by numerous demons, he listed some of Brian's more outlandish behaviour. This included turning up to consultations wearing clothing that he could only describe as flamboyant. "I think he had gold trousers and something which looked like a fur rug," recalled Neustatter. Jones' appearance in court seemed to correlate with the psychiatrist's report – arriving for the hearing wearing a sheepskin coat over his more formal attire.

Alongside Neustatter's detailed profile were reports from three other Harley Street-based psychiatrists that provided collaborative information on the musician's tormented state. Jones' personal therapist, Dr Anthony Flood, told the court of Brian's current aversion to drugs. "If one put a reefer within half a mile of Brian Jones," said the psychiatrist, "he would start running." Another physician tending to Brian, Dr Leonard Henry, recounted some of the eight meetings he'd held with Jones at his clinic, informing the court that Jones was "a very sick man", and that in "circumstances not intolerable to a less neurotic personality, might well make an attempt on his life."

With Jones' legal team supporting the psychiatrists' opinions that imprisonment would destroy him irrevocably, the Lord Chief Justice and his two colleagues adjourned for a 20-minute consultation. If any optimism could be drawn from the ominous surroundings, it was that Lord Chief Justice Parker, who'd presided over Mick and Keith's successful appeal hearings in July, and his colleagues would offer Jones a similar lifeline.

On their return, Parker and his two fellow judges overturned Jones' imprisonment, substituting it with a fine of £1,000, a three-year probation order and a condition that Jones continue his sessions with Dr Flood. While the judges had excluded some of Jones' more bizarre behaviour, equally they didn't want to diminish the charges he'd been found guilty of. In closing, Lord Parker left Brian with a severe word of warning. "Remember this is a degree of mercy which the court has shown. It is not a let off. You cannot go boasting about saying you have been let off. You are still under the control of the court. If you fail to co-operate with the probation officer or Dr. Flood, or you commit another offence of any sort, you will be brought back and punished afresh for this offence. You know the sort of punishment you will get." That said, the costs of the initial October hearing totalling 250 guineas was upheld. Parker again referred to Jones' celebrity, this time regarding his apparent wealth. "A fine is designed to hit the pocket, but no permitted fine could really hit this young man's pocket."

After a meeting with a court-appointed probation officer, Brian was free to go. One of the first to greet him was Mick. Without any fanfare, he'd watched the entire proceedings from the public gallery but, having been involved in a fracas with another driver en route to court, he was eager to get away. Nonetheless, he said a few words to the press concerning his – and the other Stones – evident relief. "We are all pleased he is free. All we want to do now is put it behind us and get down to some hard work."

Aside from the anxiety of his court appearance, Brian had been suffering from chronic toothache for the best part of two days. Given the length of the hearing and his dental problems, a planned press conference was cancelled. Nonetheless, with reporters milling outside the court, they did manage to eke a few words out of a dazed looking Jones who mumbled, "I am very happy to have my freedom. I want to be left alone to get on with my life."

Once out of the dentist's chair, Jones celebrated his freedom with a two-day bender that culminated at the hip Middle Earth in Covent Garden, where the full weight of his acquittal hit him. Mingling with the mood of considerable relief were the effects of tranquilisers he'd been prescribed for his chronic toothache, plus a further cocktail of drink and drugs. Warmly received on his arrival at the club, Brian's celebration was nothing less than spectacular, climbing up on stage with the house band, and reducing a double bass to splinters. Later collapsing at his flat he was taken by Brian Pastalanga to St George's Hospital on Hyde Park Corner. Admitted to a dedicated wing for those suffering from acute mental illness, within an hour Jones had checked himself out.

The following morning, Brian was back at The Priory in Roehampton. While the court had offered him a gesture of mercy, the rigid conditions ensured that he would be continually watching over his shoulder. Hardly helping his recovery, the *Daily Mirror* managed to infiltrate the clinic and capture shots of Jones' modest accommodation. His mercurial condition impossible to treat, Brian checked out and took off on another holiday, this time to Sri Lanka. Coldly, Jones travelled with Richards and Jimi

Hendrix's old flame, Linda Keith, leaving Suki Poitier – his most consistent partner that year – behind.

And so 1967 drew to a close. The year of the most famous drugs bust in British history was over. With Mick, Keith and Brian all undergoing their own, very public traumas, for the other two members of the Stones, it all translated into a great deal of hassle.

Bill Wyman, the Rolling Stone with the lowest public profile, articulated this feeling in his memoirs *Stone Alone* published in 1990: "Although I was strongly against drugs myself, I was put in a vulnerable position by the pushers who were constantly around the band – in the studios, on tour in dressing-rooms, hotels, planes, cars... I had to keep aware because if the cops did bust us I would have been thrown in jail together with the rest of them, as would Charlie. And who would believe that we weren't involved?... I accepted that if I was in the band, it was something that had to be tolerated. But they wouldn't lift a finger to help me in my family situation... So the 'separatism' built up... I hardly socialized with the others for ten years from about 1967."

CHAPTER 12

London II

"Anarchy is the only slight glimmer of hope. Not the popular conception of it – men in black cloaks lurking around with hidden bombs – but a freedom of every man being personally responsible for himself. There should be no such thing as private property. Anybody should be able to go where he likes and do what he likes. Politics, like the legal system, is dominated by old men. Old men who are also bugged by religion. And the law – the law's outdated and doesn't cater enough for individual cases."

Mick Jagger, September 1967

In a career that had thus far spanned five eventful years, 1967 was by far the most extraordinary for The Rolling Stones. While many would reflect warmly on the 'Summer of Love', for those intimately involved with the group, no love was lost for what had passed. Court trials, imprisonment, appeals and management upheaval had all combined to stymie their progress yet the group still managed to release two singles, an album and undertake a major European tour. Furthermore, despite mixed reviews for *Their Satanic Majesties Request*, sales for the disc topped half a million by the end of 1967.

For Jagger, one of the few benefits to arise from the turbulence was the solidification of his relationship with Marianne Faithfull. The couple holidayed in the Bahamas at the tail end of 1967, and then moved from Harley House into an apartment in Chester Square in London's Belgravia. With space an important prerequisite for Marianne's two-year-old son Nicholas, Mick then purchased a three-floor property at 48 Cheyne Walk, Chelsea. Property became something of a fad for Jagger and, eager to follow in Richards' footsteps and establish a country base of his own, he bought Stargroves, near Newbury in Berkshire. An Elizabethan manor with a history as rich as its 40 acres of surrounding woodland, he gladly stumped up the £22,000 for the largely dilapidated pile. For the most part though, Mick and Marianne kept company at their preferred Cheyne Walk property. Christopher Gibbs lived a few doors away and others of the Chelsea set were within a stone's throw.

As expected, the couple's property soon became a popular meeting point. Naturally, other members of the Stones popped by to visit. Taken with Cheyne Walk's relaxed ambiance, Keith and Anita purchased a neighbouring house the following year.

MP Tom Driberg, who'd kept tabs on Jagger's movements over the years, was another visitor to the couple's house. Desperate to engage the pop singer in Labour party politics, he attempted to woo him into standing for parliament. Jagger's popularity with the massive youth vote was potentially enormous, and he reportedly took the offer quite seriously before baulking on the idea.

Thanks to the Redlands issue, Marianne was still suffering from the character assassination generated by the media. Not only did she insist that no papers be delivered to their home, she suppressed radio and TV as well. Embarrassing moments occasionally surfaced however. According to Driberg, Faithfull was approached by the writer WH Auden at a party where, departing from his usual poetic lexicon, he asked of her, "When you're smuggling drugs, do you pack them up your arse?"

In the mood to retaliate, on February 25, 1968 Marianne appeared on the BBC television programme *Personal Choice,* a reflective late-night show that encouraged personalities to wax lyrical about their interests. She clearly rattled the suburban sensitivities of presenter Michael Barrett. After discussing her turbulent childhood and the tidal wave of attention generated from becoming a pop singer/actress, Faithfull turned her attention to the subject of drugs. "Something like LSD, if it wasn't meant to happen, it wouldn't have been invented. Because the one really explicit phrase is 'Doors of perception', and that is what drugs are, they are the doors, you don't go anywhere, you just see a crack like I am looking at you now... I think I am really powerful. They'll smash me, probably, but I want to try."

The Redlands scandal having effectively neutered her musical career, Marianne concentrated on acting, and accepted a clutch of parts that were demanding by any standards. Her role in Chekov's *The Three Sisters* in early 1967 had garnered positive notices, and two years later she played Ophelia in Tony Richardson's version of Shakespeare's *Hamlet*, which featured Anthony Hopkins as Claudius. Here too, her performance received considerable acclaim. Less artistically satisfying was her appearance alongside Alain Delon in the exploitation pic *Girl On A Motorcycle*, and a cameo in Michael Winner's *I'll Never Forget What's'isname*. However, the tabloid perception of her was never far away, causing her to look for an escape route.

"I took the drugs because we were all taking the drugs and they were around," Faithfull recalled to the BBC in 1999. "Whenever you are young and rich and successful and very powerful, there will always be creepy people coming along to give you drugs – it's one of the things that you don't realise when you are in that position. Before you can think twice you're in trouble."

The following year would prompt a sea change in attitude on every tier of the Stones' operations, all of which reflected changes going on elsewhere. If 1967 had seen a massive outpouring of optimism, 1968 favoured gritty pragmatism. Vietnam had served as a disturbing backdrop during the 'Summer Of Love' but the stark reality of opposing the war required more than just poking flowers into gun barrels. Student protests and race riots exploded around the world, and those at the cutting edges of the arts felt compelled to do something other than simply entertain. America and Europe were gearing up for an altogether more hostile year, under the watchful eye of rock's more perceptive figures.

The generally apolitical Richards rarely appeared moved (publicly at least) by what was occurring at street level, but Jagger was interested in the burgeoning resistance movement, his brief appearance on the front line at the infamous major anti-Vietnam War demonstration in Grosvenor Square on March 17 evidence of an interest first piqued during his time at the LSE. Jagger witnessed at first hand the demonstrators engaged in pitched battles with police, all of which fed into the Stones' new oeuvre of songs such as 'Street Fighting Man' and 'Gimme Shelter', their forthright lyrics a thousand light years away from the flaky incantations of the previous year. Preparing for these new recordings, Jagger and Richards went back to West Wittering to write songs and compile demos; Richards having radically converted a cottage in the grounds of Redlands into a rehearsal studio which he humourlessly called, 'The Fifth Dimension'.

Another new song paid homage to Redland's wily gardener Jack Dyer. Popping into the house at all hours, the venerable gardener had reportedly woken Jagger from his slumber in a chair in the living room. Never one to miss an opportunity, Redlands' gardener was enshrined as 'Jumpin' Jack Flash'. Now happily refocused on a proven formula, the Stones were helped considerably by producer Jimmy Miller, hot from his work with Traffic, and, previously, the Spencer Davis Group. Though *Their Satanic Majesties Request* had effectively been produced by 'The Rolling Stones' (Jagger and Richards effectively), Miller was warmly received, especially as he encouraged their realignment with a more abrasive sound. Swept up by this new direction, Brian, too, attempted to reassert his role in the group, displaying a renewed sense of optimism.

While Jones' attempt at a turnaround was met with some suspicion, his appearance was indicative of a transformation, his psychedelic finery replaced by a less challenging dress sense. The appeal hearing decision's rigid conditions neutering his penchant for hashish, he'd become more reliant on alcohol and prescribed tranquillisers. Developing a pot-belly, Brian's metamorphosis was further exaggerated with a beard.

Jones' insatiable appetite for the fair sex did not waiver, and he romanced numerous women. His more consistent attentions revolved around Suki Poitier which is what reportedly prompted Linda Keith to take an overdose of barbiturates in Jones' Belgravia apartment. Someone was evidently keeping tabs on the property, and police were called and on breaking down the door, they found her collapsed naked on the floor. She was rushed to hospital where medics were able to stabilise her. Jones was absent at an all-night recording session. Arriving home the following morning, he was informed of her transference to hospital. With reporters gathering outside, the landlord swiftly evicted Brian. Escorted by police, Jones checked into hotel accommodation in west London. Adding further controversy, a headline in one of the following day's papers read: 'Naked Girl In Stones Flat'.

While Linda Keith's suicide attempt was traumatic, Brian had scant reason to regret his eviction from Chesham Street. Although not evidenced in police or press reports, Jones' flat had allegedly been targeted by Norman Pilcher and his squad just days before the incident. On finding no drugs or Rolling Stones on the premises, Pilcher's squad retreated. Nonetheless, Jones witnessed the results of their crude entry on his return, sending him into a renewed state of paranoia.

These incidents weren't restricted to The Rolling Stones. For musicians travelling around the world, searches by overzealous customs officers were all too common. Close to the indignity facing many artists was *Melody Maker*'s Chris Welch who interviewed numerous artists accused of carrying drugs. His piece for *Melody Maker*, 'Stop Picking On Pop' (dated December 21, 1967) outlined this dilemma.

"We've had our fair share of trouble," reported Jimi Hendrix Experience drummer Mitch Mitchell. "The Stones and ourselves must be among the most searched groups in the country. It's mostly airports. I know they've got to do it, but even when I came back on my own from holiday recently I intentionally caught a plane that would land at 6:30am so I wouldn't be bothered. They held me up for 45 minutes filling in forms. Everyone else on the plane had gone by the time they'd let me go. They keep picking on us all the time. At one airport a customs officer actually said, 'Alright, where do you keep your pot and LSD?' Then they tried to turn it into a joke."

Features like Welch's did little to stymie Pilcher's crusade. With drug use rampant in London, he was well aware that a celebrity bust would generate plenty of publicity and systematically raise his team's profile. In late 1967, Pilcher's colleagues had smashed a £250,000 LSD drug ring and their efforts were praised in both High Court and the national press. During 1968–69, he was desperate to elevate his profile even further.

The quickest way to achieve this was to capitalise on the sloppy behaviour of the capital's pop musicians. While eastern mysticism momentarily took the spotlight off celebrity's private habits, Pilcher knew that despite their words to the contrary, most pop stars used drugs. Paul McCartney's LSD admission in 1967 had provoked worldwide consternation, but for the time being the police kept their distance from him and the other Beatles. However, the drug-related death of Brian Epstein in August 1967 confirmed that drugs were rife within Beatles circles. For the likes of Pilcher, this required an immediate response.

Although it was not documented in police reports or covered by the press, according to Donovan and his confidante 'Gypsy' Dave Mills, Pilcher's squad attempted a raid on John Lennon's Weybridge home, 'Kenwood', some time in early 1968. Reportedly, Lennon called the pair over after receiving a tip-off that he was about to be busted and to help dispose of any incriminating materials, flushing a few ounces of hashish down the toilet. As the story goes, the expected knock at the door soon followed, but Pilcher's team, somewhat annoyed, left without finding any drugs. On the way out Pilcher allegedly commented, "We'll get you next time."

Lennon wasn't the only rock star in Pilcher's sights. Virtuoso Cream guitarist Eric Clapton was earmarked too. In early 1968, he was living in a flat at 152 King's Road, popularly known as The Pheasantry, sharing the same block with other luminaries of the Chelsea arts set. Clapton's residence had become a popular meeting point for musicians, including his friend George Harrison. Watching the comings and goings were Pilcher and his team. Having first worked at Chelsea Police Station, he was more than familiar with the heavy concentration of artists in the area.

Through the grapevine, Cream's drummer Ginger Baker somehow heard that Pilcher was lining up his bandmate for a bust, and duly passed on the worrying news. Confirming this belief, drugs charity Release had similarly warned the guitarist that Pilcher was on his tail. "We warned

Eric Clapton," recalls Caroline Coon. "We had supporters within the local police and we got two big tip-offs – one of which was that Pilcher was going to raid the Pheasantry. We rang Eric and warned him that we'd had a tip-off, and his manager got him out to Ireland that day."

Unaware that Clapton had done a bunk, Pilcher's team raided his flat, gaining entrance by claiming to be a special delivery postman requiring a signature. The door opened, Pilcher and his team ran up the stairs screaming, "Where's Clapton?" Although Eric was at that moment en route to Ireland, the raid did succeed in busting Clapton's friend, the Australian pop artist Martin Sharp who designed the cover of Cream's *Disraeli Gears* and *Wheels Of Fire* albums.

Undeterred by Clapton having slipped the net, in May 1968 police clearly decided to undertake a further pop star hit. Brian Jones had moved to a furnished flat at Royal Avenue House, a mansion block just off King's Road. His long-term plan was to escape London for the country but in the meantime the flat – situated on the third floor – was convenient. The previous tenant was 26-year-old actress Joanna Pettet who'd become engaged to actor Alex Cord. Vacating the property in haste, she'd left many of her possessions behind.

Jones was unusually busy throughout most of May, recording and – like the rest of the Stones – on a high from their surprise appearance at the *New Musical Express* Pollwinners' show at Wembley Empire Pool on May 12, the group's first British appearance in over 18 months. The positive reaction of fans at the show seemed to give Brian a lift, and he appeared alongside Mick on radio to help promote the Stones' new single, 'Jumpin' Jack Flash'.

It wasn't to last. On the evening of May 20 Jones watched a preview of Stanley Kubrick's new film, *2001: A Space Odyssey* with the other Stones and then partied until dawn. The following morning, at 7:20 a.m., a team of drug squad officers descended on Royal Avenue House. Led by Detective Sergeant Robin Constable, they'd clearly been staking out Brian's movements during the short period that he had resided at the property. A colleague of Pilcher's, Robin Constable was well known to many of London's counterculture, jokingly referred to as 'Constable Constable'.

Five police officers buzzed the intercom and called out Jones' name. Receiving no response, Constable entered the block through a refuse hatch then opened the main door, allowing the other officers inside the building. Bounding up the communal stairway, they made their way to Brian's third-floor apartment where they found him dishevelled, sitting beside his bed, dressed in a silk kimono. On hearing the commotion he'd put a call through to Stones press agent Les Perrin to alert him of the raid.

Swarming over the flat, Constable asked Jones why he'd failed to answer the intercom. In meltdown Brian cried, "You know the scene, man. Why do I always get bugged?!" He was dispatched to the living room while detectives performed a systematic search. One Sergeant Prentice found a ball of blue wool in the top drawer of a bureau in Jones' bedroom, perversely sitting on top of a Rolling Stones' album cover. Excited by his find, Prentice took the wool over to his superior. "Is this yours?" Constable asked. "It might be," replied Brian, clearly in a quandary as to the unusual item in his possession. The wool dramatically unravelled, Brian was shown a lump of cannabis resin, weighing 144 grains. "Oh no!" said a stunned Brian. "This cannot happen again, just when we're getting on our feet. Why do you have to pick on me?" With that, Jones assumed a foetal position as the police gathered around him. Tipped off by a press source, Stones' office manager Jo Bergman had rushed over to the property to find the entrance sealed off by police.

Carted off to Chelsea Police Station in an uneven mix from his dandified wardrobe, Brian was met by waiting cameramen and reporters. Since it was less than an hour after the raid took place, it was obvious the press had been tipped off. Trevor Kempson, the *News Of The World* reporter who'd helped instigate the Redlands raid, was aware of what was driving the police's determination (and possibly others) to snare Jones. "Of course Brian was being set up," he recalled shortly before his death in 1995. "First the police would be tipped off that Brian was holding drugs, and a few minutes later the tip-off would come to me."

Under questioning, Jones maintained his innocence, telling police, "I never take this stuff. It makes me so irate." Later that day, he was formally charged at Marlborough Street Court, the same courtroom where, in 1895, the beleaguered Oscar Wilde sued the Marquis of Queensbury on a charge of criminal libel. Detectives asked for a postponement so that the substance in question could be sent for analysis, and Brian's lawyer Clive Nicholls stated, "Jones denies the charge and has a complete answer, which will be disclosed in due course." Remanded for three weeks and with bail and sureties set at £2,000, Brian was driven away from court to The Priory in Roehampton for recuperation. London's press corps gleefully ran a further instalment of the Rolling Stones' drugs saga. Reportedly, all were aware that a bust of a Stone was on the cards, and had prepared the headline, 'Rolling Stone Arrested' well in advance of the raid.

This latest incident came as a shock to those monitoring Jones' attempts to straighten himself out. While it was common knowledge that he was taking prescription drugs and drinking alcohol, he'd sworn off hashish, at least for the time being. It's certainly possible that someone from Brian's circle had left the drug behind, but the fact it was found in something as incongruous as a ball of wool – and that the police unravelled it – suggests that Jones could have been the victim of one of the drug squad's more contrived raids.

Given the strong likelihood of him being raided again, a decision was taken to remove Brian out of London to Redlands where the change of air seemed to soothe his accumulating paranoia. He certainly appeared to have reached an accommodation with Keith and Anita's relationship, and was receptive to sharing house space with them.

The peaceful atmosphere was evidently short-lived as depicted in the following alleged incident. Convinced that his excision from the group was imminent, Jones persuaded Richards to invite Jagger down to visit and for them to reassure Brian that his future with the band was secure. Reportedly, events got out of hand. Jones turned on Jagger, accusing him of attempting to lever him out of the group because his court history was preventing the Stones from fulfilling overseas obligations. When Mick retaliated, Brian ran towards Redlands' moat, screaming, "I'm going to kill myself!" Tying a rope around his waist, Mick waded in after him. The effort in itself was fairly futile as the moat was only a few feet deep, and

Jagger was reportedly more concerned about his dandy outfit that had been ruined in the process.

The party drawn to an inglorious conclusion, Jagger and Richards returned to London, leaving Tom Keylock to monitor Jones' movements around West Wittering. For Brian, the enforced extradition was tortuous, and he spent his days skulking around Redlands, all the while begging the Stones' office to allow him to leave the country. He eventually took a trip to Morocco with Suki Poitier and Christopher Gibbs but his mood swings were never far from the surface. Having viciously assaulted Poitier, Jones nursed his demons by visiting Joujouka to hear the mystical sounds of the region's pipe players. Courtesy of artist Brion Gysin, he took with him a couple of primitive tape machines to record their ethereal music. Unfortunately, technical problems meant that nothing was successfully recorded.

Back in Britain, Brian was obliged to attend a further magistrates hearing at Marlborough Street on June 11. Redlands' QC Michael Havers was summoned to act for Jones who opted for trial by jury, the hope being that a judgement from his peers would elicit some sympathy. This request was duly heard at a five-minute hearing, thus ensuring that the whole saga would be deferred to September. Adding greatly to Jones' apprehension was the fear that he might be tried by his old adversary, Judge Reginald Seaton. While clemency for Brian from the appeals court had been hard fought, any chance of mercy a second time appeared remote.

The adjournment also gave the press an opportunity to present yet another front-page story about a "Rolling Stone" appearing in court "on drugs charges", accompanied by the usual photographs of the accused scuttling from limousine to court steps in the midst of an unruly scrum. More and more adjournments meant more and more press coverage and for those unfamiliar with court procedures – and that meant most of the country – these relentless headlines gave the impression that The Rolling Stones were constantly being arrested on drugs charges even though, in reality, several court appearances might result from only one incident. It all served to seriously overstate the issue, exactly the effect the forces of law and ordered wanted.

Despite it all, the Stones forged ahead. French auteur-director Jean Luc Godard filmed the group recording at Olympic Studios during June, the idea being to merge the footage into Godard's movie *One Plus One* (later re-released as *Sympathy For The Devil).* Fired by their enthusiasm for film-making, the group announced plans for a television special which would evolve into *The Rolling Stones' Rock And Roll Circus.*

Meanwhile, offers of concert tours were pouring in, especially from abroad, but these were stymied by Jones' impending trial. In this regard a degree of frustration was trained in his direction, and Jagger, ever conscious of sustaining the group's global popularity, articulated this sense of unease during an interview in mid-1968. "There's a tour coming up and there's obvious difficulties with Brian who can't leave the country. We want to tour Japan, except Brian... he can't get into Tokyo because he is a druggie," he said with alarming callousness.

In July, Brian and Suki headed off to Morocco again. Still keen to capture Joujouka's pipe players on tape, Jones had engineer George Chkiantz ferry over professional recording equipment from London to record the tribesmen, with a view to possible release. Brion Gysin, who was present on the venture, recalls Jones' temporary assimilation with the locals: "We were sitting on the ground with Brian, under the very low eaves of this thatched farm house, and the musicians were working just four or five feet away, ahead of us in the courtyard where the animals usually are. It was getting to be time to eat, and suddenly two of the musicians came along with a snow-white goat. The goat disappeared off in the shadows with the two musicians, one of whom was holding a long knife which Brian suddenly caught the glitter of, and he started to get up, making a sort of funny noise, and he said, 'That's me!' And everybody picked up on it right at once and said, 'Yeah right, it looks just like you.' It was perfectly true, he had this fringe of blond hair hanging right down in front of his eyes, and we said, 'Of course that's you.' Then about 20 minutes later, we were eating this goat's liver on shish-kebab sticks."

Back in London, on September 26, Jones was brought for trial at Inner London Sessions. Confirming his worst fears, the presiding chairman was Reginald Seaton, the judge who'd disregarded Jones' appeal for clemency the previous year and whose reputation confirmed his adherence to dispensing the full weight of the law at every opportunity. In the event of a conviction, Jones' prior conditional discharge from the appeal court would be rendered null and void, ensuring he would be sentenced on his previous charge as well. Ushered into court, Brian cut a haunted figure in his grey suit and tie, his facial appearance betraying a torn psyche. Pleading "Not guilty" in a mumble, he confirmed his current address as "Redlands, West Wittering, Sussex". With these formalities out of the way, the prosecution called Detective Sergeant Robin Constable and two others present the morning of the raid, Detectives Prentice and Wagstaff. The three policemen painted a uniform picture of events that morning, and of how the drugs were discovered during their search. Aware that the defence would attempt to deny Jones' responsibility on the possession charge, they did their level best to depict his languid condition as representative of a seasoned drug user.

Michael Havers latched onto the ploy and in something of a gamble decided that Jones should give his side of the story. Accordingly, Havers led him through the circumstances of the raid, and dwelled on his client's abstinence of illegal substances. Most telling was Brian's complete lack of knowledge regarding the provenance of the mysterious ball of wool.

Havers: "Was the wool yours?"

Jones: "I never had a ball of wool in my life. I don't darn socks. I don't have a girlfriend who darns socks."

Havers: "Had you the slightest knowledge that the resin was in that wool?"

Jones: "No, absolutely not."

Jones was then turned over to the prosecutor Roger Frisby who focused on the defendant's apparent reluctance to open the door to the flat, suggesting Jones was occupied with hiding illegal substances. Brian denied this and proved to be tougher than his outward state suggested, refusing to be bullied into making any kind of confession.

In summing up, Havers contended that in the 10 minutes it took for the police to gain entry to the property, Jones would have had plenty of time to dispose of any illegal drugs in his possession. The fact that it was found so easily surely implied that his client had no knowledge that it was there.

There followed the all-important summing up but contrary to expectation, Seaton showed an uncharacteristic degree of mercy towards the emotionally crippled young musician standing before him. Describing the police case as purely "circumstantial" and with no evidence other than the mysterious ball of wool, he told the jury that their duty was to determine whether Jones had either decided to hide the drugs in the wool, or that he had no idea of its presence in the flat.

Seaton's surprisingly impartial summation over, the jury of ten men and two women retired while Jones, like his defence team quietly confident of the outcome, awaited the verdict in a small anteroom. If he'd cast his eyes upwards as he left the court, he would have seen that during the tail end of the hearing, Mick and Keith had made an impromptu entrance into the public gallery. Their presence drew gasps of delight from the small quorum of Stones fans present, and was a clear indication of their vested interest in Brian's well-being.

The jury returned after 45 minutes and announced that they had reached a decision. Court personnel reassembled, Jones was brought back into the dock to hear the verdict of guilty delivered. Stunned, Brian put his head in his hands and began to rock back and forth, requiring a guard to steady him. With the courtroom abuzz, a short recess was called for the magistrates to determine the appropriate sentence. A few minutes later, Jones was asked to stand to hear the bench's judgement. Facing Seaton, he looked ashen faced. He'd never fully recovered from his night at Wormwood Scrubs the year before, and with the possibility of a reactivated sentence to run concurrently with this new charge, it was likely he'd receive a custodial sentence.

With the certainty of a guilty verdict being referred on appeal to the High Court, Seaton's decision suggested that he'd either undergone a sea change in his attitude towards drugs and pop stars, or he was afraid of his judgement being scrutinised by a higher authority for a second time. Given Seaton's reputation, compassion was not something he was wholly disposed to.

"Mr. Jones," he began, "you have been found guilty. I am going to treat you as I would any other young man before this court. I am going to fine you and I will fine you relatively according to your means: £50 with 100 guineas costs. You will have one week to get up the money [sic]. Your probation order will not be changed. But you must really watch your step and stay clear of this stuff. For goodness sake do not get into trouble again. If you do there will be some real trouble."

Against the odds Jones was a free man.

Outside the court, Brian was reunited with Mick, Keith and Suki. Paparazzi photographers swarmed around the four, encouraging them to form a close huddle. Also gathered close by were the loyal fans who'd kept vigil in the public gallery. With relief written over his face, Brian chatted happily with pressmen. "When the jury announced the guilty verdict I was sure I was going to jail for at least a year," he said. "It was such a wonderful relief when I heard I was only going to be fined. I'm so happy to be free. It's wonderful." Mick, too, expressed his joy at the outcome. "We are very pleased that Brian didn't have to go to jail," he told journalists. "Money doesn't matter."

Such was Brian's elation at being shown clemency he informed the press that he would not be contesting the guilty verdict. Presumably to the chagrin of police officers monitoring his statements, Jones maintained his innocence. "Someone planted that drug in my flat," he said. "But I don't know who. I will state to my death that I did not commit this offence."

Later in the day, Brian's father Lewis Jones was asked for a statement from his home in Cheltenham. Though they rarely talked to the media, Jones' long-suffering parents were more than aware of their son's tenuous grasp on reality. On this occasion however, his father was eager to shout his corner.

Lewis Jones: "It's not for me to criticise the workings of officialdom. But I am absolutely convinced and I shall always remain convinced that Brian was unjustly convicted on the second of his drug charges. I pass no comment on the first, but on the second one I shall remain convinced for the rest of my life that Brian was innocent of that charge. And I base this mainly on the fact that the very night it happened he rang in a state of great distress because he was deeply concerned how his affairs were affecting his family, and he swore to me that he was innocent of it and he hoped that I would always believe him.

I promised him on that occasion that I believed him and nothing has ever or will ever change my mind."

Desperate to escape the attentions of London's drug squad, Jones purchased Cotchford Farm, in Hartfield, East Sussex. Forty miles from London, and well away from the likes of Norman Pilcher, Jones traded his London nightmare for a more pastoral lifestyle. Cotchford was once home to *Winnie The Pooh* author AA Milne, its sloping garden the inspiration for Hundred Acre Wood where Christopher Robin played pooh sticks with Tigger, Rabbit and the bear with a taste for honey but very little brain. There was hope yet for the most wayward Stone.

Jones was just one of numerous targets in Pilcher's crusade against musicians. In the summer of 1968 jazz trumpeter Tubby Hayes was raided at his Chelsea property, and following a systematic search, Pilcher's men found traces of diamorphine and a heroin tablet. According to testimony presented to the court, Hayes had apparently begged his arresting officer for assistance with his consuming heroin habit, whereupon Pilcher drove the musician over to Charing Cross Hospital to register him as an addict.

But Pilcher was looking for bigger fish to fry. In 1968 John Lennon was busy destroying any vestiges of his mop-top persona. Estranged from his wife and son and living with left-field Japanese artist Yoko Ono, the Beatle was now evidently fair game for opportunists such as Pilcher. Over the years Lennon had maintained superficial contact with the *Daily Mirror*'s Don Short, a reporter who covered the careers of The Beatles and The Rolling Stones. A seasoned Fleet Street man, Short was privy to gossip in watering holes where the line between reporters, informants and off-duty police was almost indivisible. In September, Short heard that Pilcher's mob was sizing up Lennon's temporary home at 34 Montagu Square just north of Marble Arch, and duly informed the Beatle to be on his guard. Subsequent events suggest that other reporters were in the loop, and were on standby for a raid.

Fearful of what might be found, Lennon and Ono cleaned the flat fastidiously, vacuuming the floors and dusting every nook and cranny. At 11:55 a.m. on Friday, October 18, the couple were waking up, rock star behaviour rarely assuming any coherency much before midday.

There was a tap on their front door that became more incessant. With their curiosity pricked, Lennon went to see who was there.

"All of a sudden," he recalled. "There was this knock on the door and a woman's voice outside. She said, 'I've got a message for you.' We said, 'Who is it? You're not the postman.' And she said, 'No, it's very personal,' and suddenly this woman starts pushing the door."

John pushed the door shut and looked out of the lounge window from where he could see the extent of the raid. Outside were eight police personnel, all primed to gain entry by force if necessary. If Lennon's view had been less obstructed, he'd also have seen a *Daily Express* cameraman.

From out of a window, John insisted that a search warrant be produced and read aloud. He was perfectly within his rights, but Pilcher saw this as a stalling tactic. When the police threatened to enter by a ground floor window, Lennon unlocked the front door and let them in. No incriminating evidence was uncovered during the initial sortie so two sniffer dogs, Boo Boo and Yogi, were called for whereupon, despite the strenuous efforts to clean the flat, 219 grains of cannabis resin were located in a "leather binocular case and suitcase". Pilcher duly charged Lennon with possession and for obstructing the police in their duty. John would later claim that Pilcher offered him a plea bargain whereby if he admitted possession to the cannabis, police would drop the obstruction charge and any action against Yoko. At 1:20 p.m., Lennon and Ono were transported to nearby Paddington Police Station where – ever the opportunist – Pilcher asked Lennon to sign a couple of Beatles albums for his children. His actions that day would dog Lennon over the next seven years.

Lennon's arrest, much like the Redlands raid and Brian Jones' trials and tribulations, was front-page news and those who believed themselves to be within Pilcher's target area felt an even greater sense of fear. Numerous rock stars were fleeing London for the relative safety of the country, but a bust by any ambitious police detective who wanted to make a name for himself remained a very real threat.

In the higher reaches of the establishment however, serious concern was being expressed at this dedicated targeting of musicians. Arthur Lewis, MP for West Ham North, tabled a parliamentary question to (then) Home Secretary James Callaghan, regarding the Lennon raid. Highlighting the "large number of police" and the presence of the "two dogs", Lewis further demanded of Callaghan to explain the strangely synchronised arrival of the media.

This question set off a lengthy trail of governmental protocol that eventually trickled down to Sergeant Pilcher's desk. Callaghan, prompted police sources, stated that the press were not present until "40 minutes after the police had knocked on the door", a statement that plainly contradicts other reports. Under Callaghan's orders, Pilcher was required to file a detailed report of the raid in which he defended the size of his posse by stating: "It is not unusual to find when executing search warrants for premises occupied by members of the entertainment world to find that there are large numbers of people present taking part in unusual parties." He evidently failed to mention that the raid took place before noon.

Although his actions were being scrutinised at the highest seat of government, Pilcher's team notched up another Beatle scalp, that of George Harrison, on March 12, 1969, and it cannot have been a coincidence that this was the same day that Paul McCartney married Linda Eastman. Pilcher's team headed over to Harrison's modish bungalow, 'Kinfauns', in Esher, Surrey, under the assumption that the Beatle guitarist would be absent and his squad would get a free run of the premises.

George was indeed in London, but instead of celebrating with the McCartneys he was at a recording session. His wife, Pattie, was at home, preparing to join her husband at a party in town later that evening after having enjoyed a fairly typical day shopping in London. On returning to her car, however, she discovered that someone had left a cigarette packet on the dashboard. Inside was a small piece of hashish with a cryptic message reading "phone me", accompanied by a telephone number. Placing the cigarette packet and its contents into her handbag, she drove back to Esher to prepare for the party later that night.

At just past 7:30 p.m., Pilcher's team of smartly dressed detectives – together with familiar sniffer dogs Boo Boo and Yogi – arrived at the Harrison residence. Faced with such a task force, Pattie allowed them inside where they conducted a systematic search of the bungalow. Permitted to make a phone call, Pattie called George at the studio. Evidently someone ear wigging on the conversation, allegedly overheard her ask, "Where in the living room?" Not surprisingly, detectives uncovered a stash of cannabis weighing 345 grains.

Harrison sped back to his house, as police continued their search. In a wardrobe they discovered another caché of cannabis weighing 304 grains, reportedly secreted in a shoe. Awaiting Harrison's return, Pilcher's team evidently made themselves at home in the Beatle's plush home, helping themselves to coffee, playing records and watching television in the lounge, a scenario Harrison would later describe as resembling a "social club". On his arrival, George was livid at what he found, ordering the TV and hi-fi to be switched off, and demanding that the detectives leave his lounge.

The officers clamoured around Pilcher as he read Harrison the formalities. Though Release lawyer Martin Poulden was on his way down to Esher, Harrison admitted the bulk of the cannabis charges, except that which was found in the shoe in his wardrobe. "I'm a tidy man," he informed Pilcher on being shown the drugs hidden in a sock in one of his shoes. "I keep my socks in the sock drawer and stash in the stash box. It's not mine."

Predictably, police found the mysterious piece of hashish in Pattie's handbag. Cautioned and taken away for the formalities, they'd later be fined £250 each. Following a court appearance Harrison sardonically told the press: "I hope the police will leave The Beatles alone now."

London's underground was closely monitoring events. Now nicknamed 'Groupie Pilcher', *Oz* magazine decided to go public and name him in their March 19 issue published just days after the Harrison raid. The headline, 'This Man Is Dangerous' was accompanied by a caricature of a policeman with the face of a pig playing a guitar. Calling Pilcher "London's deadliest male groupie", the article listed the raids he'd undertaken on the capital's music fraternity. "For god's sake," concluded the piece, "give Pilcher a lead guitar and build a group around him. It might keep him off the streets."

With Pilcher's reputation spiralling out of control, those in the Stones attempted to reassert some sort of balance. In the autumn of 1968, Mick and Marianne announced that they were expecting a child – although marriage was not on the cards. "I am still happily sinning away with Mick," said Marianne. "We won't get married for several reasons, one of which is the divorce law in this country. I am not committing adultery because I'm in love. It's the law that makes our relationship seem sordid and disgusting... I would never marry again. If I liked someone, I would live with him and have children. One hopes that society will change and stop being so stupid about these things."

Comments such as these still inflamed a nation attempting to come to terms with the revaluation of every moral tier. Faithfull's comments merely attracted more criticism in her direction. Even the Archbishop of Canterbury got in on the act, asking his congregation in Westminster Abbey to pray for her soul.

The issue something of a talking point, Mick was offered the chance to spar with the embodiment of Britain's prurience, campaigner Mary Whitehouse, on the much-watched *David Frost Show*. Pitching these polar ends of the social spectrum together made for extraordinary viewing, Jagger easily chipping away at Whitehouse's pointed moralising.

Jagger: "I don't really want to get married... I don't feel that I really need it. But if I were with a woman who really did need it, well, that's another matter. But I'm not with that kind of woman."

Whitehouse: "The fact of the matter is that if you're a Christian or a person with a faith, and you make that vow, when difficulties come, you have this basic thing you've accepted. You find your way through the difficulties."

Mick Jagger: "Your church accepts divorce. It may even accept abortion – am I right or wrong? I don't see how you can talk about this bond which is inseparable when the Christian Church itself accepts divorce."

Around this time, Keith and Anita, also expecting their first child, were out driving around West Wittering when their Bentley was pulled over by police and systematically checked. Inside, they found what was by the police's own admission "bags and bags" of substances, needles and other paraphernalia normally associated with drug use. As was customary, the caché of material was taken away for detailed analysis.

Richards and Pallenberg had the last laugh; the substances were nothing more than vitamin B12. The vitamin, especially if used intravenously, had become something of a craze during the late sixties. In fact, Pallenberg incorporated the shooting up of B12 directly into *Performance,* the film she was making with Jagger, which was co-directed by Donald Cammell and Nic Roeg.

Along with its bizarre tale of gangsters and pop stars with revolving personalities, *Performance* also served to revive elements of the Redlands saga. In September 1968, Mick, relishing the opportunity to expand his thespian skills, was confined with Anita to a film set constructed within a Knightsbridge mansion block. With interiors dressed by Christopher Gibbs, and with style and other props provided by Robert Fraser, the set veered uneasily between fantasy, fiction and the sort of lifestyle sixties rock stars were believed to engage in on a daily basis. Keith refused to visit the set, preferring to monitor proceedings from his Bentley parked outside, his paranoia spiralling out of control, with Fraser providing nuggets of information from the set. If his suspicions were correct, Jagger, Pallenberg and actress Michele Breton were engaging in a myriad of sexual permutations under the sheets at Cammell's instigation. Allegedly, some of this material was captured on film, although for obvious reasons it has been kept carefully guarded. Escaping any edits was an oblique reference to the enduring mythology of the Redlands bust. During one sequence two strategically placed Mars Bars were filmed sitting alongside the milk bottles on the film property's doorstep.

While *Performance* was being filmed, Marianne Faithfull stayed with friends in southern Ireland to ensure a safe environment for her pregnancy. Sadly, her pregnancy would not run to term and she miscarried in November of 1968. Devastated by the news, Mick flew to Ireland to comfort his grieving partner. "I cried," recalled Marianne in 1970. "Mick cried. We all cried. It was the worst 24 hours of my life."

Artistically, however, the Stones had good reason to celebrate. The back-to-basics approach employed for their seventh studio album *Beggars Banquet* successfully realigned them with their audience and the critics who'd written them off following *Their Satanic Majesties Request.*

Released in December 1968, *Beggars Banquet* was met with universally positive reviews, the estimable *Time* magazine gushing: "The album bristles with the brand of hard, raunchy rock that has helped to establish the Stones as England's most subversive roisterers since Fagin's gang in *Oliver Twist*. In keeping with a widespread mood in the pop world, *Beggars Banquet* turns back to the raw vitality of Negro R&B and the authentic simplicity of country music." Jann Wenner in *Rolling Stone* was equally effusive: "The Stones make the great comeback of their career. It is the best record they have yet done... a great rock'n'roll album, without pretence, an achievement of significance in both lyrics and music."

Courtesy of *Beggars Banquet,* the Stones' ascendancy continued throughout 1969. With tracks already in the can for their next album *Let It Bleed*, the signs were good for a further revival of fortunes. Mick, on a roll from *Performance*, was eager to build on his dramatic skills and would accept the lead part in Tony Richardson's production of *Ned Kelly*, scheduled for shooting in Australia in July. With Marianne's extraordinary presence easily transferring to the screen, she was offered a supporting role.

News of Mick and Marianne's Antipodean adventure was released to the press on May 28. That night, as the couple were entertaining close friend and Chelsea neighbour Christopher Gibbs at their Cheyne Walk residence, there was a knock on the door. Mick had barely opened it before six members of Chelsea's drug squad burst inside, the team led by Robin Constable, the detective who'd headed up Brian's bust the previous May. Scampering alongside them, as ever, were sniffer dogs Boo Boo and Yogi.

Jagger, Faithfull and Gibbs were confined to a room while the team began a thorough search, Yogi and his handler Sergeant Shearn working their way through the house. When the artful mutt began sniffing at a bureau, its lid was pulled back to reveal an envelope containing a brown substance wrapped in tin foil. Later, a few grains of cannabis were found in a box on the couple's dining room table. Constable also allegedly extracted a piece of paper from the box with white powder on it whereupon, according to Constable, Jagger went ballistic. "You bastard," he cried. "You have planted me with heroin." The officer then did a quick taste as, reportedly, did Jagger. It tasted like talcum powder but was nonetheless taken away by Constable for examination.

Some 45 minutes later, with both protesting their innocence, Jagger and Faithfull were driven to Chelsea police station for cautioning. Released on bail set at £50 each, they returned home. Police statements subsequently alleged that Mick shouted at Marianne not to open the door. "They're after the weed," he was supposed to have said. These statements were at odds with Jagger and Faithfull's sober recollection of events. "I didn't say anything like 'Marianne, it's the law, they're after the weed'," Jagger recalled. "I simply wouldn't have shouted that or used the word weed. It is [a] most archaic expression which is never used." Furthermore, Jagger claimed that police refused to allow him to use the phone, a claim that was backed up by Gibbs.

It later transpired that in the process of collecting statements, Jagger testified to the fact that he'd been taken aside by Constable and told that if he cared to hand over £1,000, the whole matter would be quietly shelved. The dialogue, as reported by Jagger, was potentially explosive.

"Where is your LSD?" Constable asked Jagger to which Mick replied, "I haven't got any." Constable then said, "We can do something about that." Taken aback Jagger asked how this was possible. According to Jagger, Constable stated, "Well, a man can be guilty and plead 'not guilty' and in that way get off. How much is it worth to you?" This alleged conversation shook Jagger to the core. "I only heard about this going on and it was difficult to take in," he later stated under oath. "I did not want to incriminate myself and I wanted him to name the figure. He named one and said '£1,000' so I just shrugged my shoulders." Constable assured, "Don't worry, you can have the money back if it doesn't work." Further to this, Jagger asserted that following the initial hearing, Constable gave Mick a telephone number to call if he wanted to avoid a charge, After consultations with his legal team, Jagger was advised to make the call. Of little surprise to him, Constable answered, saying, "Don't worry. It's all going to be sorted out. Someone will be in touch with you."

The bribe allegedly refused, Jagger and Faithfull maintained their innocence. Predictably, scheduling of the charges was delayed by objections and deferrals, all accompanied by lurid headlines, and the matter did not come to a head until January 26, 1970. With Michael Havers again drafted in to defend, and support from MP Tom Driberg as a character witness, the couple described the alleged bribe in court. Ultimately, Faithfull was cleared on the charge of possession and Jagger was found guilty and fined £200. The bribery allegations were passed to Scotland Yard and thoroughly investigated, all of which produced a massive paper trail that filled several large files. Those on both sides of the divide offered detailed statements concerning the behaviour of everyone on the night in question but following a lengthy summation by the Director of Public Prosecutions, Jagger and Faithfull's claims were dismissed on account of "insufficient evidence". As a result, Constable was exonerated from the investigation, still declaring his innocence on the charge.

With yet another blow to Jagger, and by extension The Rolling Stones, the group was struggling to assume some form of equilibrium during the early summer of 1969. Not helping was Brian Jones' ongoing instability. His infractions with the law meant it would have been hugely problematic, if not impossible, for him to obtain the necessary visas to work abroad – especially in America. This state of affairs required action, and plans were being hatched to lever the Stones' founder out.

On May 31, guitarist Mick Taylor started rehearsing with the Stones, filling in many of Jones' duties. Barely 20 years old, Taylor had proved himself in blues maestro John Mayall's Bluesbreakers; Mayall himself personally recommending him to Jagger. Before Jones was made aware of the situation Taylor was swiftly absorbed into the group. On June 8, Jones was visited at Cotchford Farm by Jagger, Richards and Charlie Watts and officially informed of his sacking. Stoically, Jones announced to the press that he'd taken the decision to leave himself, saying with an element of truth, "I no longer see eye to eye with the others over the discs we are cutting," he said. "I have a desire to play my own brand of music... We have agreed that an amicable termination of our relationship is the only answer."

Three weeks later, Jones was found dead in a swimming pool in the grounds of his Sussex cottage. As such, the Stones first headlining gig in Britain in over two years at London's Hyde Park was a miserable affair.

While drawing crowds of over 250,000, the event would be remembered more as a memorial to their founder member than as a celebration of the group's new direction. Butterflies – one of the enduring symbols of the Redlands affair – were emptied from boxes on the stage. Most just withered away as they hit the air.

With filming commitments pressing in Australia, neither Jagger nor Faithfull were present at Jones' funeral in Cheltenham. For Marianne, the trip to Australia was the final straw in an accumulation of despairing events over two horrendous years. With drug busts, the loss of her baby and now Jones' death weighing heavily on her, she teetered close to a nervous breakdown. Any hope that Australia's remoteness would act as a welcome salve was dashed the moment they arrived. "When Mick and I stepped off the plane in Sydney," she recalled to newspaper columnist Donald Zec, "I was in a complete stupor. There was a nasty demonstration against him because he was playing their hero *Ned Kelly* in a film. I was pushed and thrown to the ground."

Taken to her hotel room, Marianne – numb and devoid from reality – took 150 barbiturate tablets, washed down with hot chocolate. "I remember waking up in the morning well before Mick," she recalled the following year, "and thinking 'Who am I? Who on earth am I?' I walked over to the mirror but I didn't see myself. All I could see was a vision of Brian Jones. He was there in the mirror, I swear it, and he was dead. And I remember thinking, 'Dear God, I am dead too.' I knew nothing more until I woke up in intensive care."

Jagger had reportedly woken up to find the empty bottle of pills. He called for assistance and Faithfull was rushed to hospital where she had her stomach pumped and was put on artificial respiration. Six days later she regained consciousness, but was in a delicate condition. A stand-in took her place in *Ned Kelly*. Jagger, pulled in numerous directions, called her daily and sent letters. Some of these missives were painfully emotional, one reading, "Please forgive me for causing you all this pain. I am devastated to realise that you felt you were in such agony you had to kill yourself."

After two months' recuperating in a convent hospital, Marianne returned to London with Mick. Back in Chelsea, they attempted to reassemble the domesticity of their relationship but with Jagger fully engaged with the Stones' first tour of the States in three years, it was not to be. Seemingly innocent of the way the media might perceive it, Marianne had co-written the song 'Sister Morphine' with Jagger but when released as a single, it was removed from shops after two days, selling less than 500 copies. An erudite paean to a dying man's trauma, the press saw it differently, and ran with the title's drug reference.

Back in America with Taylor on second guitar, The Rolling Stones were elevated to new heights, selling out arena gigs and collecting a new generation of fans in the process. In response to a growing furore from the underground concerning hefty ticket prices, to placate their critics they consented to play a free concert in San Francisco at the end of the tour. While the hippie citadel of Golden Gate Park was initially chosen for the jamboree, San Francisco's city elders got cold feet, and with just hours to go, the whole caravan was unwisely shunted out to the Altamont Speedway track near Livermore. With over 300,000 revellers expected, there was no reason to suspect anything other than a joyous gathering of the tribes and since any sort of collusion with police was deemed totally unhip, the organisers engaged a local chapter of Hell's Angels to provide security for the event. Despite everyone's best intentions, the event descended into ugly chaos, leaving four dead, one murdered by an Angel. Just days away from the close of the sixties, all the negative energies of the decade were focused on the Stones as the curtain came down.

This was not the least of it. Manager Allen Klein had by now turned his attention to The Beatles, leaving the Stones with the realisation that he controlled their most valuable asset – their back catalogue and song publishing – and a huge tax bill. Their financial affairs in disarray, The Rolling Stones – one of the world's top entertainment sensations of the decade – were practically broke. Retreating abroad for the best part of two years, they would eventually regain their equilibrium, and re-establish their finances in tandem with their enormous success.

In a decade that for many was a never-ending party, the Stones left the sixties with mixed emotions. Their success had won many accolades and brought untold celebrity which ought to have translated into extraordinary wealth, but all this was counter-balanced by deep heartache and victimisation hitherto unknown in Britain. In a decade pitted with extraordinary moments, 1967 – the year that had seen three of the Stones behind bars – was unquestionably the most turbulent.

"1967 was a year of change for everybody," recalled Keith. "1967 was the explosion of the drug culture, if there is such a thing. That's when it came into the open from underground. Everyone started talking about it. And throughout this whole year we were having to put up with this incredible hassle; this sort of confrontation with policeman and judges, and I feel very uncomfortable at looking at a uniform anyway, and having to deal with these people for a whole year really did wear us down a bit. In fact, it put us on our back."

The close of the sixties also brought Norman Pilcher's vendetta on musicians to a close. Evidently scared off by the accumulating press and government interest, he continued in the drug squad, but with a lower profile. Pilcher would finally be brought to book – somewhat belatedly – in November 1973, convicted of perjury following a long-running drugs case. Resigning the force before the trial came to court, he attempted to relocate to Australia but was detained on his arrival in Freemantle. Extradition order approved, he was brought back to Britain to face justice. After an eight-week trial at the Old Bailey, Justice Melford Stevenson told Pilcher: "You poisoned the wells of criminal justice and set about it deliberately... What you have done is to provide material for the crooks, cranks and do-gooders who united to blacken the police whenever the opportunity offers."

Pilcher was sentenced to four years' imprisonment. Nonetheless, his legacy continues – maintained largely by the artist community he sought to destroy. Released from jail in the mid-seventies, and with many believing that rock's most controversial enforcer had passed away, he reportedly buried himself away in suburbia. Now in his mid-seventies and with a catalogue of famous scalps behind him, Pilcher's legend is as active as the characters he attempted to bring down. Of little surprise, his name has been referenced in a variety of satirical ways. *Monty Python's Flying Circus* canonised his notoriety as 'Spiny Norman' in their Piranha Brothers skit. In 1978, Eric Idle's Beatles pastiche, *The Rutles,* satirised

Pilcher as 'Brian Plant'. In 1993 the American band Primus released the track 'Pilcher's Squad', its lyrics overtly describing several of Pilcher's exploits. Subsequently, two of the albums signed by Lennon for Pilcher surfaced at a London auction house.

One musician that managed to escape Pilcher's hawk-like attentions during the sixties is nonetheless aware of his enduring notoriety.

"There should be a stone statue erected in memory of Sgt. Norman Pilcher," says former Animals' singer Eric Burdon. "I'm sure it would be an interesting road show attraction. Not all cops in England were snoops like Sgt Pilcher. Back then most were good ol' boys. A race apart of course, but if you didn't get too far out of line, they got on with the job of protecting the public and did their policing without firearms... Also most of them had a sense of humour. I was no angel, but I never had trouble with the law in the UK. So here's to you Sgt. Norman Pilcher, you will always be remembered as the great spoilsport."

Epilogue

"Everything one does in life, even love, occurs in an express train racing towards death. To smoke opium is to get out of the train while it is still moving; it is to concern oneself with something other than life or death."

Jean Cocteau

The enormity of the Redlands saga left an enduring impression on everyone involved. For Mick Jagger and Keith Richards, their successful appeal against conviction established them both as genuine 20th century martyrs. The trials, their brief imprisonment and the manner in which they conducted themselves before, during and after the case consolidated their position as public heroes to an entire generation. Quite why the massed ranks of the establishment, the judges and high ranking police officers didn't foresee this outcome is still astounding.

If the establishment thought that imprisoning two Rolling Stones would put an end to the group, they were badly mistaken. On the contrary, they thrived on the publicity and their fans stood by them, united in their disgust at the treatment meted out by the authorities. When the dust had settled, the whole Redlands affair proved to be merely a hiccup in a career that has seen the Stones go from strength to strength, charting a career in rock that knows no precedent. Today, if they choose to do so, they can tour the world's largest arenas and generate revenues in excess of $500 million. With the possible exception of U2, they are the biggest live rock attraction in the world.

Of little surprise to those who knew him, Jagger swiftly put the Redlands issue well behind him. In time he became part of that same establishment which in 1967 plotted his downfall. With a bank balance approaching £200 million, numerous substantial homes throughout the world and a private box at Lords cricket ground, Jagger's knighthood in December 2003 rubber-stamped his acceptance by the upper class that he'd always aspired to join.

His elevation did not please his erstwhile partner in music and, at least when they were working, his most constant companion. "I don't want to step out on stage with someone wearing a coronet and sporting the old ermine," spat Richards at Jagger via *Uncut* magazine. With Jagger claiming that he was urged to accept the honour from then Prime Minister Tony Blair, Richards was quick to respond. "Like that's an excuse. Like you can't turn down anything … I thought it was ludicrous to take one of those gongs from the establishment when they did their very best to throw us in jail."

Keith perfectly reiterated his rebel stance by adding contemptuously, "I kneel before no one."

Despite continuing to share stage space with his knighted partner, Richards has never once compromised his status as the world's greatest rock and roller. Approaching 70, he remains as uncompromising as when he first stood on that modest Ealing stage some 50 years previous. His drug busts and associated brushes with the law successfully morphed into legend, Keith maintains a cool chic that is still appealing to new generations. "I don't think I'm cool," Richards told *NME* in 2007. "It's other people that tell me I'm cool, I'm just being who I am. Just be yourself is all I can say, the rest of it's a fucking joke. 'Elegantly wasted' blah-blah-blah, I've had all of that. If you've gotta be cool – be cool with yourself. If you've gotta think about being cool, you ain't cool."

His brilliant, brutally honest autobiography *Life*, published in 2010, proved that behind the rebel exterior was a decent, thoughtful man of considerable intelligence, a consummate scholar of the music he loves and, most of all, the rock on which the Stones were built.

Others present on that February night in 1967 met mixed fortunes over the years. Robert Fraser, whose credentials were insufficient to win over the establishment, was dented by the experience of imprisonment, and fell back into heroin addiction, neutering his status as a gallery owner possessed with intuitive foresight. He succumbed to an AIDS related illness in 1985.

Michael Cooper died from a heroin overdose in 1973, another victim of the excesses of the period.

Christopher Gibbs cemented his reputation as a doyen of unusual and imaginative design. Meeting high-bohemian tastes, Gibbs became globally renowned for his unique style and flair.

Nicky Kramer, last seen being pummelled by Kray Twin associate David Litvinoff, left as anonymously as he arrived. The most enigmatic of the Redlands party circle, his whereabouts have proved impossible to trace.

Marianne Faithfull never quite recovered from the Redlands episode, and always seems to be battling the innuendo directed her way. "One does get affected by the media," she told journalist Gina Richardson soon after the scandal erupted. "People think everything I do is evil and wicked. Well I know I'm not what people think of me… I got so hung up by what people have said, and worrying whether I am beautiful or not."

Hung up or not, Faithfull decided the best way was to come out fighting. "My feminine self had been completely besmirched by this," she later recalled. "I'd accepted my role as bad girl in fur rug, and I thought, 'Right, you've cast me in this, I'm going to go for it. To hell with you all.'"

Despite Marianne's spirit, the nation's perception of her would gradually beat her down. By the time Jagger married Nicaraguan model Bianca Perez Moreno de Macias in May 1971 Faithfull was living on the streets of London, a junkie who spent her days sitting on a wall in Soho. "I think the drugs were used by me as a way of suppressing my natural spirit," she told the BBC in 1999. "And it worked. That's something that happens if you take heroin, you don't speak – you don't want to speak. You're just sort of blank. So it helped me to be a blank, and I wasn't a blank."

As is the way of such things, Marianne lost custody of her son Nicholas. Her heroin addiction all-consuming, she passed through a succession of squats and friends' houses until accepting a lifeline offer of a move to Ireland. This retreat away from London's harsh duality served to revive her music career. 1979's *Broken English* infused the anger of the punk era with the hurt she'd carried since the end of the sixties. Other albums would follow and through music she was able to process the enormity of her past.

Following more than her fair share of headlines, Marianne finally kicked her drug dependency in 1985. Ever the survivor, she regained her integrity and forged a not unsuccessful career that finally afforded her the dignity and respect she long deserved. Nonetheless, much of the gross detail of the Redlands saga endures, its sour legacy still hovering in the osmosis. "When a woman loses her reputation at 19 she loses everything," Faithfull told the *Mail On Sunday* in 2007. "What people thought of me and the Stones was downright unfair. And I so object to the Mars Bar story – it's offensive."

Nonetheless, the mud stuck – perhaps irrevocably. Deeply offensive was an approach reportedly made by the Mars confectionary company in the late nineties for her to promote their chocolate bar. At 65, Marianne has become philosophical about the fall-out of that night at Redlands. "It's happened before," she told the *Independent* in 2004, "to Oscar Wilde, where somebody just gets too grand and too successful, and is having too much fun. In Australia it's called 'Tall Poppy Syndrome'. A poppy grows up too high you cut it down. If you're not humble and grovelling enough and if you're operating outside of society they will come down on you. The clever thing they do is pick on a weakness that a person has anyway and let them hang themselves. They didn't manage to destroy Mick and Keith and, though I was the most vulnerable, they didn't manage to get me."

Others from the Redlands story met varied fates. Michael Havers QC – the hero in Jagger and Richards' hour of need – was promoted to the highest seat of English judiciary, the Lord Chancellor. He played a leading role in prosecuting celebrated cases such as the Guildford Four and the Yorkshire Ripper, and served as Tory MP for Wimbledon for over 17 years. Havers died at the relatively young age of 62 in 1992 from heart problems.

Judge Leslie Block's legal career assumed a notorious celebrity that probably not even he would have imagined possible. Despite an eminent war record, his exemplary sentencing of Jagger and Richards cemented his reputation as a latter-day Matthew Hopkins. He died in 1980, aged 74, at his West Sussex home.

Many of the police commandeered into action that February night have long since passed on. The few that survive prefer to keep their recollections to themselves, and remain cautious of any penetrating questioning. Well into retirement age – they tend their respective gardens and allotments in the Chichester area – the events of 1967 are of little consequence to them nowadays.

For well over 40 years, many have bought into the legend that the mysterious David 'Acid King' Schneiderman tipped off the police and may even have been working with the FBI and CIA. Following his rapid retreat from Britain he rebranded himself as 'David Jove', a name that he would retain for the rest of his life. He'd also retain much of his mercurial, sparkly persona, utilising his LSD collateral to prise open numerous doors throughout Europe and the Middle East. With enough time passed and countless individuals charmed with his psychobabble, he was able to slip back into America at the beginning of the seventies.

Burying himself deep in Los Angeles' unregulated media world, the vacuous landscape of Hollywood's clubland afforded him an easy mobility around town. With cocaine seemingly the emollient that bound the scene together, the former 'Acid King' satisfied many with his adroit acquisition and supply skills. If the occasion called for it, he'd namecheck a fraternisation with various pop stars while in England during the sixties. Any deeper interrogation would be stonewalled, as close friend and artistic collaborator Ed Ochs reveals. "Generally he didn't talk much about his past. Those who asked about it he would just stare at until they dropped the subject. We barely touched on it. He neither denied it, nor confirmed it, nor did he brag about it, which is something someone might have if that was his or her claim to fame."

With the punk ethic prompting a rethink of styles and values, the former David Schneiderman leapt headfirst into the Los Angeles mosh pit. Towards the end of the seventies, and courtesy of the emergence of domestic video equipment, he took to filming the hedonism on display around town. Much of what he captured at street level would be transferred – guerrilla style – to the screen courtesy of *New Wave Theatre*, a groundbreaking cable TV show. The programme was an enormous hit, and the former 'Acid King' became the toast of LA's underground.

His celebrity assured, he maintained a dilettante presence around Hollywood, dabbling in film, pop videos and even his own musical adventures. His charisma backed with a penchant for danger, he was referred to as a benign 'Charles Manson', and generated as many enemies as acolytes. The success of *New Wave Theatre* allowed him to establish his own studio cum editing workshop called The Cave. There, he'd shoot film, dispense drugs and hold court. A total reflection of the 'Acid King's' multidimensional personality, the location served as an unpredictable environment, making it a popular hang-out.

In early 1985, Marianne Faithfull was in Los Angeles doing promotional work. She'd finally kicked her heroin habit, and had regained her confidence with a series of extraordinary recordings that were garnering rave reviews. In LA with friend and agent Maggie Abbott, the pair attended a press reception in town and decided to finish off the evening with a visit to The Cave. Abbott was friendly with the rebranded Schneiderman and (like most) had no inkling of his relation to the infamous episode at Redlands back in 1967. The former 'Acid King' was in situ that night and it was inevitable that he and Faithfull would collide for the first time since the night of the Redlands raid. With Marianne processing a paranoia simmered over three decades, she reportedly asked him why he'd tipped-off the police. In his trademark double-speak, the man known previously as Schneiderman replied that he'd been forced into the set-up by various drug enforcement agencies, supposedly to rein in the likes of the Stones. Following the awkward confrontation, Faithfull begged Abbott to drive her away. "It's him, the

Acid King," she said as they left. "He set up the Redlands bust. Don't ever see him again."

Abbott would later press Schneiderman/Jove in to making a more expansive admission, but he refused to expand. Known to carry a gun, and reportedly prone to violent outbursts, she decided to abandon any further inquiries. However, following an incident where he accidently shot himself in the foot, Abbott discovered his Schneiderman origins after taking him to hospital. Nonetheless, the whole conspiracy angle only added to the man's extraordinary enigma. For friend Ed Ochs, the Acid King's adoption of the FBI/CIA/MI5 scenario was just another part of his revolving persona.

"Jove was not a CIA/MI5 plant, no way," recalls Ochs today. "But he did carry a 'hint of narc' about him and was confronted about it from time to time. Drugees can smell a narc by the look in his eye, his devious demeanour, the smell of his sweat; they can tell if he's been busted before and if he's ever ratted to escape jail. As pointed out, he could appear to act narc-like at times or could be misread as one, even though in the 30 years I knew him, he never ratted out anybody to the best of my knowledge and never broke 'the code' by calling the police or bringing them into his life in any way, for any reason. However, as there's safety in numbers, so did he feel safety in being a living contradiction, of being all things and their opposites. That way he could hide between the poles and no one would know for sure. After a while he could even convince himself that he wasn't 100% sure whether he actually did what he thought he did or not."

Despite a reputation for fleeting interests, Schneiderman/Jove maintained a long relationship with actress/comedienne Lotus Weinstock, producing a much-loved daughter, Lilli. The marriage would endure until the late eighties. At that point – even by Los Angeles standards – Schneiderman's drug use had become "voluminous". Adding to the disquiet around the sensitive artistic community, he possessed a penchant for weaponry. Following the brutal murder of *New Wave Theatre* host Peter Ivers in 1983, rumours began circulating connecting Schneiderman with his death, some suggesting that he'd retained Ivers' bloody sheets as a memento.

The variously named Acid King/David Schneiderman/Jove died of pancreatic cancer in 2004. Aged 64, he took with him a variety of secrets, not least details of his involvement with the Redlands scandal. According to his daughter Lilli (now a respected violinist), he confessed to his legend shortly before his death. "He told me he wasn't a drug dealer. He felt he was expanding the consciousness of some of the greatest minds of his day." While his legend endures, until a file surfaces that confirms Schneiderman's collusion with the world's drug authorities, the reality of what occurred will remain a mystery.

Until July 2011, the proven interloper of the Redlands episode – the *News Of The World* – appeared to have changed very little in the 44 years since the scandal erupted. Frank, crude and revelling in its role as the media's principle muckraker, its reputation was feared by indiscreet celebrities and the liberal minded who occupied positions of authority. It remained the world's most popular newspaper, continuing its mission to uncover anything deemed worthy of exposing and exploiting. Predictably, drugs remained a popular target for its reporters, with many celebrities falling foul of the paper's covert style of journalism.

In 2011, following years of accusations, private investigators employed by the paper were proven to have been hacking into the voicemails of celebrities, political figures, war widows and even the families of murder victims. Advertisers ran scared and readers reacted with revulsion. There were reports that several thousand individuals may have been unwittingly monitored and with compensation potentially running to millions, the paper – under enormous pressure – was abruptly closed down by its proprietor Rupert Murdoch, the head of News International. "The *News Of The World* is in the business of holding others to account," said Murdoch's son James. "But it failed when it came to itself."

Redlands, the house and grounds, the most enduring symbol in this extraordinary saga, is still in the ownership of Keith Richards, a stewardship that now exceeds 45 years. While the events of 1967 did little to tailor Richards' penchant for excess, the house remained a bolt hole from the transitory life of a roving rock star. Following a raid by Chelsea police in June 1973, Keith and Anita retreated back to West Wittering to recover their equilibrium. On the night of July 31, Keith's personal dealer Tony Sanchez was ensconced in the guest-house. Awoken by the sound of burning straw, Sanchez witnessed the cottage being consumed by fire. Managing to arouse Keith, Anita and their two children, they fled to see the roof reduced to a burning pyre. The rest of the cottage had to undergo considerable renovations before it was fit to live in again. In an era where fire alarms were an optional accessory, Richards and his family were lucky to survive the inferno.

Today, Redlands maintains a less sensational presence. With a family campsite established next door, its defences are considerably more secure than back in 1967. Those rabid fans still intrigued by Redlands' celebrity still occasionally turn up to pay homage to its connection with countercultural history. While from the front none of the house is visible, those more intrepid souls who venture along a nearby footpath find a less obstructed view at its rear.

In fact, these unsolicited rambles have become something of an irritant to Richards over the years. Having bought the adjoining field, he was perturbed that a footpath that ran just yards from his house couldn't be re-routed. The issue became public and Mark Hammond, the local environment and development officer, was compelled to issue a public statement. "Mr Richards is a well-known figure and so inevitably attracts a greater level of interest and attention from members of the public. He feels that on its present line the footpath causes a considerable problem in terms of the privacy and security of the property."

Scraps with the local authority are rare, however, and he occasionally turns out to support the local community. In 1998 Richards was asked to make a contribution to renovate West Wittering's aging village hall – a request he heartily acceded to. "When they said the village hall needed renovating and that there was a little bit of a shortfall, I thought, 'Here we go, they're going to hit me for quarter of a million' or something. But it was only 30 grand. I said, 'Are you kidding? Here ...' I was glad to put something back into the village because I've been there for 33 years, which makes me a local."

With its remarkable coastline less than a mile away, he recently acquired a beach hut for £60,000. Despite the saga that elevated his infamy in the area, Keith is still in awe of the locale, calling West Wittering "God's little acre… I love that village. They've always been smooth with me."

Acknowledgements

In successfully bringing my initial vision to the page, I want to thank my commissioning editor at Omnibus Press, Chris Charlesworth, who has guided and steered its passage along the way. I am grateful for his intuitive grasp of the story. Equally, I am honoured to have had the services of Andy Neill's encyclopaedic knowledge of 20th century pop culture to ensure that everything was in its place. I cannot thank them both enough.

The information contained in this book would not have appeared had it not been for the kind assistance of the following individuals who gave freely of their time to talk and/or assist in many imaginative ways: Steve Abrams, Anthony Arlidge QC, Sir John Alliott, Keith Altham, Ken Babbs, Steve Baker, Alan Barwick, Richard Bircham, Lord John Birt, Tony Bramwell, Eric Burdon, Tony Calder, David Cammell, Allan Coe, Caroline Coon, David Dalton, Christopher Gibbs, Timothy Hardacre, Nigel Havers, Philip Havers QC, Phil Hewitt, John 'Hoppy' Hopkins, Derek Jameson, Paul Krassner, Hilary Kumar, Gered Mankowitz, Leslie Mann, Sean O'Mahoney, Dave 'Gypsy' Mills, Zoot Money, Alan Readman, Lord William Rees-Mogg, Keith Robinson, John Rodway, Don Short, Rebecca Singer, Keith and Janet Smith, John Steele, Anthony Stern, Roy Stockdill,

Lord Dick Taverne, Ray Thomas, Hilton Valentine, Toni Weeks, Chris Welch, Peter Whitehead.

My thanks to Dave Hill of Tenacity Management (www.tenacitymusicpr.co.uk) for assistance well above and beyond the call of duty. Equally, Trevor Hobley and John Macgillivray who provided research and links that I'd previously considered unreachable.

Special thanks to Ed Ochs who opened up so eloquently regarding his former colleague and friend, the more than enigmatic David 'Schneiderman' Jove. Thanks Ed!

Thanks to the British Library and its newspaper division, both of which have proved invaluable for research, as has the House of Commons' information office. The Bodlean Library in Oxford, too, went out of its way for my requests. Steve Baker at the *News Of The World* and Gavin Fuller at the *Sunday Telegraph* were more than helpful with my enquiries. My thanks also to the excellent services of Westminster, Kensington and Camden libraries in London, and Chichester Library and its local history section down in West Sussex. Thanks also to the Public Record Office in Kew Garden, London.

Special thanks must go to the estimable assistance of researcher extraordinaire Peter Grimwood – librarian at Kensington Library.

Furthermore, I am grateful to those keen and precise supporters who shared in my desire to bring this book together as professionally as possible: Jane Marshall, Sara Rennison and Judith Gleeson; also thanks to Lucy Beevor for expert proofreading.

On a personal note, special thanks to literary agents David Luxton and Rebecca Winfield of Luxton Harris Ltd for easing all of this through; Paolo Hewitt for inspiration and continual wisdom; Mark 'Mumper' Baxter and Lou for kind words of support; Mark Lewisohn for uncluttered and thoughtful assistance; Adam Smith for additional help; brother Robert, father Phillip and sister Mel Wells for being at the end of the phone; Tim Poulter, Michael Collins and Phillip Watson for kind words, coffee and reassurance and not least, Forest Row's Welliez brigade – you know who you are!

Simon

Sources

BIBLIOGRAPHY

Beaton, Cecil. *Beaton in the Sixties: The Cecil Beaton Diaries As He Wrote Them, 1965–1969* (Knopf, 2004)

Birt, John. *The Harder Path* (Time Warner, 2002)

Bockris, Victor. *Keith Richards: The Biography* (Random House, 1992)

Booth, Stanley. *The True Adventures Of The Rolling Stones* (Heinemann, 1985)

Catterall, Ali & Wells, Simon. *Your Face Here: British Cult Movies Since The 1960s* (Fourth Estate, 2001)

Clayson, Alan. *Mick Jagger: The Unauthorised Biography* (Sanctuary, 2005)

Curtis, Helen & Sanderson, Mimi. *The Unsung Sixties* (Whiting & Birch, 2004)

Dalton, David. *Rolling Stones: The First Twenty Years* (Thames & Hudson, 1981)

Dalton, David & Farran, Mick. *The Rolling Stones In Their Own Words* (Omnibus Press, 1980)

Davis, Stephen. *Old Gods Almost Dead* (Aurum, 2001)

Faithfull, Marianne & Dalton, David. *Faithfull* (Michael Joseph, 1994)

Frank, Josh & Buckholtz, Charlie. *In Heaven Everything Is Fine* (Free Press, 2008)
Havers, Nigel. *Playing With Fire* (Headline, 2006)
Hewet, Tim (ed). *Rolling Stones – File Number 2* (Panther, 1967)
Hoffman, Dezo. *The Rolling Stones* (Vermilion, 1984)
Hotchner, AE. *Blown Away: The Rolling Stones And The Death Of The Sixties* (Simon & Schuster, 1990)
Lewisohn, Mark. *The Complete Beatles Chronicle* (Pyramid, 1992)
Norman, Phillip: *Symphony For The Devil: The Rolling Stones Story* (Simon & Schuster, 1984)
Rawlings, Terry. *Who Killed Christopher Robin? The Truth Behind The Murder of Brian Jones* (Boxtree, 1994)
Rawlings, Terry, Badman, Keith & Neil, Andrew. *Good Times, Bad Times – The Definitive Diary Of The Rolling Stones – 1960–1969* (Cherry Red Books, 2000)
Sandford, Christopher. *Jagger Unauthorised* (Simon & Schuster, 1993)
Sanchez, Tony. *Up And Down With The Rolling Stones* (John Blake, 2010)
Scaduto, Anthony. *Mick Jagger: A Biography* (WH Allen, 1974)
Schreuders, Piet, Lewisohn, Mark & Smith, Adam. *The Beatles' London* (Portico, 1994)
Smith, Keith & Janet. *Witterings Then And Now* (West Wittering, 1985)
Stockdill, Roy & Bainbridge, Cyril. *150 Years Of The News Of The World* (Harper Collins, 1993)
Vyner, Harriet. *Groovy Bob* (Faber & Faber, 1999)
Wells, Simon. *Rolling Stones – 365 Days* (Abrams, 2006)
Wyman, Bill, with Coleman, Ray. *Stone Alone* (Viking, 1990)

AUDIO/VISUAL SOURCES

25 x 5: The Continuing Adventures Of The Rolling Stones (CMV Entertainment, 1987)
Donald Cammell: The Ultimate Performance (BBC, 1998)
ITN Archives 1962–69
It Was Twenty Years Ago Today (Granada, 1987)
Omnibus: Video Jukebox (BBC, 1996)
The Rolling Stones: Truth And Lies (Black Hill Pictures, 2008)

The Swinging 60s – The Rolling Stones (Green Umbrella, 2009)
Under Review: Rolling Stones 1962–1966 (Music Video Distributors, 2006)
Under Review: Rolling Stones 1967–1969 (Music Video Distributors, 2006)
Who Breaks A Butterfly On A Wheel (WBBC Productions, 2007)
World In Action: Mick Jagger (Granada, July 31, 1967)

DIGITAL RESOURCES

Daily Express/Daily Mirror: UK Press Online
Guardian/Observer Online Archive: Pro Quest
The Rolling Stones Complete Works Website: www.nzentgraf.de/
Time Is On Our Side: www.timeisonourside.com
Times Digital Archive: 1785–1985, Infotrac
Who Was Who, Oxford University Press

MAGAZINES/NEWSPAPERS

Melody Maker, 1962–69
New Musical Express, 1962–69
News Of The World, 'Pop Stars And Drugs: Facts That Will Shock You', January–February, 1967
The Rolling Stones Monthly Book, 1964–66 (Beat Publications)
The Times, 'Who Breaks A Butterfly On A Wheel', Editorial, July 1, 1967
Time, 'Swinging London', April 15, 1966

Index